Henry S. Rupp

Hymns and Tunes

For public and private worship, and Sunday schools

Henry S. Rupp

Hymns and Tunes
For public and private worship, and Sunday schools

ISBN/EAN: 9783337286521

Printed in Europe, USA, Canada, Australia, Japan

Cover: Foto ©Lupo / pixelio.de

More available books at **www.hansebooks.com**

HYMNS AND TUNES

—— FOR ——

Public and Private Worship,

—— AND ——

Sunday Schools.

Compiled By A Committee.

PUBLISHED BY
Mennonite Publishing Company,
Elkhart, Indiana.
1890.

Entered according to act of Congress, in the year 1890:
By the MENNONITE PUBLISHING CO., of Elkhart, Ind.
In the office of the Librarian of Congress at Washington.

PREFACE.

In arranging HYMNS AND TUNES it was the aim of the committee to make the book as complete as possible. For the sake of convenience the matter has been condensed as much as could be done and still retain distinctness of the notes in the music, and large type in the hymns. Character notes are used because they can be read more readily than round notes.

The hymns are classed into twenty-seven subjects, in alphabetical order, beginning with "ACTIVITY" and ending with "WARNING". By this arrangement any of the subjects can be quickly found without referring to the index.

The hymns are headed with texts of Scripture, with reference to book, chapter and verse.

Both hymns and tunes are indexed according to the number of the hymns,—the tunes agreeing with the hymns immediately following them. All the hymns following a tune are of the same metre.

The beginning of a tune, found at the bottom of some of the right hand pages, is numbered the same as the full tune, which is always found toward the first part of the book. The singer who is not fully acquainted with a tune can see, at the same time, a hymn on the right hand page, and the tune on the left, holding the intervening pages directly toward him.

One of the principal objects in publishing this book is to bring about a closer union in the singing between the Sunday-school and the church. The hymns and tunes are suitable for Church and Sunday-school services, as well as worship on all occasions: a few are especially adapted to children and the Sunday-school.

It is better that the singers learn a tune before the attempt is made to use it in the congregation either in church or Sunday-school: a tune incorrectly sung makes poor music, however good it may be. The true merit of both hymns and tunes is only found when we become fully acquainted with them; and, if they are truly meritorious, will grow in favor as we continue to use them.

Adapting suitable tunes to the hymns selected has been a most careful study of the committee. Only tunes easily learned, and readily sung with a free movement, were accepted: no intricate pieces were allowed.

Thanks are hereby tendered the many friends who so kindly assisted in the compilation, in defraying the expense of the plates, and in securing the use of copyrighted hymns and tunes; also those who gratuitously favored the book with their productions of music and hymns.

That the book may be found worthy a place in the Church, and prove instrumental in the welfare and happiness of God's people, and in building up the Kingdom of our Lord, and that He who inspires every good work may receive all praise and honor, is the sincere desire of

THE COMPILING COMMITTEE.

THE COMPILING COMMITTEE was composed of the following members of the Mennonite Church, Viz: Henry S. Rupp, Shiremanstown, Pa.; Samuel Shank, Broadway, Va.; Emanuel Suter, Harrisonburg, Va.; Chr. H. Brunk, Harrisonburg, Va., and John S. Coffman, Elkhart, Ind.

THE PLATES for HYMNS AND TUNES, from page 1 to 313, were paid by collections from the churches and voluntary contributions of individual members.

LET the word of Christ dwell in you richly in all wisdom; teaching, and admonishing one another in psalms and hymns and spiritual songs, singing with grace in your hearts to the Lord. Col. 3:16.

INDEX OF THE SUBJECTS.

	Hymn Nos.
Activity	1— 17
Atonement	18— 27
Baptism	28— 31
Christmas	32— 34
Consolation	35— 48
Communion	49— 56
Crucifixion	57— 64
Death	65— 91
Evening	92—103
Heaven	104—131
Invitation	132—155
Lord's Day	156–162
Morning	163—170
New Year	171—175
Penitence	176—189
Prayer	190—238
Praise	239—294
Parting	295–301
Refuge	302—328
Resignation	329—354
Rejoicing	355—373
Resurrection	374—378
Rest	379–388
Trust	389—420
Thanksgiving	421—429
Unity	430—448
Warning	449—457
	Pages.
Index of Scripture Texts	315—324
Metrical Index of Hymns and Tunes	325—336
Index of Tunes	337—339
Index of First Lines	The End.

HYMNS AND TUNES.

ACTIVITY.

BETHLEHEM. C. M. By Committee.

If any man thirst, let him come unto me and drink. John 7: 37

1 I LONG for God, the living God;
   I hunger for his grace;
   I long to see as I have seen
     My heavenly Saviour's face.

2 The earth has not a home for me
     Where I would always stay:
   O let me take my pilgrim-staff
     And speed my upward way.

3 I would not be afraid to live,
     Nor yet afraid to die;
   Nor wish to end my working days,
     Or make them faster fly.

4 But I would hide myself beneath
     Jehovah's sheltering wing,
   And wait till his appointed hour
     Shall life immortal bring.

5 Lord, may I learn to work or wait,
     Just as thy word is given,—
   Not loitering idly at the gate
     That opens into heaven.

                    Thomas MacKellar, 1866.

ACTIVITY.

LABAN. S. M.   L. Mason.

Keep the charge of the Lord.   Lev. 8 : 35.   . S. M.

2   My soul! be on thy guard;
       Ten thousand foes arise;
   The hosts of sin are pressing hard
       To draw thee from the skies.

2 Oh, watch, and fight, and pray!
     The battle ne'er give o'er;
   Renew it boldly every day,
     And help divine implore.

3 Ne'er think the victory won,
     Nor once at ease sit down;
   Thy arduous work will not be done
     Till thou obtain thy crown.

4 Fight on, my soul, till death
     Shall bring thee to thy God!
   He'll take thee, at thy parting breath,
     Up to his blest abode.

"Watch and pray."   Mark 14 : 38.   S. M.

3   A charge to keep I have,
       A God to glorify;
   A never-dying soul to save,
     And fit it for the sky.

2 To serve the present age,
     My calling to fulfill,—
   Oh may it all my powers engage
     To do my Master's will.

ACTIVITY. 3

3 Arm me with jealous care,
  As in thy sight to live;
And oh, thy servant, Lord, prepare
  A strict account to give.

4 Help me to watch and pray,
  And on thyself rely;
Assured if I my trust betray,
  I shall forever die.

NINETY-FIFTH. C. M.

In my father's house are many mansions. John 14. 2. C. M.

4 WHEN I can read my title clear
    To mansions in the skies,
  I bid farewell to every fear,
    And wipe my weeping eyes.

2 Should earth against my soul engage,
    And fiery darts be hurled,
  Then I can smile at Satan's rage,
    And face a frowning world.

3 Let cares like a wild deluge come,
    And storms of sorrow fall!
  May I but safely reach my home,
    My God, my heaven, my all.

4 There shall I bathe my weary soul
    In seas of heavenly rest,
  And not a wave of trouble roll
    Across my peaceful breast.

                              Isaac Watts, 1700.

O HOW HAPPY. M. 20.

Lay up treasures for yourselves in heaven. Mat. 6: 20.

5 Oh! how happy are they,
   Who their Saviour obey,
And have laid up their treasures above;
   O! what tongue can express,
   The sweet comfort and peace,
Of a soul in its earliest love!

2 'Twas a heaven below,
   My Redeemer to know,
And the angels could do nothing more,
   Than to fall at his feet,
   And the story repeat,
And the lover of sinners adore.

3 Jesus all the day long,
   Was my joy and my song;
Oh! that more his salvation might see;
   He hath loved me I cried;
   He hath suffered and died,
To redeem such a rebel as me!

4 Now my remnant of days
Would I spend in his praise,
Who has died, me from death to redeem;
Whether many or few,
All my days are his due—
May they all be devoted to him.

WHITESIDE. L. M. D.   J. S. SHOEMAKER.

He is thy Lord, worship thou him. Psalm 45: 11.   L. M. D.

6 WE now have met to worship Thee,
In this, thy Holy Temple, Lord;
Help each, O Lord, attentive be,
And heed the teaching of Thy word.
Fill every heart with love divine,
Help every tongue Thy praise to sing,
Help each to say, Lord, Thou art mine,
And all to Thee an offering bring.

2 Help Thou thy servant to proclaim
The Gospel truth both strong and pure,
That all who hear, accept the same,
And make in Thee salvation sure.
In Thee alone help us to trust,
And in thy laws and love abide;
That when our bodies turn to dust,
Our souls in Heaven be glorified.

J. S. Shoemaker.

ACTIVITY.

ARLINGTON. C. M.   Thos. A. Arne.

Endure hardness as a good soldier.   2 *Tim.* 2: 3   C. M.

7   A M I a soldier of the cross,
      A follower of the Lamb?
    And shall I fear to own his cause,
      Or blush to speak his name?

   2 Must I be carried to the skies
      On flow'ry beds of ease,
    While others fought to win the prize,
      And sail'd through bloody seas?

   3 Are there no foes for me to face?
      Must I not stem the flood?
    Is this vile world a friend to grace,
      To help me on to God?

   4 Sure I must fight, if I would reign;
      Increase my courage, Lord:
    I'll bear the toil, endure the pain,
      Supported by thy word.

   5 Thy saints in all this glorious war
      Shall conquer, though they die;
    They see the triumph from afar,
      And seize it with their eye.

   6 When that illustrious day shall rise,
      And all thine armies shine
    In robes of victory through the skies,
      The glory shall be thine.

                             Isaac Watts, 1720.

ACTIVITY.

Let us worship and bow down. Ps. 95 : 6. C. M.

8 COME let us join our souls to God
In everlasting bands,
And seize the blessings he bestows
With eager hearts and hands.

2 Come let us to his temple haste,
And seek his favor there;
Before his footstool humbly bow,
And offer fervent prayer.

3 Come let us share, without delay,
The blessings of his grace;
Nor shall the years of distant life
Their memory e'er efface.

More than conquerors. Rom. 8: 37. C. M.

9 AWAKE my soul! stretch every nerve,
And press with vigor on:
A heavenly race demands thy zeal,
And an immortal crown.

2 'Tis God's all animating voice
That calls thee from on high;
'Tis he whose hand presents the prize
To thine aspiring eye.

3 A cloud of witnesses around
Hold thee in full survey:
Forget the steps already trod,
And onward urge thy way.

Hebrews II. C. M.

10 RISE, O my soul, pursue the path
By ancient worthies trod;
Aspiring, view those holy men
Who lived and walked with God.

2 'Twas through the Lamb's most precious blood
They conquered every foe;
And to his power and matchless grace
Their crowns of life they owe.

3 Lord! may I ever keep in view
The patterns thou hast given,
And ne'er forsake the blessed road
That led them safe to heaven.

Needham.

ACTIVITY.

ELM STREET. L. M.   By Com.

Well done, thou good and faithful servant. Matt 25: 21.   L. M.

11
1. Some day the word will come to me,
  Arise; the Master calls for thee,
 May I be ready then to go,
  Saying, Lord Jesus! even so.

2. Will work I've purposed in my thought,
  Be to my Master's pleasure wrought,
 And will more talents then be won,
  So that the Lord may say, Well done?

3. Will tears be shed upon my bier
  By some I've helped to comfort here?
 Will seed I've sown some fruitage bear
  Too late for me the joy to share?

4. Shall I on Jordan's farther side
  Find some redeem'd and glorified,
 To whom I pointed out the road
  Leading to that divine abode?

5. I cannot answer Yea or Nay:
  This only, Master, can I say:
 If I've done aught to honor thee,
  It was thy grace that wrought through me.

6. O blessed Lord, in me abide
  When I pass over Jordan's tide,
 That I with my last trembling breath
  May glorify thy name in death.

Thos. MacKellar, 1882.

ACTIVITY.

Zealous of good works. Titus 2: 14.   L. M.

12 So let our lives and lips express
The holy gospel we profess;
So let our works and virtues shine,
To prove the doctrine all divine.

2 Thus shall we best proclaim abroad
The honor of our Saviour God;
When the salvation reigns within,
And grace subdues the power of sin.

3 Our flesh and sense must be denied;
Passion and envy, lust and pride;
While justice, temp'rance, truth and love
Our inward piety approve.

4 Religion bears our spirits up,
While we expect that blessèd hope,
The bright appearance of the Lord,
And faith stands leaning on his word.

5 That sacred stream, thy holy Word,
That all our raging fear controls:
Sweet peace thy promises afford,
And give new strength to fainting souls.

An example that ye should follow. 1 Peter 2. 21.   L. M.

13 My dear Redeemer and my Lord,
I read my duty in thy Word;
But in thy life the law appears
Drawn out in living characters.

2 Such was thy truth, and such thy zeal,
Such deference to thy Father's will,
Such love, and meekness so divine,
I would transcribe and make them mine.

3 Cold mountains and the midnight air
Witnessed the fervor of thy prayer;
The desert thy temptations knew,
Thy conflict, and thy victory too.

4 Be thou my pattern; may I bear
More of thy gracious image here;
Then God, the Judge, shall own my name
Among the followers of the Lamb.

ACTIVITY.

MISSIONARY HYMN. M. 14 D. L. MASON, 1823.

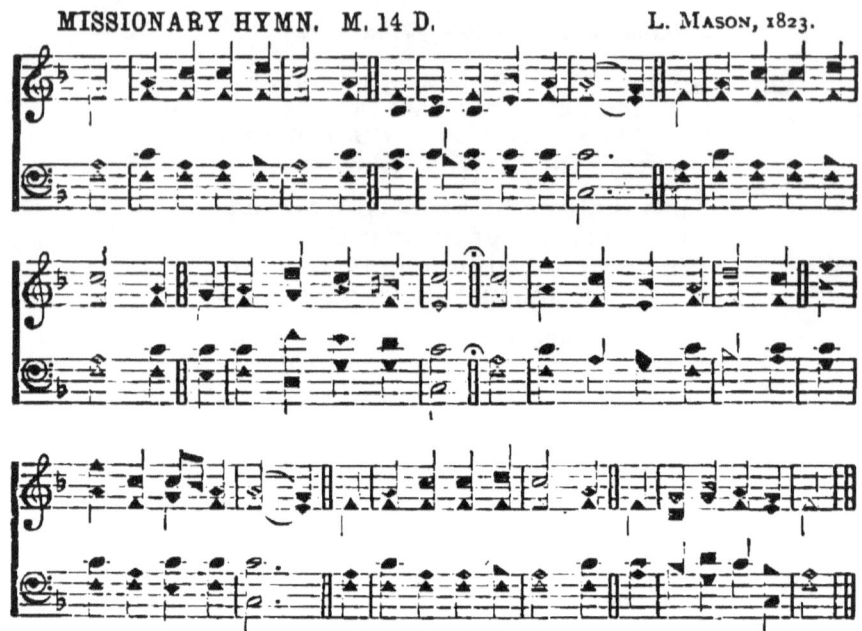

My soul longeth, yea, even fainteth for the courts of the Lord. Ps 84: 2.

14 O WHEN shall I see Jesus,
  And dwell with him above?
To drink the flowing fountains
  Of everlasting love?
When shall I be deliver'd
  From this vain world of sin,
And with my blessed Jesus,
  Drink endless pleasures in?

2 But now I am a soldier,
  My Captain's gone before;
He's given me my orders,
  And tells me not to fear.
And if I hold out faithful,
  A crown of life he'll give,
And all his valiant soldiers
  Eternal life shall have.

3 Through grace I am determin'd
  To conquer though I die;
And then away to Jesus
  On wings of love I'll fly.

ACTIVITY.

Farewell to sin and sorrow,
I bid them both adieu:
And you, my friends, prove faithful,
And on your way pursue.

BOUND BROOK. 7, 6 & 5. By Com.

"*Follow His steps.*" *1 Pet. 2: 21.* 7, 6 & 5.

15 Follow the path of Jesus,
Walk where his footsteps lead,
Keep in his beaming presence,
Every counsel heed;
Watch, while the hours are flying,
Ready some good to do;
Quick, while his voice is calling,
Yield obedience true!

2 Cling to the hand of Jesus,
All through the day and night,
Dark though the way and dreary,
He will guide you right:
Live for the good of others,
Helpless, oppressed, and wrong;
Lift them from depths of sorrow,
In his strength be strong!

ACTIVITY.

Go work in my vineyard. Mat. 21 : 28. M. 4.

16 Hark the voice of Jesus crying—
"Who will go and work to-day?
Fields are white and harvest waiting:
Who will bear the sheaves away?"
Loud and strong the Master calleth,
Rich reward he offers thee;
Who will answer, gladly saying,
"Here am I;" send me, send me.

2 If among the older people,
You may not be apt to teach,
"Feed my lambs" said Christ, our Shepherd,
"Place the food within their reach,"
And it may be that the children
You have led with trembling hand,
Will be found among your jewels
When you reach the better land.

3 Let none hear you idly saying,
  "There is nothing I can do,"
While the souls of men are dying,
  And the Master calls for you.
Take the task he gives you gladly;
  Let his work your pleasure be:
Answer quickly when he calleth,
  "Here am I: send me, send me."

Daniel March. D.D.

MAITLAND. C. M.   G. N. ALLEN.

Bear the cross after Jesus. Luke 23: 26.   C. M.

17 MUST Jesus bear the cross alone,
  And all the world go free?
No: there's a cross for every one,
  And there's a cross for me.

2 Disowned on earth, 'mid griefs and cares,
  He led his toilsome way;
But now in heaven a crown he wears,
  And reigns in endless day.

3 How happy are the saints above
  Who once went sorrowing here;
But now they taste unmingled love,
  And joy without a tear.

4 The consecrated cross I'll bear,
  Till from the cross set free,
And then go home, my crown to wear,
  For there's a crown for me.

G. N. Allen.

ATONEMENT.

MY HELPLESSNESS. L. M. H. L. HASTINGS, 1855.

Look upon the face of thine anointed. Psalm 84: 9. L. M.

18
BEFORE thy face, with lifted hands,
My helplessness, O God, I plead;
Look on the form of Him who stands
With thee, for me to intercede.

2 The marks of sin are on his brow,
Yea, in his hands, and feet, and side,
Here were the fountains whence did flow
For all my guilt, the cleansing tide.

3 My sins helped weave the thorny crown,
The nails were driven for my guilt;
On me his eyes were looking down
When freely thus his blood was spilt.

4 With broken heart and bowing head,
Fallen upon my bended knee,
I hear the words "forgive him," said,
And now I know he meaneth me.

5 His name hath led me to thy throne;
His work for me this boldness gives;
I nothing am, I gladly own,
I live redeemed because he lives.
James Albert Libby, 1876.

Him that cometh unto me, I will in no wise cast out. John 6: 37. L. M.

19
DEEP are the wounds which sin has made,
Where shall the sinner find a cure?
In vain alas, is nature's aid—
The work exceeds all nature's power.

2 And can no Sovereign balm be found,
   And is no kind physician nigh
To ease the pains and heal the wound,
   Ere life or hope forever fly?

3 There is a great physician near
   Look up, O fainting soul and live;
See, in his heavenly smiles appear
   Such ease as nature cannot give:

4 See in the Saviour's dying blood
   Life health and bliss abundant flow
'Tis only this dear sacred flood
   Can ease thy pain and heal thy woe.

Ye have put on Christ. Gal. 3: 27.   L. M.

20 JESUS, thy blood and righteousness
   My beauty are, my glorious dress:
'Midst flaming worlds, in these arrayed,
With joy shall I lift up my head.

2 Bold shall I stand in thy great day;
For who aught to my charge shall lay?
Fully through these absolved I am,
From sin and fear, from guilt and shame.

3 Empty from Satan did I flee
   To thee, my Lord, and put on thee;
And thus adorned, I wait the word,
   "He comes; arise, and meet thy Lord."

4 This spotless robe the same appears
When ruined nature sinks in years;
No age can change its glorious hue;
The robe of Christ is ever new.

5 When from the dust of earth I rise
   To claim my mansion in the skies;
Ev'n then shall this be all my plea,
Jesus hath lived and died for me.

6 Oh, let the dead now hear thy voice!
Now bid thy banished ones rejoice:
Their beauty this, their glorious dress,
Jesus, thy blood and righteousness.

                Zinzindorf.
                J. Wesley, Tr.

ATONEMENT.

DOWNS. C. M.   L. MASON.

Put away the evil of your doings from before mine eyes. Is. 1: 16.   C. M.

21
1 IN evil long I took delight,
   Unawed by shame or fear,
Till a new object struck my sight,
   And stopped my wild career.

2 I saw One hanging on a tree,
   In agonies and blood;
He fixed his languid eyes on me,
   As near his cross I stood.

3 O! never, till my latest breath,
   Shall I forget that look,
It seemed to charge me with his death,
   Though not a word he spoke.

4 My conscience felt and owned the guilt,
   It plunged me in despair;
I saw my sins his blood had spilt,
   And helped to nail him there.

5 A second look he gave, which said,
   "I freely all forgive;
This blood is for thy ransom paid;
   I die that thou may'st live."

6 Thus while his death my sin displays
   In all its darkest hue,
Such is the mystery of grace,
   It seals my pardon too.

                          John Newton, 1779.

ATONEMENT. 17

CLEANSING FOUNTAIN. C. M. WESTERN MELODY.

A fountain opened. Zech. 13: 1. C. M.

22 THERE is a fountain filled with blood,
Drawn from Immanuel's veins;
And sinners, plunged beneath that flood,
Lose all their guilty stains.

2 The dying thief rejoiced to see
That fountain in his day;
And there have I, as vile as he,
Washed all my sins away.

3 E'er since, by faith, I saw the stream
Thy flowing wounds supply,
Redeeming love has been my theme,
And shall be till I die.

4 Then in a nobler, sweeter song,
I'll sing thy power to save,
When this poor lisping, stam'ring tongue
Is ransomed from the grave.

William Cowper, 1774.

ATONEMENT.

DAWN. C. M.   A. . LANDIS, by per.

So mightily grew the word of the Lord and prevailed. Acts 19: 20.   C. M

23
1 THE morning of the centuries
    Beheld a light arise,
‖: That in their heavenly ministries
    Ne'er fell on angels' eyes. :‖

2 Through all the ancient days it seem'd
    A planet new begun;
It grew in fullness till it beam'd
    A sun beyond the sun.

3 When earth with clouds of sin was dark,
    It made an open way;
E'en where it glimmer'd as a spark,
    Some souls received the ray;

4 And they became the sons of God
    Amid a scoffing race;
While bloody was the way they trod,
    His peace lit up their face.

5 They seal'd their constancy with blood;
    And where the martyrs died
A multitude arose and stood,
    And God was glorified.

ATONEMENT.

6 That sun has never ceased to shine
  Upon the King's domain,
Pouring from heaven a light divine
  To make its pathway plain.

7 Till centuries shall be no more,
  Its light shall not grow dim;
And Christ's redeemed on heaven's shore
  Shall sing redemption's hymn.
                    Thos. MacKellar, 1881.

ALETTA. M. 5.

W. B. Bradbury.
Used by per. of Biglow and Main, owners of copyright.

"*The fountain of life.*" *Ps. 36: 9.*　　M. 5.

24 Blessed fountain full of grace!
  Grace for sinners, grace for me!
To this source alone I trace,
  What I am, and hope to be.

2 What I am, as one redeemed,
  Saved and rescued by the Lord;
Hating what I once esteemed,
  Loving what I once abhorred.

3 What I hope to be ere long,
  When I take my place above,
When I join the heavenly throng,
  When I see the God of Love.

4 Then I hope like him to be
  Who redeemed his saints from sin,
Whom I now obscurely see,
  Through a vail that stands between.
                            Kelly

ATONEMENT.

STATE STREET. S. M.   J. C. WOODMAN.

Christ the great sacrifice. Heb. 7: 27.   S. M.

25 Not all the blood of beasts
On Jewish altars slain,
Could give the guilty conscience peace,
Or wash away the stain.

2 But Christ, the heavenly Lamb,
Takes all our sins away;
A sacrifice of nobler name
And richer blood than they.

3 My faith would lay her hand
On that dear head of thine,
While like a penitent I stand,
And there confess my sin.

4 My soul looks back to see
The burdens thou didst bear,
When hanging on the cursèd tree,
And hopes her guilt was there.

5 Believing, we rejoice
To see the curse remove:
We bless the Lamb with cheerful voice,
And sing his bleeding love.
                  Isaac Watts, 1709.

Christ died for our sins. 1 Cor. 15. 3.   M. 14.

26 I lay my sins on Jesus,
The spotless Lamb of God;
He bears them all, and frees us
From the accursed load.

ATONEMENT.

2 I bring my guilt to Jesus,
  To wash my crimson stains
White in his blood most precious,
  Till not a stain remains.

3 I lay my wants on Jesus,
  All fullness dwells in him,
He heals all my diseases,
  He doth my soul redeem.

OVIO. M. 4.

Christ our friend. Prov. 18: 24.   M. 4.

27 ONE there is above all others,
  Well deserves the name of Friend;
His is love beyond a brother's,
  Costly, free, and knows no end.

2 Which of all our friends, to save us,
  Could or would have shed his blood?
But this Saviour died to have us
  Reconcil'd in him to God.

3 When he liv'd on earth abased,
  Friend of sinners was his name;
Now above all glory raised,
  He rejoices in the same.

4 Oh, for grace our hearts to soften!
  Teach us, Lord, at length to love;
We, alas! forget too often,
  What a Friend we have above.

BAPTISM.

HOWARD. C. M.   Mrs. Cuthbert.

Blessed are they that keep his testimonies. Ps. 119: 2.   C. M.

28
Come in, ye blessèd of the Lord,
   And join his children here;
Washed in the Saviour's cleansing blood,
   For him, your Lord appears.

2 Stay not within the wilderness,
   Nor waiting at the door;
For Jesus can your woes redress,
   Were they ten thousand more.

3 Though fearing, trembling, rise and come;
   Yield to the Saviour's voice,
For hung'ring thirsting souls there's room;
   O make the blissful choice.

4 Room in the Saviour's gracious breast,
   That breast which glows with love—
Room in the church, his chosen rest,
   And room in heaven above.

5 Why will you longer ling'ring stay,
   When Jesus says, "There's room?"
Now is the time, th' accepted day;—
   Arise, he bids you come.

He that believeth and is baptized shall be saved. Mark 16: 16.   C. M.

29
Proclaim, saith Christ, my wondrous grace,
   To all the sons of men;
He that believes, and is baptized,
   Salvation shall obtain.

BAPTISM. 23

2 Let plenteous grace descend on those,
  Who, hoping in thy word,
This day have solemnly declared
  That Jesus is their Lord.

3 With cheerful feet may they advance,
  And run the Christian race,
And, through the troubles of the way,
  Find all-sufficient grace.

James Newton. 1769.

HAPPY DAY. L. M.

Hap-py day, hap-py day, When Jesus washed my sins away. He taught me how to watch and pray, And live rejoicing every day.

He went on his way rejoicing. Acts 8: 39. L. M.

30
O HAPPY day, that fixed my choice
  On thee, my Saviour, and my God!
Well may this glowing heart rejoice,
  And tell its raptures all abroad.

2 O happy bond, that seals my vows
  To him who merits all my love!
Let cheerful anthems fill his house
  While to that sacred shrine I move.

3 'Tis done, the great transaction's done;
  I am my Lord's, and he is mine;
He drew me and I followed on,
  Charmed to confess the voice divine.

4 High heaven, that heard the solemn vow,
  That vow renewed shall daily hear,
Till in life's latest hour I bow,
  And bless in death a bond so dear.

Philip Doddridge, 1751.

MARLOW. C. M. JOHN CHEETHAM, arr. L. MASON, 1832.

My soul shall make her boast in the Lord. Ps. 34: 2.   C. M.

31
1 YE men and angels! witness now,
    Before the Lord we speak;
  To him we make our solemn vow,
    A vow we dare not break.

2 That long as life itself shall last,
    Ourselves to Christ we yield;
  Nor from his cause will we depart,
    Nor ever quit the field.

3 We trust not in our native strength,
    But on his grace rely;
  May he, with our returning wants,
    A needful aid supply.

4 Let plenteous grace descend on us
    Who, hoping in thy word,
  This day have solemnly declar'd
    That Jesus is our Lord.

5 With cheerful feet may we advance,
    And run the Christian race,
  And, through the troubles of the way,
    Find all-sufficient grace.

6 O! guide our doubtful feet aright,
    And keep us in thy ways;
  And while we turn our vows to pray'rs,
    Turn thou our prayers to praise.

CHRISTMAS.

HAPPY ZION. M. 7.

Glory to God in the highest, and on earth peace, good will toward men.
  Luke 2: 14, M. 7.

32 ANGELS! from the realms of glory,
   Wing your flight o'er all the earth;
Ye who sang creation's story,
  Now proclaim Messiah's birth:
Come and worship—come and worship—
  Worship Christ, the new-born King.

2 Shepherds! in the field abiding,
   Watching o'er your flocks by night,—
God with man is now residing;
  Yonder shines the heavenly light:
Come and worship —
  Worship Christ, the new-born King.

3 Saints! before the altar bending,
   Watching long in hope and fear,—
Suddenly the Lord, descending,
  In his temple shall appear:
Come and worship—
  Worship Christ, the new-born King.

4 Sinners! wrung with true repentance,
   Doomed for guilt to endless pains;
Justice now revokes the sentence,
  Mercy calls you, break your chains:
Come and worship—
  Worship Christ, the new-born King.

CHRISTMAS.

DIXON. M. 4.

Behold, I bring you good tidings of great joy. Luke 2: 10.   M. 4.

33
Hark! what mean those holy voices,
　Sweetly sounding through the skies?
Lo! th' angelic host rejoices;
　Heavenly hallelujahs rise.

2 Hear them tell the wondrous story,
　　Hear them chant in hymns of joy:
"Glory in the highest, glory!
　　Glory be to God most high!

3 " Peace on earth, good will from heaven,
　　Reaching far as man is found;
Souls redeemed, and sins forgiven!
　　Loud our golden harps shall sound.

4 "Christ is born, the great Anointed;
　　Heaven and earth his praises sing!
Oh, receive whom God appointed
　　For your Prophet, Priest, and King!

5 "Haste, ye mortals, to adore him;
　　Learn his name, and taste his joy;
Till in heaven ye sing before him,
　　"Glory be to God most high!"

6 Let us learn the wondrous story
　　Of our great Redeemer's birth;
Spread the brightness of his glory,
　　Till it cover all the earth.

　　　　　　　　　　John Cawood, 1819.

ZION'S GLAD MORNING. M. 33.

Unto you is born this day in the city of David a Saviour. Luke 2: 11. M. 33.

34 Hail the blest morn when the great Mediator,
    Down from the regions of glory descends
Shepherds, go worship the Babe in the manger;
    Lo! for his guard the bright angels attend.

2 Brightest and best of the sons of the morning,
    Dawn on our darkness and lend us thine aid;
Star of the East, the horizon adorning,
    Guide where our infant Redeemer is laid.

3 Cold on his cradle the dew-drops are shining,
    Low lies his bed with the beasts of the stall;
Angels adore him in slumber reclining,
    Maker, and Monarch, and Saviour of all.

4 Say shall we yield him, in costly devotion,
    Odors of Edom and off'rings divine—
Gems of the mountain and pearls of the ocean,
    Myrrh from the forest and gold from the mine?

5 Vainly we offer each ample oblation,
    Vainly with gold would his favor secure;
Richer by far is the heart's adoration—
    Dearer to God are the prayers of the poor.

PILGRIM. C. M. By Com.

Leaving us an example. 1 Pet. 2: 21. C. M.

35 A PILGRIM through this lonely world,
   The blessèd Saviour passed;
  A mourner all his life was he,
   A dying Lamb at last.

2 That tender heart which felt for all,
   For us its life-blood gave;
  It found on earth no resting-place,
   Save only in the grave.

3 Such was our Lord; and shall we fear
   The cross with all its scorn?
  Or love a faithless, evil world,
   That wreathed his brow with thorn?

4 No: facing all its frowns or smiles,
   Like him, obedient still,
  We homeward press through storm or calm,
   To Zion's blessèd hill.

   Denny.

Thy word is a lamp unto my feet. Psalm 119: 105. C. M.

36 HOW precious is the book divine,
   By inspiration given!
  Bright as a lamp its doctrines shine,
   To guide our souls to heaven.

2 Its light descending from above,
   Our gloomy world to cheer,
  Displays a Saviour's boundless love,
   And brings his glories near.

3 It shows to man his wandering ways,
   And where his feet have trod;
And brings to view the matchless grace
   Of a forgiving God.

4 O'er all the strait and narrow way
   Its radient beams are cast;
A light whose never-weary ray
   Grows brightest at the last.

5 It sweetly cheers our fainting hearts
   In this dark vale of tears;
Life, light, and comfort it imparts,
   And calms our anxious fears.

6 This lamp through all the dreary night
   Of life shall guide our way,
Till we behold the clearer light
   Of an eternal day.
                        John Fawcett, 1782.

Perfect through sufferings. Heb. 2: 10.   C. M.

37 THE head that once was crowned with thorns
   Is crowned with glory now;
A royal diadem adorns
   The mighty Victor's brow.

2 The highest place that heaven affords,
   Is His, is His by right—
The King of kings, the Lord of lords,
   And heaven's eternal Light.

3 The joy of all who dwell above,
   The joy of all below,
To whom he manifests his love,
   And grants his name to know.

4 To them the cross, with all its shame,
   With all its grace, is given;
Their name, an everlasting name,
   Their joy, the joy of heaven.
                        Thomas Kelly, 1802.

ARLINGTON.   No. 7.

WHAT A FRIEND. M. 4.

Chas. C. Converse, by per.

"*Ask and ye shall receive.*" *John 16: 24.*   M. 4.

38
What a friend we have in Jesus,
　All our sins and griefs to bear!
What a privilege to carry
　Every thing to God in prayer!
Oh, what peace we often forfeit,
　Oh, what needless pain we bear,—
All because we do not carry
　Every thing to God in prayer.

2 Have we trials and temptations?
　Is there trouble anywhere?
We should never be discouraged,
　Take it to the Lord in prayer.
Can we find a friend so faithful,
　Who will all our sorrows share?
Jesus knows our every weakness,—
　Take it to the Lord in prayer.

3 Are we weak and heavy laden,
　Cumbered with a load of care?
Precious Saviour, still our refuge,—
　Take it to the Lord in prayer.
Do our friends despise, forsake us?
　Take it to the Lord in prayer;
In his arms he'll take and shield us,
　We shall find a solace there.

PORTUGUESE HYMN. 11.   JOHN READING.

"Great and precious promise." 2 Pet. 1.   M. 11.

39 How firm a foundation, ye saints of the Lord,
Is laid for your faith in his excellent word!
What more can he say than to you he hath said,
Who unto the Saviour for refuge have fled :—

2 "Fear not, I am with thee, oh, be not dismayed ;
For I am thy God, I will still give thee aid ;
I'll strengthen thee, help thee, and cause thee to stand,
Upheld by my righteous, omnipotent hand.

3 "When through the deep waters I call thee to go,
The rivers of sorrow shall not overflow ;
For I will be with thee thy troubles to bless,
And sanctify to thee thy deepest distress.

4 "The soul that on Jesus hath leaned for repose
I will not, I will not, desert to his foes ;
That soul, though all hell should endeavor to shake,
I'll never—no never—no never forsake !"

Keith.

WELTON. L. M.   H. A. C. MALAN, 1830.

We walk by faith, not by sight. 2 Cor. 5: 7.   L. M.

40
"WE'VE no abiding city here "—
    This may distress the worldly mind;
But should not cost the saint a tear,
    Who hopes a better rest to find.

2 "We've no abiding city here "—
    Sad truth, were this to be our home;
But let this thought our spirits cheer,
    "We seek a city yet to come."

3 "We've no abiding city here "—
    Then let us live as pilgrims do;
Let not the world our rest appear,
    But let us haste from all below.

4 "We've no abiding city here "—
    We seek a city out of sight;
Zion its name—the Lord is there,
    It shines with everlasting light.

Believe on the Lord Jesus Christ, and thou shalt be saved. Acts 16: 31. L. M.

41
JESUS, the spring of joys divine,
    Whence all our hopes and comforts flow;
Jesus no other name but thine
Can save us from eternal woe.

2 Nor other name will heaven approve;
Thou art the true, the living Way,
Ordained by everlasting love,
To the bright realms of endless day.

3 Here let our constant feet abide,
   Nor from the heavenly path depart;
   O let thy Spirit, gracious Guide!
   Direct our steps and cheer our heart.

4 Safe lead us through this world of night,
   And bring us to the blissful plains,—
   The region of unclouded light,
   Where perfect joy forever reigns.

EFFIE. M. 4.

D. W. Click.
By per of A. S. Kieffer.

God is light, and in Him is no darkness. 1 John 1: 5.   M. 4.

42 God is love, his mercy brightens,
   All the path in which we move;
   Bliss he forms, and woe he lightens;
   God is light, and God is love.

2 Chance and change are busy ever;
   Worlds decay, and ages move;
   But his mercy waneth never;
   God is light, and God is love.

3 E'en the hour that darkest seemeth
   Will his changeless goodness prove;
   From the mist his brightness streameth;
   God is light, and God is love.

4 He with earthly cares entwineth.
   Hope and comfort from above;
   Every where his glory shineth ·
   God is light, and God is love.

CONSOLATION.

MERCY. M. 5.   By per. of O. Ditson & Co., owners of copyright.   GOTTSCHALK

Cast thy burden upon the Lord, and he shall sustain you. Ps. 55: 22.   M. 5.

43   CAST thy burden on the Lord;
Lean thou only on his word:
Ever will he be thy stay,
Though the heavens shall melt away.

2 Ever in the raging storm,
Thou shalt see his cheerful form,
Hear his pledge of coming aid:
"It is I, be not afraid."

3 Cast thy burden at his feet;
Linger near his mercy-seat:
He will lead thee by the hand
Gently to the better land.

4 He will gird thee by his power,
In thy weary, fainting hour:
Lean, then, loving, on his word;
Cast thy burden on the Lord.

Fear not little flock: for it is your Father's good pleasure to give you the Kingdom
Luke 12: 32.   M. 5.

44   FEAR not, brethren! joyful stand
On the borders of your land;
Jesus Christ, the Father's Son,
Bids you undismayed go on.

2 Lord! obediently we go,
Gladly leaving all below;
Only thou our Leader be,
And we still will follow thee.

3 For thee all things we forsake,
 We in better would partake;
 We to greater blessings soar,
 Unto joys for evermore.

SANDUSKY. S. M.   Jeremiah Ingalls.

God who is rich in mercy. Eph. 2: 4.   S. M.

45 And are we yet alive,
   And see each other's face?
 Glory and praise to Jesus give
   For his redeeming grace.

2 Preserved by power divine
   To full salvation here,
 Again in Jesus' praise we join
   And in his sight appear.

3 What troubles have we seen;
   What conflicts have we pass'd;
 Fightings without and fears within,
   Since we assembled last.

4 But out of all, the Lord
   Hath brought us by his love;
 And still he doth his help afford,
   And hides our life above.

5 Let us take up the cross
   Till we the crown obtain,
 And gladly reckon all things loss,
   So we may Jesus gain.

CONSOLATION.

ZION. M. 7. Thomas Hastings, 1830.

Comfort ye my people. Isa. 40: 1. M. 7.

46
On the mountain's top appearing,
   Lo! the sacred herald stands,
Welcome news to Zion bearing,
   Zion, long in hostile lands:
      Mourning captive!
   God himself shall loose thy bands.

2 Has thy night been long and mournful?
   Have thy friends unfaithful proved?
Have thy foes been proud and scornful,
   By thy sighs and tears unmoved?
      Cease thy mourning;
   Zion still is well beloved.

3 God, thy God, will now restore thee;
   He himself appears thy Friend;
All thy foes shall flee before thee;
   Here their boasts and triumphs end;
      Great deliverance
   Zion's King will surely send.

4 Enemies no more shall trouble,
   All thy wrongs shall be redress'd,
For thy shame thou shalt have double,
   In thy Maker's favor bless'd.
      All thy conflicts
   End in everlasting rest.

Thomas Kelly.

COME, YE DISCONSOLATE. M. 33.

Samuel Webbe, 1800.

To heal the broken-hearted. Luke 4: 18. M. 33.

47 Come, ye disconsolate, where'er ye languish;
   Come to the mercy seat, fervently kneel;
Here bring your wounded hearts, here tell your anguish;
   Earth has no sorrow that heav'n cannot heal.

2 Joy of the desolate, light of the straying,
   Hope of the penitent, fadeless and pure,
Here speaks the Comforter, tenderly saying,
   "Earth has no sorrow that heaven cannot cure."

3 Here see the bread of life; see waters flowing
   Forth from the throne of God, pure from above;
Come to the feast of love; come ever knowing
   Earth has no sorrow but heaven can remove.
       V. 1, 2, Thomas Moore, 1816; v. 3, Thomas Hastings, d. 1872.

Who shall separate us? Rom. 8: 35. M. 33.

48 Rock of my strength! to thee my soul is clinging,
   Assailed by doubt, beset by care and fear;
Smiling through tears, and in my sorrow singing,
   I hear thy welcome voice, "Be of good cheer."

2 What though my foes break out in bitter taunting,
   What tho' their curses crown my humbled head?
Yet, while their insults they at me are flaunting,
   Jesus stands near, and says, "Be not afraid."

3 Who shall divide me from that deep affection
   Felt by the loving Father for his own?
Who shall disturb me under his protection,
   Resting in God, and trusting him alone?

COMMUNION.

SOLON. C. M.

Ye show forth the Lord's death till he come. 1 Cor. 11: 26.   C. M.

49 THAT doleful night before his death,
　　The Lamb, for sinners slain,
Did, almost with his latest breath
　　This solemn feast ordain.

2 To keep the feast, Lord, we are met,
　　And to remember thee:
Help each poor trembler to repeat,
　　"The Saviour died for me."

3 Thy sufferings, Lord, each sacred sign
　　To our remembrance brings;
We eat the bread and drink the wine,
　　But think on nobler things.

4 O tune our tongues, and set in frame
　　Each heart that pants for thee,
To sing, "Hosanna to the Lamb,
　　The Lamb that died for me."

　　　　　　　　　　　　　Jas. Hart.

He is brought as a lamb to the slaughter. Is. 53: 7.   C. M.

50 HOW condescending and how kind
　　Was God's eternal Son!
Our misery reached his heavenly mind,
　　And pity brought him down.

2 When justice by our sins provoked,
　　Drew forth its dreadful sword,
He gave his soul up to the stroke,
　　Without a murm'ring word.

COMMUNION.   39

3 He sank beneath our heavy woes,
    To raise us to his throne;
There's ne'er a gift his hand bestows,
    But cost his heart a groan.

4 This was compassion like a God,
    That, when the Saviour knew
The price of pardon was his blood,
    His pity ne'er withdrew.

5 Here let our hearts begin to melt,
    While we his death record,
And with our joy for pardoned guilt,
    Mourn that we pierced the Lord.

For as often as ye eat this bread, and drink this cup, ye proclaim the Lord's death till he come. 1 Cor. 11: 26.   C. M.

51 As children dwelling in their home
        By right of grace divine,
Unto thy table, Lord, we come
    To take of bread and wine.

2 The bread shows forth thy body slain,
    The wine thy blood out-pour'd:
To take away our sin and stain
    Cost thy dear life, O Lord.

3 O may the Holy Ghost descend
    With blessings from above,
That grateful praise may now ascend
    For thine amazing love.

4 Abide with us this holy day,
    And fill us with thy peace,
And while we gladly praise and pray,
    Dear Lord, our faith increase.

5 Sit with us at the blessèd feast,
    As in the day of old,
Our high and sovereign Saviour-Priest,
    Thy glory to behold.

                                Thos. MacKellar.

ARLINGTON.   No. 7.

COMMUNION.

TURIN. M. 13. Pec. 7s & 6s.

Do this in remembrance of me. Luke 22: 19   M. 13. Pec.

52 LAMB of God! whose dying love
　　We now recall to mind,
Send the answer from above,
　　And let us mercy find;
Think on us who think on thee;
　　Every struggling soul release;
Oh, remember Calvary,
　　And bid us go in peace!

2 By thine agonizing pain
　　And bloody sweat, we pray;
By thy dying love to man,
　　Take all our sins away;
Break our bonds and set us free;
　　From iniquity release;
Oh, remember Calvary,
　　And bid us go in peace!

3 Let thy blood, by faith applied,
　　The sinner's pardon seal;
Speak us freely justified,
　　Our wounded spirits heal;
By thy passion on the tree,
　　Let our griefs and troubles cease;
Oh, remember Calvary,
　　And bid us go in peace!

　　　　　　　　　　　Charles Wesley

FEDERAL STREET L. M.
H. K. Oliver.

I have given you an example. John 13: 15.   L. M.

53
Christ in the night he was betrayed
For us a plain example laid;
He to a private room retired
With those he afterwards inspired.

2 The Paschal Feast was there prepared,
And Lord and servants mutual shared;
Before he suffered 'twas his will
This great desire he should fulfill.

3 He rose and laid his garments by,
When towel and water were brought nigh;
To prove his love divinely sweet,
He stooped to wash his servant's feet.

4 So after he had washed their feet,
Resumed his garment, took his seat,
He asked them if they now had thought
What lesson plain he here had taught.

5 "Ye call me Master and your Lord,
Which is according to my word;
If I have done this unto you,
Ye ought to serve each other too.

6 Example give I unto you,
As I have done so ye should do,
And if ye then my servants be,
Obey my word and follow me."

AZMON. C. M.   Arr. from GLÄSER.

Desiring an entire cleansing. John 13: 9.   C. M.

54 For ever here my rest shall be,
    Close to thy bleeding side;
This all my hope, and all my plea,
    For me the Saviour died.

2 My dying Saviour, and my God,
    Fountain for guilt and sin,
Sprinkle me ever with thy blood,
    And cleanse and keep me clean.

3 Wash me, and make me thus thine own;
    Wash me, and mine thou art:
Wash me, but not my feet alone,
    My hands, my head, my heart.

4 Th' atonement of thy blood apply,
    Till faith to sight improve;
Till hope in full fruition die,
    And all my soul be love.

I am the Bread of Life. John 6: 35.   C. M.

55 Let us adore the eternal Word,
    'Tis He our souls has fed;
Thou art our living stream, O Lord,
    And thou the immortal bread.

2 The manna came from lower skies,
    But Jesus from above,
Where the fresh springs of pleasure rise,
    And rivers flow with love.

3 The Jews, the fathers, died at last,
   Who ate that heavenly bread;
But these provisions which we taste
   Can raise us from the dead.

4 Bless'd be the Lord, that gives his flesh
   To nourish dying men;
And often spreads his table fresh,
   Lest we should faint again.

5 Our souls shall draw their heav'nly breath,
   While Jesus finds supplies;
Nor shall our graces sink to death,
   For Jesus never dies.

In remembrance of me. Luke 22: 19.   C. M.

56
IN memory of the Saviour's love,
   We keep the sacred feast,
Where every humble, contrite heart
   Is made a welcome guest.

2 Here let our ransom'd pow'rs unite
   His honor'd name to raise;
Let grateful joy fill ev'ry mind,
   And ev'ry voice be praise.

3 One fold, one faith, one hope, one Lord,
   One God alone we know;
Brethren we are; let ev'ry heart
   With kind affections glow.

4 By faith we take the bread of life,
   With which our souls are fed;
And cup, in token of His blood
   That was for sinners shed.

5 Under his banner thus we sing
   The wonders of his love,
And thus anticipate by faith
   The heavenly feast above.

      Thomas Cotterill, 1812.   Richard Whittingham, 1835.

DOWNS.   No. 21.

BALERMA. C. M.   Arr. from HUGH WILSON.

Christ died for our sins. 1 Cor. 15: 3.   C. M.

57
  ALAS! and did my Saviour bleed?
    And did my Sovereign die?
  Would he devote that sacred head
    For such a worm as I?

2 Was it for crimes that I had done
    He groaned upon the tree?
  Amazing pity! grace unknown!
    And love beyond degree!

3 Well might the sun in darkness hide,
    And shut his glories in,
  When Christ the glorious Saviour died
    For man the creature's sin.

4 Thus might I hide my blushing face,
    While his dear cross appears;
  Dissolve my heart in thankfulness,
    And melt mine eyes to tears.

5 But drops of grief can ne'er repay
    The debt of love I owe:
  Here, Lord, I give myself away:
    'Tis all that I can do.
                            Watts.

To-day thou shalt be with me in Paradise. Luke 23: 43.   C. M.

58
  AS on the cross the Saviour hung,
    And wept, and bled, and died,
  He poured salvation on a wretch,
    That languished at his side.

2 His crimes, with inward grief and shame,
    The penitent confessed;
Then turned his dying eyes to Christ,
    And thus his prayer addressed:

3 "Jesus, thou Son and Heir of Heaven,
    Thou spotless Lamb of God,
I see thee bathed in sweat and tears,
    And weltering in thy blood.

4 Yet quickly from these scenes of woe,
    In triumph thou shalt rise,
Burst thro' the gloomy shades of death,
    And shine above the skies.

5 "Amid the glories of thy home
    May I a sharer be?
When thou dost in thy kingdom come,
    O Lord, remember me."

6 "Truly to-day, I say to thee,"
    The suffering Lord replies,
"Thou shalt in peace and glory be
    With me in paradise."
                      Samuel Stennett, 1727-1795.

Father, into thy hands I commend my spirit. Luke 23: 46   C. M.

59 Behold the Saviour of mankind
    Nailed to the shameful tree;
How great the love that him inclined
    To bleed and die for thee!

2 Hark! how he groans while nature shakes,
    And earth's strong pillars bend;
The temple's vail in sunder breaks,
    The solid marbles rend.

3 'Tis done! the precious ransom's paid!
    "Receive my soul!" he cries:
See where he bows his sacred head!
    He bows his head, and dies.

4 But soon he'll break death's envious chain,
    And in full glory shine,
O Lamb of God, was ever pain,
    Was ever love, like thine!

CRUCIFIXION.

SAW YE MY SAVIOUR. 10, 7, 7, 7, 9.

And they crucified him. Matt. 27 : 35.

60
Saw ye my Saviour? saw ye my Saviour?
Saw ye my Saviour and God?
Oh, he died on Calvary,
To atone for you and me,
And to purchase our pardon with blood.

2 He was extended, he was extended,
Painfully nailed to the cross;
There he bowed his head and died,
There my Lord was crucified,
To atone for a world that was lost.

3 Jesus hung bleeding, Jesus hung bleeding
Three dreadful hours in pain;
And the solid rocks were rent,
Through creation's vast extent,
When the Jews crucified the Lamb.

4 Darkness prevailed, darkness prevailed,
Darkness prevailed o'er the land,
And the sun refused to shine
When his Majesty divine
Was derided, insulted, and slain.

GETHSEMANE. M. 5.

C. H. Brunk.

Then sayeth he unto them, my soul is exceeding sorrowful even unto death.
Matt. 26: 38. M. 5

61
O THE agonizing prayer
  Rising on the midnight air!
"Let this cup pass from thy Son:
Not my will, but thine be done!"
    Jesus in Gethsemane!

2 O the tears and bloody sweat
  Falling fast on Olivet!
In thy lonely agony,
Shedding crimson tears for me,
    Jesus in Gethsemane!

3 O what wrath of earth and hell
  On thy head unpitying fell,
When thy passion-time began,
Bearer of the sin of man,
    Jesus in Gethsemane!

4 Sorrow none had ever known
  Came upon thy soul alone;
While its billows o'er thee swept,
Near at hand thy followers slept,
    Jesus in Gethsemane!

5 Waken me from sinful sleep:
  Faithful, loving, make me keep,
Watching every hour with thee
Who didst agonize for me,
    Jesus in Gethsemane!

Thos MacKellar.

CRUCIFIXION.

MISSIONARY CHANT. L. M. CHARLES ZEUNER, 1832.

And being in an agony he prayed more earnestly. Luke 22: 44. L. M.

62 'Tis midnight; and on Olive's brow
The star is dimmed that lately shone;
'Tis midnight; in the garden now
The suffering Saviour prays alone.

2 'Tis midnight; and, from all removed,
The Saviour wrestles lone with fears;
E'en that disciple whom he loved
Heeds not his Master's grief and tears.

3 'Tis midnight; and, for other's guilt,
The Man of Sorrows weeps in blood;
Yet he, who hath in anguish knelt,
Is not forsaken by his God.

4 'Tis midnight; and from ether-plains
Is borne the song that angels know;
Unheard by mortals are the strains
That sweetly soothe the Saviour's woe.

William Bingham Tappan, 1829.

God forbid that I should glory. Save in the cross of the Lord Jesus Christ
Gal. 6: 14. L. M.

63 When I survey the wondrous cross,
On which the prince of glory died,
My richest gain I count but loss,
And pour contempt on all my pride.

2 Forbid it, Lord that I should boast,
Save in the death of Christ, my God;
All the vain things that charm me most,
I sacrifice them to his blood.

3 See, from his head, his hands, his feet,
    Sorrow and love flow mingled down;
Did e'er such love and sorrow meet,
    Or thorns compose so rich a crown?

4 His dying crimson, like a robe,
    Spreads o'er his body on the tree;
Then am I dead to all the globe,
    And all the globe is dead to me.

5 Were the whole realm of nature mine,
    That were a present far too small;
Love so amazing, so divine,
    Demands my soul, my life, my all.

Who gave himself a ransom for all.   *1 Tim. 2: 6.*   L. M.

64   JESUS, be endless praise to thee,
    Whose boundless mercy hath for me—
For me and all thy hands have made,
An everlasting ransom paid.

2 The holy, meek, unspotted Lamb,
Who from the Father's bosom came,
Who died for me, even me to atone,
Now for my Lord and Master own.

3 Lord, I believe the precious blood
Which at the mercy seat of God
Forever doth for sinners plead,
For me, even for my soul was shed.

4 Ah, give me now, all-gracious Lord,
With power to speak thy quickening word;
That all who to thy words will flee
May find eternal life in thee.

5 Then shall heaven's hosts with loud acclaim
Give praise and glory to the Lamb
Who bore our sins, and by his blood
Hath made us kings and priests to God.
    N. L. Zinzendorf. ab. 1739.   Tr. J. Wesley, 1740, ab.

HEBRON.   No. 95.

DEATH.

MORN. S. M.
Slow.
H. S. RUPP.

Suffer little children, and forbid them not, to come unto me. Matt. 10: 14.

S. M.
65 Go to thy rest, fair child!
　　Go to thy dreamless bed,
While yet so gentle, undefil'd,
　　With blessings on thy head.

2 Before thy heart had learn'd
　　In waywardness to stray;
Before thy feet had ever turn'd
　　The dark and downward way;

3 Ere sin had sear'd the breast,
　　Or sorrow woke the tear;
Rise to thy throne of changeless rest,
　　In yon celestial sphere!

4 Because thy smile was fair,
　　Thy lip and eye so bright,
Because thy loving cradle-care
　　Was such a dear delight;

5 Shall love, with weak embrace,
　　Thy upward wing detain?
No! gentle angel, seek thy place
　　Amid the cherub train.

S. M.
66 Lord, what a feeble piece,
　　Is this our mortal frame!
Our life! How poor a trifle 'tis,
　　That scarce deserves the name!

DEATH. 51

2 Alas, this brittle clay
   That built our bodies first!
And every month, and every day,
   'Tis mould'ring back to dust.

3 Our moments fly apace,
   Our feeble powers decay;
Swift as a flood our hasty days
   Are sweeping us away.

4 Yet if our days must fly,
   We'll keep their end in sight,
We'll spend them all in wisdom's ways,
   And let them speed their flight.

5 They'll waft us sooner o'er
   This life's tempestuous sea;
Soon we shall reach the peaceful shore
   Of bless'd eternity.
                                   Watts.

Who shall change our vile body. Phil. 3: 21.   S. M.

67 AND must this body die?
   This mortal frame decay?
And must these active limbs of mine
   Lie mold'ring in the clay?

2 Corruption, earth, and worms,
   Shall but refine this flesh,
Till my triumphant spirit comes
   To put it on afresh.

3 God, my Redeemer, lives,
   And often from the skies,
Looks down and watches all my dust,
   Till he shall bid it rise.

4 Array'd in glorious grace
   Shall these vile bodies shine,
And ev'ry form and ev'ry face
   Look heav'nly and divine.

5 These lively hopes we owe
   To Jesus' dying love;
We would adore his grace below,
   And sing his power above.
                                   Watts.

DEATH.

HATTIE. L. M. H. S. RUPP.

Death of a mother. L. M.

68 THE bosom where I oft have lain,
And slept my infant hours away,
Will never beat for me again,
'Tis still in death! 'tis senseless clay.

2 How many were the silent prayers
My mother offered up for me,
How many were the bitter cares
She felt when none but God could see.

3 Well, she is gone, and now in heaven,
She sings his praise, who died for her,
And in her hand a harp is given,
And she's a heavenly worshiper.

4 Oft let me think of what she said,
And of the kind advice she gave;
O let me do it, as she's dead,
And sleeping in her lowly grave.

5 And let me choose the path she chose,
And her I soon again may see,
Beyond this world of sin and woes
With Jesus in Eternity.

The widow's God. L. M.

69 IN this lone hour of deep distress,
When heavy sorrows round me press,
Encourag'd by thy gracious word,
I trust thee as the widow's God.

2 A husband lies in death's embrace,
  The grave is now his resting-place;
  O, as I pass beneath thy rod,
  Reveal thyself the widow's God.

3 Assuage my grief, remove my fears,
  Suppress my murm'ring, dry my tears,
  Help me to own thee as my Lord,
  And bless thee as the widow's God.

4 Be thou my counsellor and stay,
  Protect by night, and guide by day;
  Then, as I travel life's rough road,
  I'll praise thee as the widow's God.

The flower fadeth. Is. 40: 7.   L. M.

70 So fades the lovely, blooming flow'r,
  Frail, smiling solace of an hour;
  So soon our transient comforts fly,
  And pleasure only blooms to die.

2 Is there no kind, no healing art,
  To soothe the anguish of the heart?
  Divine Redeemer, be thou nigh:
  Thy comforts were not made to die.

3 Then gentle patience smiles on pain,
  And dying hope revives again;
  Hope wipes the tear from sorrow's eye,
  And faith points upward to the sky.

My heart is sore pained within me: and the terrors of death are fallen upon me.
                            Ps. 55: 4.   L. M.

71 Why should we start and fear to die?
  What tim'rous worms we mortals are,
  Death is the gate to endless joy,
  And yet we dread to enter there.

2 The pains, the groans, and dying strife
  Fright our approaching souls away;
  Still we shrink back again to life,
  Fond of our prison and our clay.

3 Oh! if my Lord would come and meet,
  My soul should stretch her wings in haste,
  Fly fearless through death's iron gate,
  Nor feel the terrors as they pass'd.

REST. L. M.   W. B. BRADBURY, 1843.

Them also which sleep in Jesus will God bring with him. 1 Thess 4: 14.
L. M.

72 ASLEEP in Jesus! blesséd sleep!
From which none ever wake to weep;
A calm and undisturbed repose,
Unbroken by the last of foes.

2 Asleep in Jesus! oh, how sweet
To be for such a slumber meet!
With holy confidence to sing
That death has lost its venomed sting.

3 Asleep in Jesus! peaceful rest!
Whose waking is supremely blest;
No fear, no woe shall dim that hour
Which manifests the Saviour's power.

4 Asleep in Jesus! oh, for me
May such a blissful refuge be!
Securely shall my ashes lie,
And wait the summons from on high.
Mrs. Mackay.

"*Which die in the Lord. Rev. 14: 13.*   L. M.

73 HOW blest the righteous when he dies!
When sinks a weary soul to rest,
How mildly beam the closing eyes,
How gently heaves th' expiring breast.

2 So fades a summer cloud away;
So sinks the gale when storms are o'er;
So gently shuts the eye of day;
So dies a wave along the shore.

DEATH.

3 A holy quiet reigns around,—
 A calm which life nor death destroys;
And naught disturbs that peace profound
 Which his unfettered soul enjoys.

4 Life's labor done, as sinks the clay,
 Light from its load the spirit flies;
While heaven and earth combine to say,
 "How blest the righteous when he dies."
    Mrs. Barbauld.

DUBLIN. C. M.

Blessed is every one that feareth the Lord. Ps. 128: 1.   C. M.

74 WHY do we mourn departing friends,
  Or shake at death's alarms?
'Tis but the voice that Jesus sends,
 To call them to his arms.

2 Are we not tending upward too,
 As fast as time can move?
Nor should we wish the hours more slow,
 To keep us from our love.

3 The graves of all his saints he blest,
 And softened every bed;
Where should the dying members rest,
 But with their dying Head?

4 Then let the last loud trumpet sound,
 And bid our kindred rise;
Awake, ye nations under ground,
 Ye saints ascend the skies.
    Isaac Watts.

56　　　　　　　　　DEATH.

MEAR. C. M.　　　　　　　　　　　　　A. WILLIAMS.

A funeral thought.　　　　　　　　　C. M.

75 Hark! from the tomb a doleful sound;
My ears attend the cry:
"Ye living men, come view the ground,
Where you must shortly lie."

2 "Princes, this clay must be your bed,
In spite of all your tow'rs!
The tall, the wise, the rev'rend head
Must lie as low as ours."

3 Great God! is this our certain doom?
And are we still secure?
Still walking downward to our tomb,
And yet prepare no more?

4 Grant us the pow'r of quick'ning grace,
To fit our souls to fly;
Then when we drop this dying flesh,
We'll rise above the sky.

Lo, children are a heritage of the Lord. Ps. 127: 3.　　C. M.

76 Thy life I read, my dearest Lord,
With transport all divine;
Thine image trace in every word,—
Thy love in every line.

2 Methinks I see a thousand charms
Spread o'er thy lovely face,
While infants in thy tender arms,
Receive the smiling grace.

DEATH.

3 "I take these little Lambs," said he,
   And lay them in my breast;
Protection they shall find in me,
   In me be ever blest.

4 "Death may the bands of life unloose,
   But can't dissolve my love;
Millions of infant souls compose
   The family above.

Hope in prospect of eternity. C. M.

77 AND let this feeble body fail,
      And let it droop or die;
   My soul shall quit this mournful vale,
      And soar to worlds on high.

2 Shall join the disembodied saints,
      And find its long-sought rest,
   That only bliss for which it pants,
      In the Redeemer's breast.

3 In hope of that immortal crown,
      I now the cross sustain,
   And gladly wander up and down,
      And smile at toil and pain.

4 I suffer on my threescore years,
      Till my Deliv'rer come,
   And wipe away his servant's tears,
      And take his exile home.

5 O, what hath Jesus bought for me!
      Before my raptur'd eyes
   Rivers of life divine I see,
      And trees of paradise!

6 I see a world of spirits bright,
      Who taste the pleasures there;
   They all are rob'd in spotless white,
      And conquering palms they bear.

BALERMA. C. M.   No. 57.

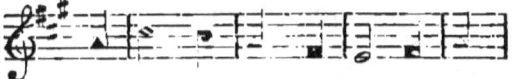

DEATH.

MOUNT VERNON. M. 4. L. MASON.

Sister, thou wast mild and lovely. M. 4.

78 SISTER, thou wast mild and lovely,
  Gentle as the summer breeze,
Pleasant as the air of ev'ning,
  When it floats among the trees.

2 Peaceful be thy silent slumber—
  Peaceful in the grave so low:
Thou no more wilt join our number;
  Thou no more our songs shalt know.

3 Dearest sister, thou hast left us;
  Here thy loss we deeply feel;
But 'tis God that hath bereft us:
  He can all our sorrows heal.

4 Yet again we hope to meet thee,
  When the day of life is fled,
Then in heaven with joy to greet thee,
  Where no farewell tear is shed.

Blessed be the name of the Lord. Job 1 : 21. M. 4.

79 JESUS, while our hearts are bleeding
  O'er the spoils that death has won,
We would, at this solemn meeting,
  Calmly say, "Thy will be done."

2 Tho' cast down, we're not forsaken;
  Though afflicted, not alone:
Thou didst give, and thou hast taken;
  Blessèd Lord, "Thy will be done."

DEATH.

3 Tho' to-day we're filled with mourning,
   Mercy still is on the throne;
   With thy smiles of love returning,
   We can sing, "Thy will be done."

4 By thy hands the boon was given;
   Thou hast taken but thine own:
   Lord of earth, and God of heaven,
   Evermore, "Thy will be done."
                          Thomas Hastings, 1850.

BROTHER, SWEETLY REST. M. 4.   G. R. STREET.

Blessed Jesus give as-surance,
We are weeping, sadly weeping, For this loss is hard to bear;
That thy glo-ry we may share.

Death of a brother.   M. 4.

80 BROTHER, thou hast left us lonely,
        Sorrow fills our hearts to-day;
     But beyond this vale of sorrow
        Tears will all be wiped away.

2 Brother, thou art sweetly resting,
    Cold may be this earthly tomb;
  But the angels sweetly whispered,
    Come and live with us at home.

3 Brother, thou art sweetly resting
    On the lovely Saviour's breast,
  Where the wicked cease from troubling,
    And the weary are at rest.

4 Brother, thou art sweetly resting,
    Here thy toils and cares are o'er;
  Pain and sickness death and sorrow,
    Never can distress thee more.

DEATH.

AVON. C. M.   HUGH WILSON.

Death of a youth.   C. M.

81 WHEN blooming youth is snatch'd away
    By death's resistless hand,
Our hearts the mournful tribute pay,
    Which pity must demand.

2 While pity prompts the rising sigh,
    O may this truth, imprest
With awful pow'r—I too must die—
    Sink deep in ev'ry breast.

3 Let this vain world engage no more;
    Behold the gaping tomb!
It bids us seize the present hour,
    To-morrow death may come.

4 The voice of this alarming scene,
    May ev'ry heart obey;
Nor be the heav'nly warning vain,
    Which calls to watch and pray.

And the truth shall make you free.   *John 8: 32.*   C. M.

82 FAR from affliction, toil and care,
    The happy soul is fled;
The breathless clay shall slumber here,
    Among the silent dead.

2 The Gospel was his joy and song,
    E'en to his latest breath;
The truth he had proclaimed so long
    Was his support in death.

3 Now he resides where Jesus is,
　　Above this dusky sphere;
　His soul was ripen'd for that bliss,
　　While yet he sojourn'd here.

4 The Church's loss we all deplore,
　　And shed the falling tear;
　Since we shall see his face no more,
　　Till Jesus shall appear.

5 But we are hast'ning to the tomb;
　　Oh, may we ready stand;
　Then, dearest Lord, receive us home,
　　To dwell at thy right hand.

Jesus in whom you have redemption through his blood. Eph. 1: 7. C. M.

83 How happy are these little ones
　　　Which Jesus Christ has blest;
　Come, let us praise him with our songs,
　　For taking them to rest.

2 Yes, happy are these little lambs—
　　Of such the kingdom is;
　The Lord our praise and thanks demands,
　　Who made them heirs of bliss.

3 With his own blood he made them free
　　From sin and every stain;
　For them he suffered on the tree—
　　Yes, for them he was slain.

4 He takes them home, where pain and woe
　　Will ne'er disturb them more;
　Oh let us all prepare to go,
　　And with them Christ adore.

5 However painful it may be,
　　To know that they are gone,
　The thought is sweet that we may see
　　Them in that heavenly home.

SOLON.　　　　　　　　　　　　No. 49.

DEATH.

DUNDEE. C. M.   GUILLAUME FRANCK.

Ye are not your own. *1 Cor. 6: 19.*   C. M.

84   WHY should our tears in sorrow flow,
      When God recalls his own,
  And bids them leave a world of woe
      For an immortal crown?

2 Is not e'en death a gain to those
     Whose life to God was giv'n?
  Gladly to earth their eyes they close,
     To open them in heav'n.

3 Their toils are past, their work is done,
     And they are fully blest:
  They fought the fight, the vict'ry won,
     And enter'd into rest.

4 Then let our sorrows cease to flow—
     God has recall'd his own;
  And let our hearts, in every woe,
     Still say—"Thy will be done!"

Which hope we have as an anchor of the soul, both sure and steadfast.
                                     Heb. 6: 19.   C. M.

85   FOND parents, calm the heaving breast,
      The Saviour called him home;
  Grieve not, your darling is at rest
      Beyond this vale of gloom.

2 Let hope's bright beams dispel the **gloom**,
     That fills your throbbing breast;
  'Twas Jesus kindly bade him **come**,
     And called him to his rest.

DEATH.   63

Lord, make me to know mine end.   Psalm 39: 4.   C. M.

86 TEACH me the measure of my days,
         Thou Maker of my frame;
      I would survey life's narrow space,
         And learn how frail I am.

2 A span is all that we can boast;
      How short the fleeting time!
   Man is but vanity and dust,
      In all his flower and prime.

3 What should I wish, or wait for, then,
      From creatures—earth and dust?
   They make our expectations vain,
      And disappoint our trust.

4 Now I forbid my carnal hope,
      My fond desire recall;
   I give my mortal interest up,
      And make my God my all.
                          Isaac Watts.

Your fathers, where are they?   Zech 1: 5.   C. M.

87. WHAT though the arm of conquering death
            Does God's own house invade;
         What though the prophet and the priest
            In the dark grave are laid.

2 The eternal Shepherd still survives,
      New comfort to impart:
   His eye still guides us, and his voice
      Still animates the heart.

3 "Lo, I am with you," saith the Lord,
      "My Church shall safe abide;
   For I will ne'er forsake my own,
      Whose souls in me confide."

4 Through every scene of life and death
      This promise is our trust;
   And this shall be our children's song,
      When we are cold in dust.
                  Philip Doddridge, 1755.

ARLINGTON.   No. 7.

DEATH.

JUNIATA. L. M.

It is sown in weakness. 1 Cor. 15: 43.   L. M.

88
  Soft be the turf on thy dear breast,
  And heavenly calm thy lone retreat;
  How longed the weary frame for rest!
  That rest is come, and, oh, how sweet!

2 Why should we ever shrink from death?
  'Tis but to cast our robes away,
  And sleep at night without a breath
  To break repose, till dawn of day.

3 'Tis not a night without a morn,
  Though glooms impregnable surround;
  Nor lies the buried saint forlorn,
  A hopeless prisoner in the ground.

4 The darkest night to day gives birth,
  And sunshine comes when storms are fled;
  The seed, though buried in the earth,
  Springs from its grave as from its bed.

5 So shall the bodies of the just,
  In weakness sown, be raised in power;
  The precious seed shall leave the dust,
  A glorious and immortal flower.

Comfort one another with these words. 1 Thess. 4: 18.   L. M.

89
  There is a glorious world on high,
  Resplendent with eternal day;
  Faith views the blissful prospects nigh,
  While God's own word reveals the way.

DEATH.

2 How blest are those, how truly wise,
   Who learn and keep the sacred road!
Happy the men whom heaven employs
   To turn rebellious hearts to God!

3 The shining firmament shall fade,
   And sparkling stars resign their light;
But these shall know no change nor shade,
   For ever fair, for ever bright.

4 On wings of faith, and strong desire,
   Oh, may our spirits daily rise;
And reach at last the shining choir,
   In the bright mansions of the skies!

Mag auch die Liebe weinen. L. M.

90 Though love may weep with breaking heart,
   There comes, O Christ, a day of thine!
There is a Morning Star must shine,
   And all these shadows shall depart.

2 Though faith may droop and tremble here,
   That day of light shall surely come;
The shadowy path leads safely home;
   When twilight breaks, the dawn is near.

3 Though hope seem now to hope in vain,
   And death seem king of all below,
There yet shall come the morning glow,
   And wake our slumberers once again.
       Fred. Adolphus Krummacher, 1805. Tr. C. Winkworth, 1858.

Come ye blessed of my Father inherit the kingdom. Matt. 25: 34. L. M.

91 The time is short ere all that live
   Shall hence be called their God to meet,
And each a strict account must give,
   At Jesus' awful judgment seat.

2 The time is short: sinner, beware!
   Nor squander these brief hours away;
Oh, flee to Christ by faith and prayer,
   Ere yet shall close this fleeting day.

3 The time is short; ye saints, rejoice
   Your Saviour-Judge will quickly come;
Soon shall you hear the Bridegroom's voice
   Invite you to His heavenly home.
                    Joseph Hoskins, ab, 1789.

EVENING HYMN. M. 4.

J. H. Hall, by per.

Not too fast.

If God be for us, who can be against us. Rom. 8: 31.   M. 4.

92 Saviour, breathe an evening blessing,
　　Ere repose our spirits seal;
　Sin and want we come confessing;
　　Thou canst save and thou canst heal.
　Though destruction walk around us,
　　Though the arrows past us fly,
　Angel guards from thee surround us;
　　We are safe if thou art nigh.

2 Though the night be dark and dreary,
　　Darkness can not hide from thee;
　Thou art He, who, never weary,
　　Watchest where thy people be.

Should swift death this night o'ertake us,
  And command us to the tomb,
May the morn in heaven awake us,
  Clad in bright, eternal bloom.

VESPER. S. M.   JEREMIAH INGALLS, 1804.

Thou Lord makest me dwell in safety. Ps. 4: 8.   S. M.

93
  THE day is past and gone:
    The evening shades appear;
  Oh, may we all remember well
    The night of death draws near.

2 Lord, keep us safe this night,
  Secure from all our fears;
May angels guard us while we sleep,
  Till morning light appears.

3 And when our days are past,
  And we from time remove,
O may we in thy bosom rest,
  The bosom of thy love.
                John Leland, 1792.

The evening sacrifice. Psalm 141. 2.   S. M.

94
  THE day is past and gone:
    Great God, we bow to thee;
  Again, as shades of night steal on,
    Unto thy side we flee.

2 We are, preserved beneath
  The shelter of thy wing,
Forevermore thy praise shall breathe,
  And of thy mercy sing!
           Latin. Tr. William John Blew, 1849.

HEBRON. L. M.   L. MASON, 1830.

I will lay me down in peace, and sleep. Psalm 4: 8.   L. M.

95 Thus far the Lord has led me on;
Thus far his power prolongs my days;
And every evening shall make known
Some fresh memorial of his grace.

2 Much of my time has run to waste,
And I, perhaps, am near my home;
But he forgives my follies past:
He gives me strength for days to come.

3 I lay my body down to sleep;
Peace is the pillow for my head;
While well-appointed angels keep
Their watchful stations round my bed.

4 Faith in thy name forbids my fear;
Oh, may thy presence ne'er depart!
And in the morning make me hear
The love and kindness of thy heart.
                                    Watts.

Thou wilt keep him in perfect peace. Is. 26: 3.   L. M.

96 Glory to thee, my God, this night,
For all the blessings of the light;
Keep me, O keep me, King of kings,
Beneath the shadow of thy wings.

2 Forgive me, Lord, for thy dear Son,
The ill that I this day have done,
That with the world, myself and thee,
I, ere I sleep, at peace may be.

3 Teach me to live, that I may dread
　The grave as little as my bed;
　Teach me to die, so that I may
　Triumphant rise at the last day.

4 O let my soul on thee repose,
　And may sweet sleep mine eye-lids close:
　Sleep that shall me more vig'rous make,
　To serve my God when I awake.
　　　　　　　　　　　　　Kenn.

ENON. M. 55.　　　　　　Rev. E. S. WIDDEMAN.

Abide with us. Luke 24: 29.　　　M. 55.

97 ABIDE with me! fast falls the even tide,
　　The darkness deepens— Lord, with me abide!
　When other helpers fail, and comforts flee,
　Help of the helpless, oh, abide with me!

2 Swift to its close ebbs out life's little day;
　Earth's joys grow dim, its glories pass away;
　Change and decay in all around I see;
　O thou who changest not, abide with me!

3 I need thy presence every passing hour,
　What but thy grace can foil the tempter's power?
　Who, like thyself, my guide and stay can be?
　Through cloud and sunshine, oh, abide with me!

4 Hold thou thy cross before my closing eyes;
　Shine through the gloom, and point me to the skies;
　Heaven's morning breaks, and earth's vain shadows
　In life, in death, O Lord, abide with me!　　[flee!
　　　　　　　　　　　　　　　　　　　　Lyte.

EVAN. C. M.   Arr. by W. H. HAVERGAL.

With my soul have I desired thee in the night.   Is. 26: 9.   C. M.

98 IN mercy, Lord, remember me
    Through all the hours of night,
And grant to me most graciously
    The safeguard of thy might.

2 With cheerful heart I close my eyes,
    Since thou wilt not remove:
Oh, in the morning let me rise
    Rejoicing in thy love.

3 Or if this night should prove the last,
    And end my transient days,
Then take me to thy promised rest,
    Where I may sing thy praise.

So that I might finish my course with joy.   Acts 20: 24.   C. M.

99 INDULGENT Father, by whose care,
    I've passed another day,
Let me this night thy mercy share,
    And teach me how to pray.

2 Show me my sins, and how to mourn
    My guilt before thy face;
Direct me, Lord, to Christ alone,
    And save me by thy grace.

3 Let each returning night declare
    The tokens of thy love;
And every hour thy grace prepare
    My soul for joys above.

Yea, thou shalt lie down, and thy sleep shall be sweet. Prov. 3: 24. C. M.

100 Upon the pillow of thy love
 My weary head I lay,
Assured that watchers from above
 Will round about me stay.

2 The weanéd child, subdued and still,
 Sleeps on its mother's breast;
So I, submissive to thy will,
 Lean on thy strength for rest.

3 The sighs, and tears, and agony
 That marr'd the hours of day,
Subside as tempests on the sea
 In silence die away.

4 The restful peace of answer'd prayer
 Is in my chasten'd heart:
My fears, my sorrows, and my care
 At thy command depart.
     Thos. MacKellar.

To meditate in the field at eventide. Gen. 24: 63. C. M.

101 I love to steal awhile away
 From every cumbering care,
And spend the hour of setting day
 In humble, grateful prayer.

2 I love in solitude to shed
 The penitential tear,
And all his promises to plead,
 Where none but God can hear.

3 I love to think on mercies past,
 And future good implore,
And all my cares and sorrows cast
 On Him whom I adore.

4 I love by faith to take a view
 Of brighter scenes in heaven;
The prospect doth my strength renew
 While here by tempests driven.

5 Thus, when life's toilsome day is o'er,
 May its departing ray
Be calm as this impressive hour;
 And lead to endless day.
     Phœbe Hinsdale Brown.

EVE. M. 5.   By per. of O. Ditson & Co.
                                          Owners of Copyright.

The peace of God. Phil. 4: 7.   M. 5.

102 SOFTLY fades the twilight ray
          Of the holy Sabbath day:
    Gently as life's setting sun,
    When the Christian's course is run.

  2 Peace is on the world abroad;
    'Tis the holy peace of God,
    Symbol of the peace within,
    When the spirit rests from sin.

  3 Still the Spirit lingers near
    Where the evening worshiper
    Seeks communion with the skies,
    Pressing onward to the prize.

  4 Saviour, may our Sabbaths be
    Days of peace and joy in thee!
    Till in heaven our souls repose,
    Where the Sabbath ne'er shall close.
                                                S. F. Smith.

             The night cometh.   M. 5.

103 SOFTLY now the light of day
          Fades upon my sight away:
    Free from care, from labor free,
    Lord! I would commune with thee.

  2 Soon for me the light of day
    Shall forever pass away;
    Then, from sin and sorrow free,
    Take, me, Lord! to dwell with thee.
                                                Doane.

HEAVEN.

DOTHAN. 6s, & 4s. By Com.

"Strangers and pilgrims." Heb. 11: 13.   6s, & 4s.

104 I'M but a stranger here,
　　Heaven is my home;
　Earth is a desert drear,
　　Heaven is my home:
　Danger and sorrow stand
　Round me on every hand;
　Heaven is my fatherland—
　　Heaven is my home.

2 There, at my Saviour's side,
　　Heaven is my home;
　I shall be glorified—
　　Heaven is my home:
　There are the good and blest,
　Those I loved most and best,
　And there I, too, shall rest;—
　　Heaven is my home.
　　　　　　　　T R. Taylor.

HEAVEN.

VARINA. C. M. D.   RINK.

There remaineth therefore a rest. Heb. 4: 9.   C. M.

105 O LAND of rest, for thee I sigh!
    When will the moment come,
When I shall lay my armor by,
    And dwell with Christ at home?
No tranquil joys on earth I know,
    No peaceful, sheltering dome;
This world's a wilderness of woe,
    This world is not my home.

2 When by afflictions sharply tried,
    I view the gaping tomb;
Although I dread death's chilling flood,
    Yet still I sigh for home.
Weary of wandering round and round
    This vale of sin and gloom,
I long to leave th'unhallowed ground,
    And dwell with Christ at home.
                     Elizabeth Mills, 1805-1829.

Seek those things which are above. Col. 3: 1.   C. M.

106 THERE is a land of pure delight,
    Where saints immortal reign;
Infinite day excludes the night,
    And pleasures banish pain:

There everlasting spring abides,
  And never-withering flowers;
Death, like a narrow sea, divides
  This heavenly land from ours.

2 Sweet fields beyond the swelling flood,
    Stand dressed in living green;
  So to the Jews old Canaan stood,
    While Jordan rolled between;
  But tim'rous mortals start and shrink
    To cross the narrow sea,
  And linger shiv'ring on the brink,
    And fear to launch away.

3 Oh, could we make our doubts remove,
    Those gloomy doubts that rise,
  And see the Canaan that we love,
    With unbeclouded eyes!
  Could we but climb where Moses stood,
    And view the landscape o'er,
  Not Jordan's stream, nor death's cold flood,
    Should fright us from the shore.
                              Low.

Fear the Lord, serve him in sincerity. Josh. 24: 14.   C. M.

107 Come, let us now forget our mirth,
    And think that we must die:
  What are our best delights on earth,
    Compared with those on high?
  Our pleasures here will soon be past,
    Our brightest joys decay:
  But pleasures there forever last,
    And cannot fade away.

2 Here sins and sorrows we deplore,
    With many cares distressed;
  But there the mourners weep no more,
    And there the weary rest.
  Then let us love and serve the Lord,
    With all our youthful powers,
  And we shall gain the great reward,
    The glory shall be ours.

HEAVEN.

HEBER. C. M.   Geo. Kingsley.

My soul shall be joyful in the Lord. Ps. 35: 9.   C. M.

108 From thee, my God, my joys shall rise,
    And run eternal rounds,
Beyond the limits of the skies,
    And all created bounds.

2 The holy triumph of my soul
    Shall death itself outbrave;
Leave dull mortality behind,
    And fly beyond the grave.

3 There, where my blessèd Jesus reigns,
    In heaven's unmeasured space,
I'll spend a long eternity
    In pleasure and in praise.

4 Millions of years my wond'ring eyes
    Shall o'er thy beauties rove,
And endless ages I'll adore
    The glories of thy love.

5 Sweet Jesus! every smile of thine
    Shall fresh endearments bring;
Ten thousand tastes of new delight
    From all thy graces spring.

There is a house not made with hands, eternal in the heavens. 2 Cor 5: 1.
                                                                                     C. M.

109 There is a house not made with hands,
    Eternal, and on high;
And here my spirit waiting stands
    Till God shall bid it fly.

HEAVEN. 77

2 Shortly this prison of my clay
   Must be dissolved and fall;
Then, O my soul, with joy obey
   Thy heavenly father's call.

3 'Tis he, by his Almighty grace,
   That forms thee fit for heaven;
And as an earnest of the place,
   Has his own Spirit given.

4 We walk by faith of joys to come;
   Faith lives upon his word;
But while the body is our home,
   We're absent from the Lord.

Prospect of heaven.   C. M.

110 On Jordan's stormy banks I stand,
   And cast a wishful eye
To Canaan's fair and happy land,
   Where my possessions lie.

2 Oh the transporting, rapt'rous scene,
   That rises to my sight!
Sweet fields array'd in living green,
   And rivers of delight.

3 There gen'rous fruits that never fail,
   On trees immortal grow:
There rocks and hills, and brooks and vales
   With milk and honey flow.

4 All o'er those wide extended plains
   Shines one eternal day;
There God the Sun for ever reigns,
   And scatters night away.

5 No chilling winds, nor pois'nous breath
   Can reach that healthful shore;
Sickness and sorrow, pain and death
   Are felt and fear'd no more.

6 When shall I reach that happy place,
   And be for ever blest?
When shall I see my Father's face,
   And in his bosom rest?

                                    Stennett.

HEAVEN.

DUNBAR. S. M.   E. W. Dunbar.

The ransomed of the Lord shall come to Zion with songs and everlasting joy.
Is. 35: 10.   S. M.

111 OH, sing to me of heav'n,
    When I am called to die;
Sing songs of holy ecstacy,
    To waft my soul on high.

2 When cold and sluggish drops
    Roll off my sweaty brow,
Burst forth in strains of joyfulness,—
    Let heav'n begin below.

3 When the last moment comes,
    O watch my dying face,
And catch the bright seraphic gleam
    That on each feature plays.

4 Then to my ravished ear,
    Let one sweet song be giv'n;
Let music charm me last on earth,
    And greet me first in heav'n.

5 Then close my sightless eyes,
    And lay me down to rest,
And clasp my cold and icy hands,
    Across my peaceful breast.

6 Then round my senseless clay
    Assemble those I love,
And sing of heav'n, delightful heav'n,
    My glorious home above.

HEAVEN.

A house not made with hands, eternal in the heavens. 2 Cor. 5: 1. S. M.

112
1 I HAVE a home above,
  From sin and sorrow free;
A mansion which eternal love
  Design'd and form'd for me.

2 My Saviour's precious blood
  Has made my title sure;
He pass'd through death's dark raging flood
  To make my rest secure.

3 The Comforter is come,
  The earnest has been given,
He leads me onward to the home
  Reserved for me in heaven.

4 Loved ones are gone before,
  Whose pilgrim days are done;
I soon shall greet them on that shore
  Where partings are unknown.

Be thou faithful unto death, and I will give thee a crown of life. Rev. 2: 10
S. M

113
1 OH, FOR the death of those
  Who slumber in the Lord!
Oh, be like theirs my last repose,
  Like theirs my last reward.

2 Their bodies in the ground,
  In silent hope may lie,
Till the last trumpet's joyful sound
  Shall call them to the sky.

3 Their ransomed spirits soar,
  On wings of faith and love,
To meet the Saviour they adore,
  And reign with him above.

4 Oh, for the death of those
  Who slumber in the Lord!
Oh, be like theirs my last repose,
  Like theirs my last reward.

STATE STREET.   No. 25.

And the city had no need of the sun, for the Glory of God did lighten it.
Rev. 21: 23.

114
1. There's a beautiful, beautiful land,—
'Tis the home of the blest;
Where with Jesus, a glorified band,
They forever shall rest.

2. In that land is the city of light,
Bright and fair, we are told:
All its mansions are dazzling and white,
And its streets are of gold.

3. There's no need of the sun in that land,
For the Lamb is its light;
And He sits at his Father's right hand,
Crowned with glory and might.

HEAVEN.   81

4 Oh, how glorious and sweet it must be,
   In that peaceful abode !
 Where from sin and from misery free,
   We shall dwell with our God !

5 There we hope many loved ones to meet,
   And in tender embrace
 We in triumph each other shall greet,
   In that beautiful place.

6 When we get to that Home of the Blest,
   From all pain to be free,
 And with Jesus forever to rest,
   Oh, how sweet it will be.

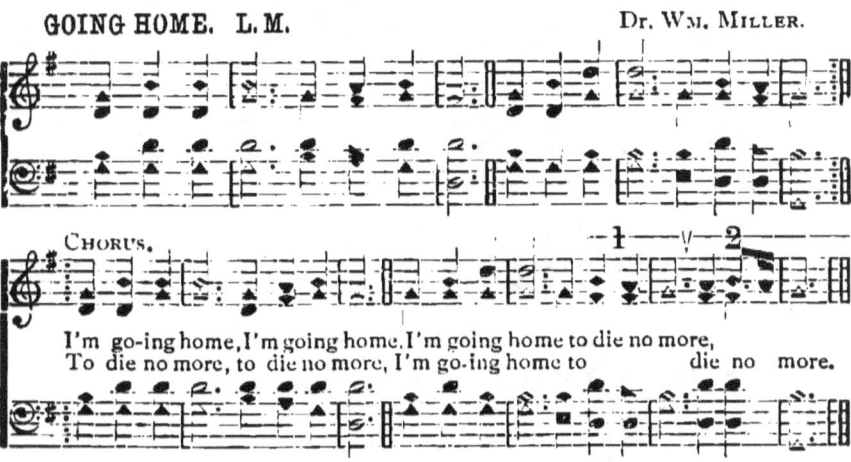

GOING HOME. L. M.   Dr. Wm. Miller.

I'm go-ing home, I'm going home, I'm going home to die no more,
To die no more, to die no more, I'm go-ing home to die no more.

Whose builder and maker is God.   Heb. 11: 10.   L. M.

115 My heavenly home is bright and fair,
       No pain nor death can enter there;
    Its glittering towers the sun outshine;
    That heavenly mansion shall be mine.

  2 While here, a stranger far from home,
    Affliction's waves may round me foam;
    And tho', like Lazarus, sick and poor,
    My heavenly mansion is secure.

  3 Let others seek a home below,
    Which flames devour, or waves o'erflow;
    Be mine a happier lot to own
    A heavenly mansion near the throne.

HEAVEN.

ANGEL BAND. C. M.   By per. of Biglow and Main, owners of copyright.   W. B. Bradbury.

O come, an-gel band, come and around me stand, O bear me a-way on your snowy wings, To my immortal home, O bear me away on your snowy wings To my immortal home.

Let us run with patience the race that is set before us. Heb. 12: 1.   C. M.

116 My latest sun is sinking fast,
    My race is almost run;
My strongest trials now are past,
    My triumph is begun.

2 I know I'm near the holy ranks
    Of friends and kindred dear,
For I brush the dews on Jordan's banks,
    The crossing must be near.

3 I've almost gained my heavenly home,
    My spirit loudly sings;
The holy ones, behold, they come!
    I hear the noise of wings.

4 O, bear my longing heart to him
    Who bled and died for me;
Whose blood now cleanses from all sin,
    And gives me victory.

HEAVEN.

ELTHAM. M. 5. L. MASON.

Where I am, there ye may be also. John 14: 3   M. 5.

117 High in yonder realms of light
   Dwell the raptured saints above,
Far beyond our feeble sight,
   Happy in Immanuel's love;
Once they knew, like us below,
   Pilgrims in this vale of tears,
Torturing pain and heavy woe,
   Gloomy doubts, distressing fears.

2 Often the unbidden tear,
   Stealing down the furrowed cheek,
Told in eloquence sincere
   Tales of woe they could not speak;
But these days of weeping o'er,
   Past this scene of toil and pain,
They shall feel distress no more—
   Never, never weep again.

3 All is tranquil and serene,
   Calm and undisturbed repose;
There no cloud can intervene,
   There no angry tempest blows;
Every tear is wiped away,
   Sighs no more shall heave **the breast,**
Night is lost in endless day,
   Sorrow—in eternal rest.

HEAVENLY DESIRE. M. 14.

Thou art with me; Thy rod and thy staff they comfort me. Ps. 23: 4. M. 14.

118 There is a land immortal,
　　The beautiful of lands;
　Beside its ancient portal
　　A sentry grimly stands;
　He only can undo it,
　　And open wide the door;
　And mortals who pass through it
　　Are mortals nevermore.

2 That glorious land is Heaven,
　　And death the sentry grim:
　The Lord thereof has given
　　The opening keys to him;
　And ransom'd spirits, sighing
　　And sorrowful for sin,
　Pass through the gate in dying,
　　And freely enter in.

3 Though dark and drear the passage
　　That leads unto the gate,
　Yet grace attends the message
　　To souls that watch and wait;
　And at the time appointed
　　A messenger comes down,
　And guides the Lord's anointed
　　From cross to glory's crown.

HEAVEN.

4 Their sighs are lost in singing;
  They're blesséd in their tears:
Their journey heavenward winging,
  They leave on earth their fears.
Death like an angel seeming,
  "We welcome thee;" they cry:
Their eyes with glory gleaming,
  'Tis life for them to die.
                    Thos. MacKellar. 1845.

UXBRIDGE. L. M.   L. MASON.

It is even a vapor. Jas. 4: 14.   L. M.

119 How vain is all beneath the skies!
       How transient every earthly bliss!
     How slender all the earthly ties
       That bind us to a world like this!

2 The evening cloud, the morning dew,
    The withering grass, the fading flower,
  Of earthly hopes are emblems true—
    The glory of a passing hour!

3 But though earth's fairest blossoms die,
    And all beneath the skies is vain,
  There is a land whose confines lie
    Beyond the reach of care and pain.

4 Then let the hope of joys to come
    Dispel our cares, and chase our fears:
  If God be ours, we're traveling home,
    Though passing through a vale of tears.
                              D. E. Ford.

HEAVEN.

ABNER. M. 4.   H. S. RUPP.

In my Father's house are many mansions. Jno. 14: 2.   M. 4.

120 LET me go where saints are going,
    To the mansions of the blest;
Let me go where my Redeemer
    Has prepared his people's rest;
I would gain the realms of brightness,
    Where they dwell forevermore;
I would join the friends that wait me
    Over on the other shore.

2 Let me go where none are weary,
    Where is raised no wail of woe;
Let me go and bathe my spirit
    In the raptures angels know:
Let me go, for bliss eternal,
    Lures my soul away, away,
And the victor's song triumphant
    Thrills my heart, I cannot stay.

3 Let me go, why should I tarry?
    What has earth to bind me here?
What but cares, and toils, and sorrows?
    What but death, and pain, and fear?
Let me go, for hopes most cherished,
    Blasted round me often lie:
O! I've gathered brightest flowers,
    But to see them fade and die.

HEAVEN.

SHALL WE MEET? M. 4.   ELIHU S. RICE, 1866, by per.

Then shall we also appear with him in glory. Col. 3: 4.   M. 4.

121 SHALL we meet beyond the river,
    Where the surges cease to roll?
Where, in all the bright forever,
    Sorrow ne'er shall press the soul?

2 Shall we meet in that blest harbor,
    When our stormy voyage is o'er?
Shall we meet and cast the anchor
    By the fair, celestial shore?

3 Shall we meet in yonder city
    Where the tow'rs of crystal shine?
Where the walls are all of jasper,
    Built by workmanship divine?--

4 Shall we meet the shining myriads
    Who the songs of glory sing?
Shall our voices join their praises
    To the everlasting King?

5 Shall we meet with Christ our Saviour,
    When he comes to claim his own?
Shall we know his blesséd favor,
    And sit down upon his throne?

        H. L. Hastings, 1858. From Songs of Pilgrimage.

HEAVEN.

HOME OF THE SOUL. 12s & 8s.
Philip Phillips.
Used by per. of The Phillips Pub Co., owners of copyright.

In my Father's house are many mansions. John 14: 2.   12s & 8s.

122
1. I WILL sing you a song of that beautiful land,
   The far away home of the soul,
   Where no storms ever beat on the glittering strand,
   ‖: While the years of eternity roll.:‖
   Where no storms, etc.

2. Oh, that home of the soul in my visions and dreams,
   Its bright jasper walls I can see ;
   Till I fancy but thinly the veil intervenes
   ‖: Between the fair city and me.:‖   Till I fancy, etc.

3. That unchangable home is for you and for me,
   Where Jesus of Nazareth stands ;
   The King of all kingdoms forever, is He,
   ‖: And He holdeth our crowns in His hands.:‖
   The King, etc.

HEAVEN. 89

4 Oh, how sweet it will be in that beautiful land,
   So free from all sorrow and pain;
   With songs on our lips and with harps in our hands
   ‖: To meet one another again. :‖ With songs, etc.
                                     Mrs. Ellen H. Gates.

ONE SWEETLY SOLEMN THOUGHT. S. M.   PHILIP PHILLIPS.
         Used by per. of THE P. PHILLIPS Pub. Co., owners of copyright.

Now they desire a better country, that is, an heavenly. Heb. 11: 16. S. M.

123 ONE sweetly-solemn thought
         Comes to me o'er and o'er,
       Nearer my home am I to-day,
         Than e'er I was before.—CHORUS.

   2 Nearer my Father's house,
        Where many mansions be;
      Nearer the throne where Jesus reigns,
        Nearer the crystal sea.

   3 Nearer the bound of life,
        Where burdens are laid down;
      Nearer leaving my heavy cross,
        Wearing my starry crown.
                              Phœbe Cary, 1852.

HEAVEN.

THE HOME OVER THERE. Pec. M. — TULLIUS C. O'KANE.

Used by per. of the P. Phillips Pub. Co., owners of Copyright.

Oh that I had wings like a dove, for then would I fly away and be at rest.
Ps. 55:6. Pec. M.

124 OH, THINK of the home over there,
By the side of the river of light,
Where the saints all immortal and fair,
Are robed in their garments of white,
Over there, over there,
Oh, think of the home over there.

2 Oh, think of the friends over there,
　　Who before us the journey have trod,
　Of the songs that they breathe on the air,
　　In their home in the palace of God,
　　　Over there, over there,
　Oh, think of the friends over there.

3 My Saviour is now over there,
　　There my kindred and friends are at rest;
　Then away from my sorrow and care,
　　Let me fly to the land of the blest,
　　　Over there, over there,
　My Saviour is now over there.

Rev. D. W. C. Huntingdon.

STAR OF DAY. L. M.　　　　　By Com.
With Gentleness.

For if we believe that Jesus died, and rose again, even so them also which sleep in Jesus will God bring with him. 1 Thess 4:14.　　L. M.

125 THERE is a calm for those who weep,
　　A rest for weary pilgrims found;
　They softly lie, and sweetly sleep,
　　Low in the ground, low in the ground.

2 The storm that sweeps the wintry sky
　　No more disturbs their deep repose
　Than Summer evening's latest sigh,
　　That shuts the rose, that shuts the rose.

3 Thy soul, renewed by grace divine,
　　In God's own image, freed from clay,
　In heaven's eternal sphere shall shine,
　　; star of day, a star of day.

MIFFLIN. M. 52.

Now is our salvation nearer. Rom. 13: 11. M. 52.

126 How bright is the day when the Christian
Receives the sweet message to come
‖: To rise to the mansions of glory,
‖: And be there forever at Home.:‖ And be there.

2 The Angels stand ready and waiting
The moment the Spirit is gone,
‖: To carry it upward to heaven,
‖: And welcome it safely at Home.:‖ And welcome.

3 The saints that have gone up before us
All raise a new song as we come,
‖: And sing Hallelujah the louder
‖: To welcome the travelers Home. :‖ To welcome.

4 And there are our friends and companions
Escaped from the evil to come,
‖: And crowding the gates of fair Zion
‖: To wait our arrival at Home.:‖ To wait.

5 And there is the blessed Redeemer,
So mild on His merciful Throne,
‖: With heart and hands widely extended
‖: To welcome his ransom'd ones Home.:‖ To welcome.

6 Then let us go onward rejoicing
Till Jesus invites us to come
‖: To share in his glorious kingdom,
‖: And rest in his bosom at Home.:‖ And rest.

CANAAN. C. M. H. S. Rupp.

The holy city, New Jerusalem. Rev. 21: 2. C. M.

127 Jerusalem, my happy home!
  Name ever dear to me!
When shall my labors have an end,
  In joy and peace in thee?

2 When shall these eyes thy heaven-built walls
  And pearly gates behold?
Thy bulwarks with salvation strong,
  And streets of shining gold?

3 Oh, when, thou city of my God,
  Shall I thy courts ascend,
Where congregations ne'er break up,
  And Sabbaths have no end?

4 There happier bow'rs than Eden's bloom,
  Nor sin nor sorrow know:
Blest seats! thro' rude and stormy scenes
  I onward press to you.

5 Jerusalem, my happy home!
  My soul still pants for thee;
Then shall my labors have an end,
  When I thy joys shall see.

Montgomery.

WALES. C. M.   Arr. by Com.

For now we see through a glass darkly; but then face to face. 1 Cor 13: 12.

C. M.

128 WHILE through this changing world I roam,
    From infancy to age,
Heaven is the Christian Pilgrim's home,
    His rest at every stage.

2 Thither his raptured thought ascends,
    Eternal joys to share,
There his adoring spirit bends,
    While here he kneels in prayer.

3 Oh! there may we our treasure place,
    There let our hearts be found,
That still where sin abounded, grace
    May more and more abound.

4 Henceforth our conversation be
    With Christ before the throne,
Ere long, we eye to eye shall see,
    And know as we are known.

The things which are not seen. 2 Cor. 4: 18.   C. M.

129 OH! could our thoughts and wishes fly
    Above these gloomy shades,
To those bright worlds beyond the sky
    Which sorrow ne'er invades!

2 There joys, unseen by mortal eyes,
    Or reason's feeble ray,
In ever-blooming prospects rise
    Unconscious of decay.

HEAVEN. 95

3 Lord, send a beam of light divine
  To guide our upward aim;
With one reviving touch of thine
  Our languid hearts inflame.

4 Oh, then, on faith's sublimest wing,
  Our ardent hope shall rise
To those bright scenes where pleasures spring
  Immortal, in the skies.
                    Anne Steele, ab. 1716-1788.

Your sorrow shall be turned into joy. John 16: 20. C. M.

130 THERE is an hour of hallow'd peace
      For those with care oppress'd,
When sighs and sorrowing tears shall cease,
  And all be hush'd to rest.

2 'Tis then the soul is freed from fears
  And doubts that here annoy:
Then they that oft had sown in tears
  Shall reap again in joy.

3 There is a home of sweet repose,
  Where storms assail no more;
The stream of endless pleasure flows
  On that celestial shore:

4 There purity with love appears,
  And bliss without alloy;
There they that oft had sown in tears
  Shall reap eternal joy.

O that I had wings like a dove. Psalm 55: 6. C. M.

131 AWAKE, ye saints, and raise your eyes,
      And lift your voices high;
Awake, and praise the sovereign love,
  That shows salvation nigh.

2 Swift on the wings of time it flies,
  Each moment brings it near;
Then welcome, each declining day;
  Welcome, each closing year.

3 Not many years their round shall **run,**
  Not many mornings rise,
Ere all its glories stand revealed
  To our admiring eyes.
                    Philip Doddridge, ab. 1755.

INVITATION.

HERALD. L. M.   T. C. Cook.

Come unto me, all ye that labor, and are heavy laden. Matt. 11: 28.   L. M.

132
Come hither, all ye weary souls,
  Ye heavy-laden sinners, come,
I'll give you rest from all your toils,
  And bring you to my heavenly home.

2 They shall find rest that learn of me;
  I'm of a meek and lowly mind;
But passion rages like the sea,
  And pride is restless as the wind.

3 Bless'd is the man whose shoulders take
  My yoke, and bear it with delight;
My yoke is easy to his neck;
  My grace shall make the burden light.

4 Jesus, we come at thy command,
  With faith, and hope, and humble zeal,
Resign our spirits to thy hand,
  To mould and guide us at thy will.

Now is the accepted time. 2 Cor. 6: 2.   L. M.

133
Say, sinner, hath a voice within,
  Oft whispered to thy secret soul,
Urged thee to leave the ways of sin,
  And yield thy heart to God's control?

2 Sinner, it was a heavenly voice,—
  It was the Spirit's gracious call;
It bade thee make the better choice,
  And haste to seek in Christ thine all.

3 Spurn not the call to life and light;
   Regard in time the warning kind;
 That call thou mayest not always slight,
   And yet the gate of mercy find.

4 God's Spirit will not always strive
   With hardened, self-destroying man;
 Ye, who persist his love to grieve,
   May never hear his voice again.

5 Sinner, perhaps this very day
   Thy last accepted time may be;
 O, shouldst thou grieve him now away,
   Then hope may never beam on thee.
                    Abigail Bradley Hyde, 1824.

Choose you this day whom ye will serve. Joshua 24: 15.   L. M.

134
 OH, do not let the word depart,
   And close thine eyes against the light;
 Poor sinner, harden not thy heart;
   Thou wouldst be saved,—why not **to-night**?

2 To-morrow's sun may never rise
   To bless thy long-deluded sight;
 This is the time; oh, then, be wise!
   Thou wouldst be saved,—why not **to-night**?

3 Our God in pity lingers still;
   And wilt thou thus his love requite?
 Renounce at once thy stubborn will;
   Thou wouldst be saved,—why not to-night?

4 The world has nothing left to give;
   It has no new, no pure delight;
 Oh, try the life which Christians live!
   Thou wouldst be saved,—why not to-night?

5 Our blessèd Lord refuses none
   Who would to him their souls unite;
 Then be the work of grace begun;
   Thou wouldst be saved,—why not to-night?
                    Elizabeth Holmes Reed, 1842.

WELTON.   No. 40.

INVITATION.

WARD. L. M.   Scotch, arr. L. Mason, 1830.

And the blood of Christ cleanseth us from all sin. 1 *John* 1: 7.   L. M.

135   JESUS, dear name! how sweet it sounds,
Replete with balm for all our wounds!
His word declares his grace is free;
Come, needy sinner, "Come and see."

2 He left the shining courts on high,
Came to our world to bleed and die;
Jesus the Lord hung on a tree;
Come, thoughtless sinner, "Come and see."

3 Your sins did pierce his bleeding heart,
Till death had done its dreadful part;
His boundless love extends to thee;
Come, trembling sinner, "Come and see."

4 His blood can cleanse the foulest stain,
Can make the vilest sinner clean;
This fountain open stands for thee;
Come, guilty sinner, "Come and see."

To-day if ye will hear his voice. Heb. 3: 7.   L. M.

136   WHILE life prolongs its precious light,
Mercy is found and peace is given;
But soon, ah, soon, approaching night
Shall blot out every hope of heaven.

2 While God invites, how blest the day!
How sweet the gospel's joyful sound!
Come sinners, haste, Oh, haste away,
While yet a pardoning God is found.

INVITATION.

3 Soon borne on time's most rapid wing,
    Shall death command you to the grave,
Before his bar your spirits bring,
    And none be found to hear or save.

4 In that lone land of deep despair,
    No Sabbath's heavenly light shall rise;
No God regard your bitter prayer,
    Nor Saviour call you to the skies.

5 Silence, and solitude, and gloom,
    In these forgetful realms appear,
Deep sorrows fill the dismal tomb,
    And hope shall never enter there.

Him that cometh to me I will in no wise cast out. John 6: 37. L. M.

137 With tearful eyes I look around,
    Life seems a dark and stormy sea;
Yet, 'midst the gloom, I hear a sound,
    A heav'nly whisper, "Come to me."

2 It tells me of a place of rest—
    It tells me where my soul may flee;
O! to the weary, faint, oppress'd,
    How sweet the bidding, "Come to me."

3 When nature shudders, loth to part
    From all I love, enjoy, and see;
When a faint chill steals o'er my heart
    A sweet voice utters, "Come to me."

4 Come, for all else must fail and die;
    Earth is no resting-place for thee;
Heav'nward direct thy weeping eye,
    I am thy portion, "Come to me."

5 O, voice of mercy! voice of love!
    In conflict, grief, and agony,
Support me, cheer me from above!
    And gently whisper, "Come to me."

HEBRON. No. 95.

DUNLAP'S CREEK. C. M.

So will I go in unto the king. Esther 4: 16.   C. M.

138
Come, humble sinner, in whose breast
  A thousand thoughts revolve,
Come, with your guilt and fear oppressed,
  And make this last resolve:

2 "I'll go to Jesus, though my sin
  Hath like a mountain rose;
I know his courts, I'll enter in,
  Whatever may oppose.

3 "I'll to the gracious King approach,
  Whose sceptre pardon gives;
Oh, that he may command my touch,
  And then the suppliant lives.

4 "Prostrate I'll lie before his throne,
  And there my guilt confess;
I'll tell him I'm a wretch undone,
  Without his soverign grace.

5 "I shall not perish, if I go—
  I am resolved to try;
For if I stay away, I know
  I must forever die.

6 "My Saviour will not spurn my cry,
  My King will hear my prayer;
In safety at his feet I lie,
  For none can perish there."

Edmond Jones.

INVITATION.   101

Let him return unto the Lord. Is. 55: 7.   C. M.

139 RETURN, O wanderer, now return,
   And seek thy Father's face!
Those new desires which in thee burn,
   Were kindled by his grace.

2 Return, O wanderer, now return,
   Thy Saviour bids thee live;
Go to his bleeding feet, and learn
   How freely he'll forgive.

3 Return, O wanderer, now return,
   And wipe the falling tear!
Thy Father calls—no longer mourn:
   His love invites thee near.
                              Collyer.

Come unto me, and I will give you rest. Matt. 11: 28.   C. M.

140 OH, what amazing words of grace
   Are in the gospel found,
Suited to every sinner's case
   Who knows the joyful sound.

2 Poor, sinful, thirsty, fainting souls,
   Are freely welcome here;
Salvation, like a river rolls,
   Abundant, free, and clear.

3 Come then, with all your wants and wounds;
   Your every burden bring,
Here love, unchanging love abounds,—
   A deep celestial spring!

4 Whoever will—O gracious word!
   Shall of this stream partake:
Come thirsty souls, and bless the Lord,
   And drink, for Jesus' sake!

5 Millions of sinners, vile as you,
   Have here found life and peace;
Come then, and prove its virtues too,
   And drink, adore, and bless.

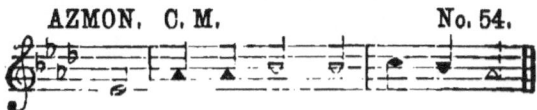
AZMON. C. M.   No. 54.

ATHENS C. M.

If any man thirst, let him come unto me, and drink. John 7: 37.   C. M.

141 I HEARD the voice of Jesus say,
"Come unto me and rest;
Lay down, thou weary one, lay down
Thy head upon my breast:"

2 I came to Jesus as I was,
Weary, and worn, and sad;
I found in him a resting-place,
And he has made me glad.

3 I heard the voice of Jesus say,
"Behold, I freely give
The living water! thirsty one
Stoop down, and drink, and live:"

4 I came to Jesus, and I drank
Of that life-giving stream:
My thirst was quenched, my soul revived,
And now I live in him.

5 I heard the voice of Jesus say,
"I am this dark world's light:
Look unto me; thy morn shall rise,
And all thy day be bright:"

6 I looked to Jesus, and I found
In him my Star, my Sun;
And in that light of life I'll walk
Till all my journey's done.

Bonar.

INVITATION.

BARR. C. M. J. S. COFFMAN.

I will arise and go to my Father. Luke 15: 18. C. M.

142 O WEARY wanderer, come home,
　　Thy Saviour bids thee come,
Thou long in sin didst love to roam,
　　Yet still he calls thee, come.

2 Think of thy Father's house to-day,
　　So blest with plenteous store ;
Think of thy sinful, wandering way,
　　Then come, and roam no more.

3 Poor prodigal, come home and rest,
　　Come and be reconciled ;
Here lean upon thy Father's breast,
　　He loves his wandering child.
　　　　　　　　　J. S. Coffman.

The fear of the Lord is the beginning of wisdom. Ps. III: 10. C. M.

143 COME children learn to fear the Lord:
　　And, that your days be long,
Let not a false or spiteful word
　　Be found upon your tongue.

2 Depart from mischief, practice love,
　　Pursue the works of peace,
So shall the Lord your ways approve,
　　And set your souls at ease.

3 His eyes awake to guard the just,
　　His ears attend the cry ;
When broken Spirits dwell in dust,
　　The God of grace is nigh.

INVITATION.

MANOAH. M. 14. By Com.

Remember thy Creator in the days of thy youth. Eccl. 12: 1. M. 14.

144   "REMEMBER thy Creator,"
  While youth's fair spring is bright,
Before thy cares are greater,
  Before comes age's night.
While yet the sun shines o'er thee,
  While stars the darkness cheer,
While life is all before thee,
  Thy great Creator fear.

2 "Remember thy Creator,"
  E'er life resigns its trust,
E'er sinks dissolving nature,
  And dust returns to dust.
Before, with God, who gave it,
  The spirit shall appear,
He cries, who died to save it,
  "Thy great Creator fear."

Buy the truth, and sell it not. Pr. 23: 23. M. 14

145   GO thou in life's fair morning,
  Go, in thy bloom of youth,
And seek, for thine adorning,
  The precious pearl of truth;
Secure the heav'nly treasure,
  And bind it on thy heart;
And let no earthly pleasure
  E'er cause it to depart.

INVITATION. 105

2 Go, while the day-star shineth,
  Go, while thy heart is light,
Go, ere thy strength declineth,
  While every sense is bright:
Sell all thou hast and buy it;
  'Tis worth all earthly things—
Rubies, and gold, and diamonds,
  Scepters and crowns of kings.

3 Go, ere the cloud of sorrow
  Steals o'er thy bloom of youth;
Defer not till to-morrow;
  Go now, and buy the truth.
Go, seek thy great Creator;
  Learn early to be wise;
Go place upon the altar
  A morning sacrifice.

AMOY. 6s & 4s.   LOWELL MASON, 1831.

The day of salvation. 2 Cor. 6: 2.   6s & 4s.

146 TO-DAY the Saviour calls:
        Ye wand'rers, come;
    Oh ye benighted souls,
        Why longer roam?

2 To-day the Saviour calls:
    Oh, hear him now;
  Within these sacred walls,
    To Jesus bow.

3 To-day the Saviour calls:
    For refuge fly;
  The storm of justice falls,
    And death is nigh.

4 The Spirit calls to-day:
    Yield to his power;
  Oh, grieve him not away,
    'Tis mercy's hour.
                    Samuel Francis Smith.

INVITATION.

PHŒBE. S. M.   By Com.

Grieve not the Holy Spirit. Eph. 4: 30.   S. M.

147 AND canst thou, sinner, slight
    The call of love divine!
Shall God with tenderness invite,
    And gain no thought of thine?

2 Wilt thou not cease to grieve
    The Spirit from thy breast,
Till he thy wretched soul shall leave,
    With all thy sins oppressed?

3 To-day, a pardoning God
    Will hear the suppliant pray;
To-day, a Saviour's cleansing blood
    Will wash thy guilt away.

                                Hyde.

To-day if ye will hear his voice, harden not your hearts. Psalm 95: 7-8.
                                            S. M.

148 YE sinners fear the Lord,
    While yet 'tis called to-day,
Soon will the awful voice of death
    Command your souls away.

2 Soon will the harvest close;
    The summer soon be o'er;
And soon your injured, angry God
    Will hear your prayers no more.

3 Then while 'tis called to-day,
    Oh hear the gospel sound:
Come, sinner, haste—oh haste away,
    While pardon may be found

INVITATION.   107

Behold, now is the accepted time. 2 Cor. 6: 2.   S. M.

149
1 Now is th' accepted time,
      Now is the day of grace;
   Now, sinners, come, without delay,
      And seek the Saviour's face.

2 Now is th' accepted time,
      The Saviour calls to-day;
   To-morrow it may be too late,
      Then why should you delay?

3 Now is th' accepted time,
      The gospel bids you come;
   And every promise in his word
      Declares there yet is room.

4 Now is th' accepted time,
      O sinners! why delay?
   Come while the gospel trumpet sounds,
      Come in th' accepted day.

My Son give me thine heart. Prov. 23: 26.   S. M.

150
1 Give to the Lord thine heart;
      In him all pleasures meet;
   Oh, come, and choose the better part,
      Low at the Saviour's feet.

2 Hear, and your soul shall live;
      His peace shall be your stay—
   Peace, which the world can never give,
      Can never take away.

3 Go with him to his cross,
      Go with him to his tomb;
   Your richest gain account but loss,
      And tarry till he come.

4 Then, when you hear his voice,
      Your faithful Shepherd's call,
   Lift up your heads, in him rejoice,
      Your God, your Guide, your all.

LABAN.   No. 2.

INVITATION.

GREENVILLE. M. 4. J. J. ROUSSEAU, 1750.

Christ came into the world to save sinners. 1 Tim. 1: 15.   M. 4.

151 Come, ye sinners, poor and needy,
　　Weak and wounded, sick and sore;
Jesus ready stands to save you,
　　Full of pity, love, and power:
‖: He is able, He is able,
　　He is willing, doubt no more. :‖

2 Now, ye needy, come, and welcome:
　　God's free bounty glorify;
True belief and true repentance,
　　Every grace that brings you nigh,
‖: Without money, without money,
　Come to Jesus Christ and buy. :‖

3 Let not conscience make you linger,
　　Nor of fitness fondly dream;
All the fitness he requireth
　　Is to feel your need of him:
‖: This He gives you, this He gives you,
　'Tis the Spirit's glimmering beam.:‖

4 Come, ye weary, heavy-laden,
　　Bruised and mangled by the fall;
If you tarry till you're better,
　　You will never come at all;
‖: Not the righteous, not the righteous,
　　Sinners Jesus came to call. :‖

INVITATION.

Come thou, for there is peace. 1 Sam. 20: 21.   M. 4.

152 SINNERS, will you scorn the message
Sent in mercy from above?
Every sentence, oh, how tender!
Every line is full of love;
‖: Hear, oh, hear it! :‖
Every line is full of love.

2 Hear the heralds of the Gospel,
News from Zion's King proclaim,
To each rebel sinner—"Pardon,
Free forgiveness in his name:"
‖: Oh, receive it! :‖
Free forgiveness in his name!

3 Tempted souls, they bring you succor:
Fearful hearts, they quell your fears,
And with news of consolation,
Chase away the falling tears:
‖: Tender heralds—:‖
Chase away the falling tears.

Allen.

AVA. 10s & 4s.   T. HASTINGS.

"*Yet there is room.*" Luke 14: 22.   10s & 4s.

153 CHILD of sin and sorrow, filled with dismay,
Wait not for to-morrow, yield thee to-day;
Heaven bids thee come,
While yet there's room;
Child of sin and sorrow, hear and obey.

2 Child of sin and sorrow, why wilt thou die!
Come, while thou canst borrow help from on **high;**
Grieve not that love,
Which from above,
Child of sin and sorrow, would bring thee **nigh.**

3 Child of sin and sorrow, thy moments glide,
Like the flitting arrow or the rushing tide;
Ere time is o'er,
Heaven's grace implore;
Child of sin and sorrow, in Christ confide.

Hastings.

WELLS. L. M.   Arr. I. HOLDROYD.

Do it with thy might. Eccl. 9: 10.   L. M.

154 LIFE is the time to serve the Lord,
The time to insure the great reward;
And while the lamp holds out to burn,
The vilest sinner may return.

2 Life is the hour that God hath given
To escape from hell, and fly to heaven;
The day of grace, and mortals may
Secure the blessings of the day.

3 The living know that they must die,
But all the dead forgotten lie;
Their memory and their sense is gone,
Alike unknowing and unknown.

4 Their hatred and their love is lost,
Their envy buried in the dust;
They have no share in all that's done
Beneath the circuit of the sun.

5 Then what my thoughts design to do,
My hands with all your might pursue,
Since no device nor work is found,
Nor faith, nor hope, beneath the ground.

6 There are no acts of pardon passed
In the cold grave to which we haste;
But darkness, death, and long despair,
Reign in eternal silence, there.

                                    I. Watts.

INVITATION.

LANCASTER. M. 5.   J. S. SHOEMAKER.

Why will you die. Ezek. 18: 31.   M. 5.

155 Tell us sinner, tell us why
Will you grieve the Lord and die?
Why not give your heart to Him,
While he suffered for your sin?
He has now in store for thee,
Grace and love, both full and free;
He can fill thy heart with peace,
And thy soul from sin release.

2 "It is finished" Jesus cried;
Then he bowed His head and died;
Finished, all is now, that we
From our sins can be made free.
He who loved thee, sets thee free,
For He died to ransom thee,
And for thee does intercede,
Then why not for mercy plead.

3 Better come before too late,
Death may seal thy endless fate;
And the sentence you most fear,
Depart from me, you will hear.
If to-day you heed His voice,
And make him your only choice,
He will lead you safely on,
Till you reach the heavenly home.

J. S. Shoemaker.

The Lord is my light and my salvation. Psalm 27: 1.   C. M.

156
1 Sweet Sabbath School! more dear to me
    Than fairest palace dome,
  My heart e'er turns with joy to thee,
    My own dear Sabbath Home.

2 Here first my wilful, wand'ring heart,
    The way of life was shown;
  Here first I sought the better part,
    And gained a Sabbath Home.

3 Here shall I offer my requests,
    And see thy beauties still;
  Shall share thy messages of love,
    And here inquire thy will.

4 Here I would find a settled rest,
    While others outside roam;
  No more a stranger or a guest,
    But like a child at Home.

THE LORD'S DAY.

SABBATH. 7s.   L. Mason

Enter into his gates with thanksgiving. Psalm 100: 4.   7s.

157   Safely through another week,
    God has brought us on our way;
Let us now a blessing seek,
    Waiting in his courts to-day:
Day of all the week the best,
Emblem of eternal rest.

2 While we pray for pardoning grace,
    Through the dear Reedemer's name,
Show thy reconciling face;
    Take away our sin and shame:
From our worldly cares set free,
May we rest this day in thee.

3 Here we come, thy name to praise;
    Let us feel thy presence near;
May thy glories meet our eyes,
    While we in thy house appear:
Here afford us, Lord, a taste
Of our everlasting feast.

                                Newton.

THE LORD'S DAY.

HAMBURG. L. M.   Gregorian. Arr. L. MASON, 1825.

As it began to dawn. Matt. 28: 1.   L. M.

158
MY op'ning eyes with rapture see
  The dawn of thy returning day;
My thoughts, O God, ascend to thee,
  While thus my early vows I pay.

2 I yield my heart to thee alone,
  Nor would receive another guest:
Eternal King, erect thy throne,
  And reign sole monarch in my breast.

3 O bid this trifling world retire,
  And drive each carnal thought away,
Nor let me feel one vain desire,
  One sinful thought, through all the day.

4 Then, to thy courts when I repair,
  My soul shall rise on joyful wing,
The wonders of thy love declare,
  And join the strains which angels sing.

Abide with us, for it is toward evening. Luke 24: 29.   L. M.

159
ANOTHER day has passed along,
  And we are nearer to the tomb,—
Nearer to join the heavenly song,
  Or hear the last eternal doom.

2 Sweet is the light of Sabbath eve,
  And soft the sun-beams lingering there;
For these blest hours, the world I leave,
  Wafted on wings of faith and prayer.

THE LORD'S DAY.

3 The time, how lovely and how still;
   Peace shines and smiles on all below—
The plain, the stream, the wood, the hill—
   All fair with evening's setting glow.

4 Season of rest! the tranquil soul
   Feels the sweet calm, and melts to love;
And while these sacred moments roll
   Faith sees a smiling heav'n above.

5 Nor will our days of toil be long,
   Our pilgrimage will soon be trod;
And we shall join the ceaseless song—
   The endless Sabbath of our God.

HOLY REST. M. 55.

The day which the Lord hath made.   Psalm 118: 24.   M. 55.

160 AGAIN the day returns of holy rest,
Which, when He made the world, Jehovah blest;
When, like His own, He bade our labors cease,
And all be piety, and all be peace.

2 Let us devote this consecrated day
To learn His will, and all we learn obey;
So shall He hear, when fervently we raise
Our choral harmony in hymns of praise.

3 Father in heaven! in whom our hopes confide,
Whose power defends us, and whose precepts guide;
In life our Guardian, and in death our Friend;
Glory supreme be thine, till time shall end.
                    William Mason, 1725-1796.

THE LORD'S DAY.

WELCOME. M. 5.

Return unto thy rest, O my soul. Psalm 116: 7. M. 5.

161 WELCOME, welcome day of rest,
  To the world in kindness given;
Welcome to this care-worn breast,
  As the beaming light from heaven;
Day of soft and sweet repose,
  Gently now thy moments run;
As the peaceful streamlet flows,
  Radiant with a summer's sun.

2 Day of tidings from the skies,
  Day of solemn praise and prayer,
Day to make the simple wise,
  O how great thy blessings are.
Welcome, welcome day of rest,
  With thy influence divine;
May thy hallowed hours be blest,
  To this feeble heart of mine.

3 Welcome, welcome day of rest,
  Songs of praise ascend on high,
Day of joy and day of rest,
  Hallelujahs fill the sky.
Let the Sabbath day be blest,
  Humble prayer to God ascend,
Day of joy and day of rest,
  God our Father and our Friend.

HOLY SABBATH EVE. 6s & 5s. F. D. Jacobs, by per.

Grace, mercy, and peace. 1 Tim. 1: 2. 6s & 5s.

162 Holy Sabbath evening,
    Peaceful hour of rest,
Now thy presence bringing
    Peace to every breast.

2 Holy Sabbath evening,
    Ever calm and still,
With sweet thoughts thy presence,
    Ev'ry heart shall fill.

3 Holy Sabbath evening,
    Bringing sweet repose,
Peacefully in slumber
    May our eyelids close

4 Jesus, grant thy children
    Calm and sweet repose;
With thy tenderest blessing
    Let our eyelids close.

5 Through the long night watches,
    May thine angels spread
Their white wings above us,
    Standing round our bed.

6 When the morning wakens,
    Then may we arise
Pure, and fresh, and sinless,
    In thy holy eyes.

PETERBORO. C. M. — RALPH HARRISON, 1786.

Day unto day uttereth speech. Ps. 19: 2.   C. M.

163
Once more, my soul, the rising day
  Salutes thy waking eyes;
Once more, my voice, thy tribute pay
  To him that rules the skies.

2 Night unto night his name repeats,
  The day renews the sound,
Wide as the heaven on which he sits,
  To turn the seasons round.

3 'Tis he supports my mortal frame;
  My tongue shall speak his praise;
My sins would rouse his wrath to flame,
  And yet his wrath delays.

4 On a poor worm thy power might tread,
  And I could ne'er withstand;
Thy justice might have crushed me dead,
  But mercy held thy hand.

5 A thousand wretched souls are fled
  Since the last setting sun,
And yet thou lengthenest out my thread,
  And yet my moments run.

6 O God, let all my hours be thine,
  Whilst I enjoy the light:
Then shall my sun in smiles decline,
  And bring a peaceful night.

Divine protection acknowledged. Psalm 3: 5.   C. M.

164
   My God was with me all the night,
     And gave me sweet repose;
   His angels watch'd me while I slept,
     Or I had never rose.

2 Now for the mercies of the night
   My humble thanks I'll pay,
And unto God I'll dedicate
   The first fruits of the day.

3 In pressing dangers, fears and death,
   Thy goodness I'll adore,
And praise thee for thy mercies past,
   And humbly hope for more.

4 My life, if thou preserve my life,
   Thy sacrifice shall be;
And death, when death must be my lot,
   Shall join my soul to thee.

For the Lord preserveth the faithful. Psalm 31: 23.   C. M.

165
   God of my life, my morning song
     To thee I gladly raise;
   Thy act of love 'tis good to sing,
     And pleasant 'tis to praise.

2 Preserved by thy Almighty arm,
   I passed the shades of night,
Serene—and safe from every harm,
   To see the morning light.

3 While numbers spent the night in sighs,
   And restless pains and woes,
In gentle sleep I closed my eyes,
   And rose from sweet repose.

4 When sleep, death's image, o'er me spread,
   And I unconscious lay,
Thy watchful care was round my bed,
   To guard my feeble clay.

5 O let the same Almighty care
   Through all this day attend;
From every danger, every snare,
   My heedless steps defend.

WARWICK. C. M. Samuel Stanley, 1773

My voice shalt thou hear in the morning. Ps. 5: 3.   C. M.

166 Lord, in the morning thou shalt hear
My voice ascending high;
To thee will I direct my prayer,
To thee lift up mine eye;

2 Up to the hills where Christ is gone
To plead for all his saints,
Presenting at his Father's throne
Our songs and our complaints.

3 Thou art a God before whose sight
The wicked shall not stand;
Sinners shall ne'er be thy delight,
Nor dwell at thy right hand.

4 But to thy house will I resort,
To taste thy mercies there;
I will frequent thy holy court,
And worship in thy fear.

5 Oh, may thy Spirit guide my feet
In ways of righteousness;
Make every path of duty straight
And plain before my face.

The Lord sustained me. Ps. 3: 5.   C. M.

167 Great God, preserved by thine arm,
I passed the shades of night;
Serene—and safe from every harm,
And see returning light.

2 Oh! let the same Almighty care
  My wakeful hours defend;
  From every danger, every snare,
  My heedless steps defend.

3 Smile on my minutes as they roll,
  And guide my future days;
  And let thy goodness fill my soul
  With gratitude and praise.

TRUSTING. M. 5.   W. G. FISCHER.

I will instruct thee in the way which thou shalt go: I will guide thee.
Ps. 32: 8. M. 5.

168 Now the shades of night are gone;
  Now the morning light is come;
  Lord, may I be thine to-day—
  Drive the shades of sin away.

2 Fill my soul with heavenly light,
  Banish doubt, and cleanse my sight;
  In thy service, Lord, to-day,
  Help me labor, help me pray.

3 Keep my haughty passions bound—
  Save me from my foes around;
  Going out and coming in,
  Keep me safe from every sin.

4 When my work of life is past,
  Oh! receive me then at last!
  Night of sin will be no more
  When I reach the heavenly shore.

MORNING HYMN.

GRATITUDE. C. M.   By Com.

I will sing aloud of thy mercy in the morning. Ps. 59: 16.   C. M.

169 I owe the Lord a morning song
    Of gratitude and praise,
For the kind mercy He has shown
    In lengthening out my days.

2 He kept me safe another night;
    I see another day,
Now may His Spirit as the light
    Direct me in His way.

3 Keep me from danger and from sin;
    Help me thy will to do,
So that my heart be pure within;
    And I thy goodness know.

4 Keep me till thou wilt call me hence,
    Where never night can be,
And save me, Lord, for Jesus' sake,—
    He shed his blood for me.
Amos Herr.

The Lord sustained me. Ps. 3: 5.   C. M.

170 Lord, for the mercies of the night
    My humble thanks I pay;
And unto thee I dedicate
    The first-fruits of the day.

2 Let this day praise thee, O my God,
    And so let all my days;
And oh, let mine eternal day
    Be thine eternal praise.
John Mason, 1683.

RANTOLS. L. M.

"We spend our years as a tale. Psalm 90." L. M.

171 ANOTHER year, another year,
Hath sped its flight on silent wing,
And all that marked its brief career
Hath passed from mortal reckoning.

2 Lord, for thy grace and patient love,
Unwearied still, and still the same,
For all our hopes of joy above,
We laud and bless thy holy name.

3 Still bear with us, and bless us still;
And, while in this dark world we stay,
Oh, let us love thy sacred will,
Oh, let us keep thy narrow way.

Littledale.

Thou crownest the year. Psalm 65. L. M.

172 GREAT God! we sing that mighty hand,
By which supported still we stand;
The opening year thy mercy shows,
That mercy crowns it till its close.

2 By day, by night, at home, abroad,
Still we are guarded by our God,
By his incessant bounty fed,
By his unerring counsel led.

3 With grateful hearts the past we own;
The future, all to us unknown,
We to thy guardian care commit,
And peaceful leave before thy feet.

ELIDA. C. M.

Reflection at the end of the year.   C. M.

173
    AND now, my soul, another year,
        Of thy short life is past;
    I can not long continue here,
        And this may be my last.

2 Much of my hasty life is gone,
    Nor will return again;
And swift my passing moments run—
    The few that yet remain.

3 Awake, my soul, with utmost care
    Thy true condition learn:
What are thy hopes? how sure? how fair?
    What is thy great concern?

4 Behold another year begins;
    Set out afresh for heav'n;
Seek pardon for thy former sins,
    In Christ so freely given.

5 Devoutly yield thyself to God,
    And on his grace depend;
With zeal pursue the heav'nly road,
    Nor doubt a happy end.

We spend our years as a tale that is told. Psalm 90: 9.   C. M.

174
    OUR life is ever on the wing,
        And death is ever nigh;
    The moment when our lives begin
        We all begin to die.

2 Yet, mighty God, our fleeting days
   Thy lasting favors share;
Yet with the bounties of thy grace,
   Thou load'st the rolling year.

3 'Tis sov'reign mercy finds us food,
   And we are clothed with love;
While grace stands pointing out the road
   That leads our souls above.

4 His goodness runs on endless round,
   All glory to the Lord!
His mercy never knows a bound,
   And be his name adored!

5 Thus we begin the lasting song,
   And when we close our eyes,
Let future ages praise prolong,
   Till time and nature dies.

Remember, O Lord, thy tender mercies. Psalm 25: 6.   **C. M.**

175 Now, gracious Lord, thine arm reveal,
   And make thy glory known:
Now let us all thy presence feel,
   And soften hearts of stone.

2 From all the guilt and former sin,
   May mercy set us free;
And let the year we now begin,
   Begin and end with thee.

3 Send down thy Spirit from above,
   That saints may love thee more;
And sinners now may learn to love,
   Who never loved before.

4 And when before thee we appear,
   In our eternal home,
May growing numbers worship here,
   And praise thee in our room.

PETERBORO.   No. 163.

PENITENCE.

THE PENITENT. M. 4.

C. G. ALLEN.

By per. of BIGLOW and MAIN, owners of copyright.

Blessed are they that mourn: for they shall be comforted. Matt. 5: 4.   M. 4.

176 Can my soul find rest from sorrow?
  Can my sins forgiven be?
Must I wait until to-morrow
  Ere my Saviour speaks to me?
Will he speak in words of kindness,
  Will he wash away my sin?
Will he lift this veil of blindness,
  And remove this deadly pain?

2 O the darkness, how it thickens,
  Like the brooding of despair!
And my soul within me sickens—
  God, in mercy, hear my prayer!
Give me but a hope to cherish,
  Give me just one ray of light—
Help me, save me, or I perish,
  Take away this awful night!

God forbid that I should glory, save in the cross of our Lord Jesus Christ.
Gal. 6: 14.   M. 4.

177 Lamb of God, we fall before Thee,
  Humbly trusting in Thy cross;
That alone be all our glory,
  All things else are only dross.
Thee we own a perfect Saviour,
  Only source of all that's good:
Ev'ry grace and ev'ry favor
  Comes to us through Jesus' blood.

PENITENCE.

2 Jesus gives us true repentance,
　By His Spirit sent from heaven;
Whispers this transporting sentence,
　"Son, thy sins are all forgiven."
Faith He grants us to believe it,
　Grateful hearts His love to prize:
Want we wisdom? He must give it;
　Hearing ears, and seeing eyes.

3 Jesus gives us pure affections,
　Wills to do what he requires;
Makes us follow His directions,
　And what He commands—inspires.
All our prayers, and all our praises,
　Rightly offer'd in His name,
He that dictates them is Jesus;
　He that answers is the same.

Behold what manner of love. 1 John 3: 1.　　M. 4.

178　Love divine, all love excelling,
　Joy of heaven, to earth come down!
Fix in us thy humble dwelling;
　All thy faithful mercies crown.
Jesus, thou art all compassion,
　Pure, unbounded love thou art;
Visit us with thy salvation;
　Enter every trembling heart.

2 Breathe, oh, breathe thy loving Spirit
　Into every troubled breast!
Let us all in thee inherit,
　Let us find that second rest.
Take away our power of sinning;
　Alpha and Omega be;
End of faith, as its beginning,
　Set our hearts at liberty.
　　　　　　　　　　Wesley, 1757.

GREENVILLE.　　　　No. 151.

PENITENCE.

CRYSTAL FOUNTAIN. M. 4.
A. L. LANDIS.

Come unto me, all ye that labor and are heavy laden, and I will give you rest.
Matt. 11: 28. M. 4.

179
At the door of mercy sighing
  With the burden of my sin,
Day and night my soul is crying,
  "Open, Lord, and let me in."
Waiting mid the darkness dreary,
  Stretching out my hands to Thee,
In the refuge for the weary
  Is there not a place for me?

2 I have sought to earn thy favor,
  Caring not for toil or cost;
Yet I find not him my Saviour,
  Him who came to seek the lost.
Blessed Master! in thy pity
  Teach me what I ought to do,
So that in the holy city
  I may gain an entrance too.

3 Hark! what sounds mine ear **receiveth,**
　　Sweet as songs of seraphim!
"He that in the Lord believeth
　　Life eternal hath in Him.
At the outer door why staying?
　　Nothing, soul! hast thou to pay:
Christ in love to thee is saying,
　　Weary child, come in to-day."

4 I knew not of Jesus' kindness!
　　I knew not of Jesus' grace!
Oh, the blackness of the blindness
　　That could not behold his face!
I saw not the door was open,
　　Nor my Lord invite me in:
Grace is mine beyond my hoping,
　　Mercy mightier than my sin.
　　　　　　　　　　Thos. MacKellar, 1871.

Thou knowest that I love thee. John 21 : 17.　　M. 4.

180 Art thou in thy spirit lowly,
　　Like the man of Nazareth?
Art thou seeking to be wholly
　　Join'd to him, come life, come death?
　　　Lov'st thou Jesus
　　More than thine own vital breath?

2 Is thy bosom full of sorrow?
　　Is a cloud upon thy way?
Why the worldling's burden borrow?
　　Child of grace and promise, say!
　　　Lov'st thou Jesus?
　　Joy should be thy guest to-day.

3 Hath God made all men to praise **thee?**
　　Or art thou to fame unknown?
Only seek that he should raise thee
　　Up to an immortal throne.
　　　Lov'st thou Jesus?
　　He'll provide for all his own.

4 Care not thou how low thy station,
　　If thy God hath chosen thee
Heir of glory and salvation
　　Now and evermore to be!
　　　Lov'st thou Jesus?
　　Life is thine eternally.
　　　　　　　　　　Thos. MacKellar, 1870.

PENITENCE.

WOODWORTH. L. M.   WILLIAM B. BRADBURY, 1840.

Behold the lamb of God. John 1: 29.   L. M.

181 JUST as I am, without one plea,
But that thy blood was shed for me,
And that thou bid'st me come to thee,
  O Lamb of God, I come! I come!

2 Just as I am, and waiting not
To rid my soul of one dark blot,
To thee, whose blood can cleanse each spot,
  O Lamb of God, I come! I come!

3 Just as I am, though tossed about
With many a conflict, many a doubt,
Fightings within, and fears without,
  O Lamb of God, I come! I come!

4 Just as I am—poor, wretched, blind;
Sight, riches, healing of the mind,
Yea, all I need, in thee to find,
  O Lamb of God, I come! I come!

5 Just as I am—thou wilt receive,
Wilt welcome, pardon, cleanse, relieve,
Because thy promise I believe,
  O Lamb of God, I come! I come!

6 Just as I am—thy love unknown
Hath broken every barrier down:
Now, to be thine, yea, thine alone,
  O Lamb of God, I come! I come!

                              Charlotte Elliott, 1841.

PENITENCE.

A broken heart God's sacrifice.   Psalm 51: 17.   L. M.

182 A BROKEN heart, my God, my King,
Is all the sacrifice I bring;
The God of grace will ne'er despise
A broken heart for sacrifice.

2 My soul is humbled in the dust,
And owns thy dreadful sentence just;
Look down, O Lord, with pitying eye,
And save the soul condemn'd to die.

3 Then will I teach the world thy ways;
Sinners shall learn thy sov'reign grace;
I'll lead them to my Saviour's blood,
And they shall praise a pard'ning God.

4 Oh, may thy love inspire my tongue;
Salvation shall be all my song;
And all my pow'rs shall join to bless
The Lord, my strength and right eousness.

Speak, Lord, thy servant heareth. 1 Sam. 3: 10.   L. M.

183 WHILE now thy throne of grace we seek,
O God! within our spirits speak;
For we will hear thy voice to-day,
Nor turn our harden'd hearts away.

2 Speak in thy gentlest tones of love,
Till all our best affections move;
We long to hear thy gentle call,
And feel that thou art all in all.

3 To conscience speak thy quick'ning word,
Till all its sense of sin is stirr'd;
For we would leave no stain of guile,
To cloud the radiance of thy smile.

4 Speak to convince, forgive, console:
Childlike we yield to thy control:
These hearts, too often clos'd before,
Would grieve thy patient love no more.

HATTIE.   No. 68.

YARBROUGH. M. 5. Used by per. of R. M. McIntosh, Owner of Copyright.

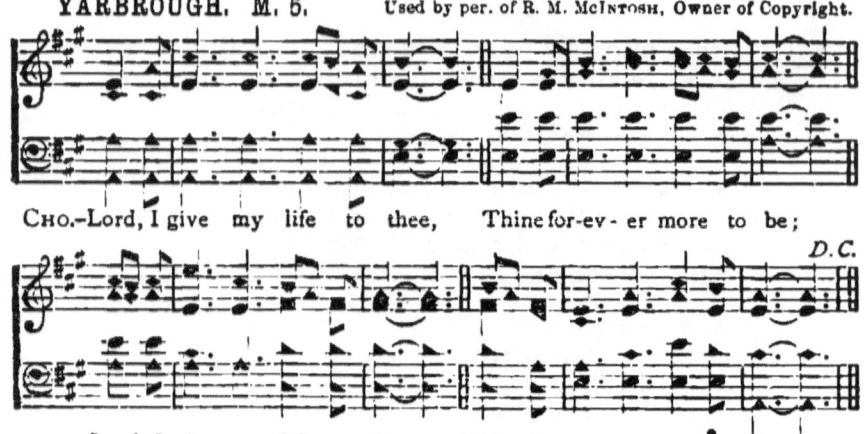

Cho.—Lord, I give my life to thee, Thine for-ev-er more to be;

Lord, I give my life to thee, Thine for-ev-er more to be.

He died that we should live unto Him which died and rose again.
2 Cor. 5: 15.   M. 5.

184 TAKE my life and let it be
Consecrated, Lord, to thee;
Take my hands, and let them move
At the impulse of thy love.

2 Take my feet, and let them be
Swift and beautiful for thee;
Take my voice, and let me sing
Always, only for my King.

3 Take my silver and my gold,
Not a mite would I withhold;
Take my moments and my days,
Let them flow in ceaseless praise.

4 Take my will and make it thine,
It shall be no longer mine;
Take my heart, it is thine own,
It shall be thy royal throne.

5 Take my love; my Lord, I pour
At thy feet its treasure-store;
Take myself, and I will be
Ever, only, all for thee.
            Miss Frances R. Havergal.

Christ Jesus came into the world to save sinners. 1 Tim. 1: 15.   M. 5.

185 DEPTH of mercy! can there be
Mercy still reserved for me?
Can my God his wrath forbear?
Me, the chief of sinners, spare?

2 I have scorned the Son of God,
   Trampled on his precious blood,
   Would not hearken to his calls,
   Grieved him by a thousand falls.

3 Lord, incline me to repent;
   Let me now my fall lament—
   Deeply my revolt deplore,
   Weep, believe, and sin no more.

4 Still for me the Saviour stands,
   Shows his wounds, and spreads his hands:
   God is love, I know, I feel;
   Jesus weeps, and loves me still.
                        C. Wesley, 1740.

Prepare to meet thy God. Amos 4: 12.　　M. 5.

186 SINNER, art thou still secure?
   Wilt thou still refuse to pray?
   Can thy heart or hands endure
   In the Lord's avenging day?

2 Who His advent may abide?
   You that glory in your shame,
   Will you find a place to hide
   When the world is wrapt in flame?

3 Then the rich, the great, the wise,
   Trembling, guilty, self-condemned,
   Must behold the wrathful eyes
   Of the Judge they once blasphemed.

4 Where are now their haughty looks?
   Oh, their horror and despair,
   When they see the opened books,
   And their dreadful sentence hear!

5 Oh, when flesh and heart shall fail,
   Let Thy love our spirits cheer,
   Strengthened thus, we shall prevail
   Over Satan, sin, and fear.

6 Trusting in Thy precious name,
   May we thus our journey end;
   Then our foes shall lose their aim,
   And the Judge shall be our Friend.
                        John Newton, 1779.

PENITENCE.

LOTTIE. S. M.

He beheld the city, and wept over it. Luke 19: 41. S. M.

187 DID Christ o'er sinners weep,
And shall our cheeks be dry?
Let tears of penitential grief
Flow forth from ev'ry eye.

2 The Son of God in tears,
The wond'ring angels see;
Be thou astonish'd, O my soul!
He shed those tears for thee.

3 He wept that we might weep;
Each sin demands a tear;
In heav'n alone no sin is found,
And there's no weeping there.

Thou son of David have mercy. Mark 10: 47. S. M.

188 HAVE mercy, Lord, on me,
As thou wert ever kind;
Let me, oppress'd with loads of guilt,
The wonted pardon find.

2 Against thee, Lord, alone,
And only in thy sight,
Have I transgressed; and tho' condemned,
Must own thy judgments right.

3 Blot out my crying sins,
Nor me in anger view;
Create in me a heart that's clean—
An upright mind renew.

PENITENCE.

I NEED THEE. M. 14. H. S. RUPP.

Lo I am with you always. Matt. 28: 20. M. 14.

189
I NEED thee, precious Jesus,
  For I am very poor;
A stranger and a pilgrim,
  I have no earthly store;
I need the love of Jesus
  To cheer me on my way,
To guide my doubting footsteps,
  To be my strength and stay.

2 I need thee, precious Jesus,
  I need a friend like thee,
A friend to soothe and pity,
  A friend to care for me:
I need the heart of Jesus
  To feel each anxious care,
To tell my every trial,
  And all my sorrows share.

3 I need thee, precious Jesus,
  I need thee day by day,
To fill me with thy fullness,
  To lead me on my way;
I need thy Holy Spirit
  To teach me what I am,
To show me more of Jesus,
  And point me to the Lamb.

LAKE ENON. S. M.

To seek and to save. Luke 19: 10.   S. M.

190 Assist thy servant, Lord,
    The gospel to proclaim;
Let power and love attend thy word,
    And every breast inflame.

2 Bid unbelief depart;
    With love his soul inflame;
Take full posession of his heart,
    And glorify thy name.

3 May stubborn sinners bend
    To thy divine control;
Constrain the wandering to attend,
    And make the wounded whole.

4 Extend thy conquering arm,
    With banner wide unfurled,
Until thy glorious grace shall charm,
    And harmonize the world.

Casting our cares upon him. 1 Pet. 5: 7.   S. M.

191 Jesus, who knows full well
    The heart of every saint,
Invites us all our griefs to tell,
    To pray, and never faint.

2 He bows his gracious ear—
    We never plead in vain;
Then let us wait till he appear,
    And pray, and pray again.

3 Jesus, the Lord, will hear
   His chosen when they cry;
Yes, though he may awhile forbear,
   He'll help them from on high.

4 Then let us earnest cry,
   And never faint in prayer;
He sees, he hears, and from on high
   Will make our cause his care.
                          Newton.

Thou art the guide of my youth. Jer. 3: 4.   S. M.

192 With humble heart and tongue,
   My God, to thee I pray;
Oh make me learn, while I am young,
   How I may cleanse my way.

2 Make an unguarded youth
   The object of thy care;
Help me to choose the way of truth,
   And fly from every snare.

3 My heart to folly prone,
   Renew by power divine;
Unite it to thyself alone,
   And make me wholly thine.

4 Oh, let thy word of grace
   My warmest thoughts employ;
Be this through my remaining days,
   My treasure and my joy.

5 To what thy laws impart,
   Be my whole soul inclined;
Oh, let them dwell within my heart,
   And sanctify my mind.

6 May thy young servant learn,
   By these to cleanse his way;
And may I here the path discern,
   That leads to endless day.

LOTTIE.   No. 187.

ELIZABETHTOWN. C. M.

Geo. Kingsley.

Enoch walked with God. Gen. 5: 22.   C. M.

193
O for a closer walk with God,
  A calm and heavenly frame!
A light to shine upon the road
  That leads me to the Lamb.

2 Where is the blessedness I knew
  When first I saw the Lord?
Where is the soul-refreshing view
  Of Jesus and his word?

3 What peaceful hours I once onjoyed;
  How sweet their memory still!
But they have left an aching void
  The world can never fill.

4 Return, O holy Dove, return,
  Sweet messenger of rest!
I hate the sins that made thee mourn,
  And drove thee from my breast.

5 The dearest idol I have known,
  Whate'er that idol be,
Help me to tear it from thy throne,
  And worship only Thee.

6 So shall my walk be close with God,
  Calm and serene my frame;
So purer light shall mark the road
  That leads me to the Lamb.
                    William Cowper, 1772.

"Deliver my feet from falling." Psalm 56: 13. C. M.

194
ALAS! what hourly dangers rise,
    What snares beset my way!
To heaven, oh, let me lift mine eyes,
    And hourly watch and pray.

2 Increase my faith, increase my hope,
    When fears and foes prevail;
And bear my fainting spirit up,
    Or soon my strength will fail.

3 Oh! keep me in thy heavenly way,
    And bid the tempter flee;
And let me never, never stray
    From happiness and thee.

Mrs. Steele.

The Lord is my Shepherd. Psalm 23: 1. C. M

195
SHEPHERD divine, our wants relieve,
    In this our evil day;
To all thy tempted foll'wers give
    The power to watch and pray.

2 Long as our fiery trials last,
    Long as the cross we bear;
Oh, let our souls on thee be cast
    In never-ceasing prayer!

3 The spirit of redeeming grace,
    Give us in faith to claim;
To wrestle till we see thy face,
    And know thy hidden name.

4 Till thou thy perfect love impart,
    Till thou thyself bestow;
Be this the cry of every heart,
    "I will not let thee go."

5 Then let me on the mountain top
    Behold thy open face,
Where faith in sight is swallowed up,
    And prayer in endless praise.

SOLON.   No. 49.

NAOMI. C. M.   H. G. NÆGELI, 1832.

Let the peace of God rule in your hearts. Col. 3: 15.   C. M.

196 FATHER, whate'er of earthly bliss
    Thy sov'reign will denies,
Accepted at thy throne of grace
    Let this petition rise:—

2 Give me a calm, a thankful heart,
    From every murmur free;
The blessings of thy grace impart,
    And make me live to thee.

3 Let the sweet hope that thou art mine,
    My life and death attend;
Thy presence thro' my journey shine,
    And crown my journey's end.

Anne Steele.

Order my steps in thy word: and let not any iniqity have dominion over me.
Psalm 119: 133.   C. M.

197 GIVE me to know thy will, O God,
    And may I see to-day
A light from heaven upon my road
    To clearly point the way:

2 That I may know just what to do,
    And what to leave undone,
And be unto thy service true
    From dawn to setting sun:

3 That I may speak the timely word,
    And timely silence keep,—
By passion's hasty words unstirr'd
    That cause the soul to weep:

4 That I may hold my thoughts in check,
    And every wild desire
That rises quick at pleasure's beck
    And flames into a fire:

5 That I may kiss the needed rod,
    And patient bear the blow;
And say, 'Tis from the love of God;
    My Father wills it so.

6 Lord Jesus! from thy holy place
    The Spirit on me breathe:
Open the mantle of thy grace
    And keep my soul beneath.
                  Thos. MacKellar, 1880.

Thy mercy, O Lord, is in the heavens. Psalm 36: 5.   C. M.

198
    Above the trembling elements,
      Above life's restless sea,
  Dear Saviour, lift my spirit up,—
    Oh, lift me up to thee!

2 Great calmness there, sweet patience too
    Upon thy face I see:
I would be calm and patient, Lord,
    Oh, lift me up to thee!

3 I am not weary of thy work,
    From earth I would not flee;
But while I walk, and while I serve,
    Oh, lift me up to thee!

4 That I may bless my tender friends,
    And those who love not me;
Oh, lift me high above myself,
    Dear Jesus, up to thee!

5 Whatever falls, of good or ill,
    Thy hand, thy care I see,
And while these varied dealings pass,
    Oh, lift me up to thee!

6 And when my eyes close for the last,
    Still this my prayer shall be,—
Dear Saviour, lift my spirit up,
    And lift me up to thee.

142 PRAYER.

MEMPHIS. C. M.

I have stretched out my hands unto thee. Psalm 88: 9. C. M.

199 Father, I stretch my hands to thee,
No other help I know;
If thou withdraw thyself from me,
Ah, whither shall I go?

2 What did thy only Son endure,
Before I drew my breath!
What pain, what labor to secure
My soul from endless death!

3 O Jesus, could I this believe,
I now should feel thy power;
Now my poor soul thou would'st retrieve,
Nor let me wait one hour.

4 Author of faith, to thee I lift
My weary longing eyes;
O may I now receive that gift,
My soul without it dies.

Descending from heaven like a dove. John 1: 32. C. M.

200 Come, Holy Spirit, heavenly Dove,
With all thy quick'ning powers;
Kindle a flame of sacred love
In these cold hearts of ours.

2 Look how we grovel here below,
Fond of these earthly toys;
Our souls can neither fly nor go,
To reach eternal joys!

3 In vain we tune our formal songs,
    In vain we strive to rise;
  Hosannas languish on our tongues,
    And our devotion dies.

4 Father, and shall we ever live,
    At this poor, dying rate?
  Our love so faint, so cold to thee,
    And thine to us so great?

5 Come, Holy Spirit, heavenly Dove,
    With all thy quick'ning powers;
  Come, shed abroad a Saviour's love,
    And that shall kindle ours.
                  Isaac Watts, 1809.

The Father seeketh such to worship him. John 4: 23.   C. M.

201 PRAYER is the soul's sincere desire,
    Unuttered or expressed;
  The motion of a hidden fire
    That trembles in the breast.

2 Prayer is the burden of a sigh,
    The falling of a tear;
  The upward glancing of an eye,
    When none but God is near.

3 Prayer is the simplest form of speech
    That infant lips can try;
  Prayer, the sublimest strains that reach,
    The Majesty on high.

4 Prayer is the contrite sinner's voice
    Returning from his ways,
  While angels in their songs rejoice,
    And say, "Behold, he prays!"

5 Prayer is the Christian's vital breath,
    The Christian's native air,
  His watchword at the gate of death—
    He enters heaven with prayer.

EVAN.   No. 93.

SOLITUDE. C. M. A. J. SHOWALTER.

Create in me a clean heart. Ps. 51: 10.   C. M.

202 OH, FOR a heart to praise my God,
　　A heart from sin set free!
　A heart that's sprinkled with the blood
　　So freely shed for me.

2 A heart resigned, submissive, meek—
　　My dear Redeemer's throne;
　Where only Christ is heard to speak,
　　Where Jesus reigns alone.

3 A heart in every thought renewed,
　　And full of love divine;
　Perfect, and right, and pure, and good—
　　A copy, Lord, of thine.

4 An humble, lowly, contrite heart,
　　Believing, true and clean,
　Which neither life nor death can part
　　From him that dwells within.
　　　　　　　　　　C. Wesley.

In spirit and in truth. John 4: 23.   C. M.

203 ONCE more we come before our God,
　　Once more his blessing ask.
　Oh, may not duty seem a load,
　　Nor worship prove a task.

2 Father, thy quickening Spirit send
　　On us in Jesus' name;
　To make our waiting minds attend,
　　And put our souls in frame.

3 May we receive the word we hear,
    Each in an honest heart;
  Hoard up the precious treasure there,
    And never with it part.

4 To seek thee all our hearts dispose,
    To each thy blessings suit;
  And let the seed thy servant sows,
    Produce abundant fruit.

5 The thirsty bless with heavenly showers,
    The cold with warmth divine;
  And as the benefit is ours,
    Be all the glory thine.
                                Joseph Hart, 1768.

"He shall hide me." Psalm 27: 5–9.   C. M.

204 DEAR Father, to thy mercy-seat
         My soul for shelter flies,
       'Tis here I find a safe retreat
         When storms and tempests rise.

2 My cheerful hope can never die,
    If thou, my God, art near;
  Thy grace can raise my comforts high,
    And banish every fear.

3 Oh, never let my soul remove
    From this divine retreat!
  Still let me trust thy power and love,
    And dwell beneath thy feet.
                                    Mrs. Steele.

Be renewed in the spirit of your mind. Eph. 4: 23.   C. M.

205 OH, could I find from day to day
         A nearness to my God!
       Then would my hours glide sweet away,
         While leaning on his word.

2 Lord, I desire with Thee to live
    Anew from day to day,
  In joys the world can never give
    Nor ever take away.

3 Blest Jesus, come, and rule my heart,
    And make me wholly thine,
  That I may never more depart,
    Nor grieve thy love divine.
                          Benjamin Cleveland, ab. 1790.

GIVE ME A FOOTHOLD. C. M. D.

H. S. Rupp.

And the rock was Christ. 1 Cor 10: 4.   C. M. D.

206 Give me a foothold on the rock:
    The billows round me roll;
Let not their wild, impetuous shock
    O'erwhelm my trembling soul.
O thou that walkest on the wave,
    Thou Ruler of the sea,
Stretch forth thy mighty arm to save
    The soul that calls on thee.

2 Give me a foothold on the rock,
    O Saviour of the lost!
The world and sin my struggles mock,
    And I am tempest-tost.
I strive to reach an anchoring place:
    My God, give me a stay;
Extend to me thy hand of grace,
    Lest I be cast away.

3 Give me a foothold on the rock,
    Till voices 'yond the sea,
Like evening chimings of the clock,
    Bid welcome home to me.

PRAYER. 147

The day of toil and watching o'er,
The night of sorrow past,
I step upon the eternal shore,
And rest in peace at last.
Thos. MacKellar.

PRAYER. C. M.

Lord, remember me. Luke 23: 42.   C. M.

207 Jesus, thou art the sinner's Friend;
As such I look to thee;
Now in the fullness of thy love,
O Lord! remember me.

2 Remember thy pure word of grace,
Remember Calvary;
Remember all thy dying groans,
And then remember me.

3 Thou wondrous Advocate with God!
I yield myself to thee;
While thou art sitting on thy throne,
O Lord! remember me.

4 I own I'm guilty, own I'm vile,
Yet thy salvation's free;
Then in thy all-abounding grace,
O Lord! remember me.

5 Howe'er forsaken or distressed,
Howe'er oppressed I be,
Howe'er afflicted here on earth,
Do thou remember me.
Richard Burnham, 1783.

URVILLA. L. M.   C. J. MILLER.

Take heed, therefore, how ye hear. Luke 8: 18.   L. M.

208 Thy presence, gracious God, afford;
Prepare us to receive thy word;
Now let thy voice engage our ear,
And faith be mix'd with what we hear.

2 Distracting thoughts and cares remove,
And fix our hearts and hopes above;
With food divine may we be fed,
And satisfied with living bread.

3 To us thy sacred word apply,
With sov'reign pow'r and energy,
And may we, in thy faith and fear
Reduce to practice what we hear.

4 Father, in us thy Son reveal;
Teach us to know and do thy will;
Thy saving pow'r and love display,
And guide us to the realms of day.

Be kind to one another. Eph. 4: 32.   L. M.

209 Jesus, my Saviour, let me be
More perfectly conformed to thee,
Implant each grace, each sin dethrone,
And form my temper like thine own.

2 My foe, when hungry, let me feed,
Share in his grief, supply his need;
The haughty frown may I not fear,
But with a lowly meekness bear.

3 Let the envenomed heart and tongue,
  The hand outstretched to do me wrong,
  Excite no feelings in my breast,
  But such as Jesus once expressed.

4 To others let me always give
  What I from others would receive;
  Good deeds for evil ones return,
  Nor, when provoked, with anger burn.

5 This will proclaim how bright and fair
  The precepts of the gospel are;
  And God himself, the God of love,
  His own resemblance will approve.

First of all, supplications. 1 Tim. 2: 1. L. M.

210 WE pray for those who do not pray!
  Who waste, O Lord, salvation's day:
  For those we love who love not thee;—
  Our grief, their danger, pitying see.

2 Those for whom many tears are shed,
  And blessings breathed upon their head;
  The children of thy people save,
  From godless life and hopeless grave.

3 Hear fathers, mothers, as they pray
  For sons, for daughters, far away—
  Brother for brother, friend for friend—
  Hear all our prayers that upward blend.

4 We pray for those who long have heard,
  But still neglect thy gracious word;
  Soften the hearts obdurate made
  By calls unheeded, vows delayed.

5 Release the drunkard from his chain,
  Save those beguiled by pleasure vain,
  Set free the slaves of lust, and bring
  Back to their home the wandering.

6 The hopeless cheer; guide those who doubt;
  Restore the lost; cast no one out;
  For all that are far off we pray,
  Since we were once far off as they.

Christopher Newman Hall, b. 1816.

PRAYER.

SHARON. L. M. By Com.
Slow

He will guide you into all truth. John 16: 13.   L. M.

211 COME, gracious Spirit, heavenly Dove,
With light and comfort from above;
Be thou our guardian, thou our guide,
O'er every thought and step preside.

2 The light of truth to us display,
And make us know and choose thy way;
Plant holy fear in every heart,
That we from God may ne'er depart.

3 Lead us to holiness—the road
Which we must take to dwell with God;
Lead us to Christ, the living way;
Nor let us from his pastures stray.

4 Lead us to God, our final rest,
To be with him for ever blest;
Lead us to heaven, its bliss to share—
Fullness of joy for ever there.

S. Browne.

"Denying ungodliness." Tit. 2: 12.   L. M.

212 MY God, permit me not to be
A stranger to myself and thee:
Amid a thousand thoughts I rove,
Forgetful of my highest love.

2 Why should my passions mix with earth,
And thus debase my heavenly birth?
Why should I cleave to things below,
And let my God, my Saviour, go?

3 Call me away from flesh and sense;
One sovereign word can draw me thence;
I would obey the voice divine,
And all inferior joys resign.

4 Be earth, with all her scenes, withdrawn;
Let noise and vanity be gone;
In secret silence of the mind
My heaven, and there my God, I find.

Gathered together in my name. Matt. 18: 20.   L. M.

213 WITH thankful hearts we meet, O Lord,
To sing thy praise and hear thy word,
To seek thy face in earnest prayer,
To cast on thee each earthly care.

2 Dear Shepherd of thy chosen flock,
Thy people's shield, their shadowing rock,
Once more we meet to hear thy voice,
Once more before Thee to rejoice.

3 Oh, may thy servants, by thy word,
Refresh each wearied heart, dear Lord,
Wearied of earth's vain strife and woe,
Wearied of sin and all below.

4 Thy presence, Saviour, now we seek,
Confirm the strong, sustain the weak,
Way-worn and tried, we hither come,
Give us a foretaste of our home.

The Lord shall command the blessing. Deut. 28: 8.   L. M.

214 DISMISS us with thy blessing, Lord—
Help us to feed upon thy word;
All that has been amiss forgive,
And let thy truth within us live.

2 Though we are guilty, thou art good—
Wash all our works in Jesus' blood;
Give every fettered soul release,
And bid us all depart in peace.

Jas. Hart.

WOODWORTH.   No. 181.

PURITY. M. 5.

We love him, because he first loved us. 1 John 4: 19. M. 5.

215 Saviour, teach me day by day,
Love's sweet lesson to obey;
Sweeter lesson cannot be:
Loving him who first loved me.

2 With a childlike heart of love,
At thy bidding may I move,
Prompt to serve and follow thee—
Loving him who first loved me.

3 Love in loving finds employ—
In obedience all her joy;
Ever new that joy will be:
Loving him who first loved me.

4 Thus may I rejoice to show
That I feel the love I owe;
Singing till thy face I see,
Of his love who first loved me.

Ask and it shall be given you. Matt. 7: 7. M. 5

216 Come, my soul, thy suit prepare,
Jesus loves to answer prayer;
He himself has bid thee pray,
Therefore will not say thee nay.

2 With my burden I begin,
Lord remove this load of sin;
Let thy blood, for sinners spilt,
Set my conscience free from guilt.

3 Lord, I come to thee for rest,
　Take possession of my breast;
　There thy blood-bought right maintain,
　And without a rival reign.

4 While I am a pilgrim here,
　Let thy love my spirit cheer;
　As my Guide, my Guard, my Friend,
　Lead me to my journey's end.

5 Show me what I have to do,
　Every hour my strength renew;
　Let me live a life of faith,
　Let me die thy people's death.

A blessing humbly and earnestly sought. Gen. 32: 26.   M. 5.

217
1 Lord, we come before thee now,
　At thy feet we humbly bow;
　Oh! do not our suit disdain,
　Shall we seek thee, Lord, in vain?

2 In thine own appointed way,
　Now we seek thee, here we stay:
　Lord, we know not how to go,
　Till a blessing thou bestow.

3 Send some message from thy word,
　That may peace and joy afford;
　Let thy Spirit now impart,
　Full salvation to each heart.

4 Comfort those who weep and mourn,
　Let the time of joy return;
　Those that are cast down lift up,
　Make them strong in faith and hope.

5 Grant that all may seek and find
　Thee a gracious God and kind;
　Heal the sick, the captive free,
　Let us all rejoice in Thee.

EVE.　　　　　　　　　　　　　　No. 102.

PRAYER.

EVENING. M. 4. P. S. Good.

I will fear no evil. Ps. 23: 4.   M. 4.

218   Tarry with me, O my Saviour!
   For the day is passing by;
See! the shades of evening gather,
   And the night is drawing nigh.
Deeper, deeper grow the shadows,
   Paler now the glowing west,
Swift the night of death advances,
   Shall it be the night of rest?

2 Feeble, trembling, fainting, dying,
   Lord, I cast myself on Thee;
Tarry with me thro' the darkness;
   While I sleep, still watch o'er me.
Tarry with me, O my Saviour!
   Lay my head upon Thy breast
Till the morning; then awake me—
   Morning of eternal rest.

Blessed are the meek. Matt. 5: 5.   M. 4.

219   Let thy grace, Lord, make me lowly,
   Humble all my swelling pride;
Fallen, guilty and unholy,
   Greatness from mine eyes I'll hide:
I'll forbid my vain aspiring,
   Nor at earthly honors aim,
No ambitious heights desiring,
   Far above my humble claim.

2 Weaned from earth's delusive pleasures,
   In thy love I'll seek for mine:
Placed in heav'n my nobler treasures,
   Earth I quietly resign:
Thus the transient world despising,
   On the Lord my hopes rely;
Thus my joys from him arising,
   Like himself shall never die.

He leadeth me.   Psalm 23: 2.   M. 4.

220   TAKE my heart, O Father, take it,
   Make and keep it all thine own,
Let thy Spirit melt and break it,
   This proud heart of sin and stone.

2 Father, make it pure and holy,
   Fond of peace and far from strife,
Turning from the paths unholy,
   Of this vain and sinful life.

I will not let thee go except thou bless me.   Gen. 32: 26.   M. 4.

221   JESUS, grant us all a blessing,
   Send it down, Lord, from above;
Give us each a heart of prayer,
   Help us to rejoice in love!
Farewell, brethren—farewell, sisters
   Till we all shall meet above.

2 Jesus, pardon all our follies
   While together we have been;
Make us humble, make us holy,
   Cleanse us all from every sin:
Farewell, brethren—farewell, sisters,
   Till we all shall meet again.

3 May thy blessings, Lord, go with us,
   To each one's respective home,
And the presence of our Jesus
   Rest upon us every one!
Farewell, brethren—farewell sisters,
   Till we all shall meet at home.

                              Atkins.

GREENVILLE.   No. 151.

PRAYER.

GORTON. M. 7.   C. H. BRUNK.

Wilt thou not from this time cry unto me, My Father, thou art the guide of my youth? Jer. 3: 4.   M. 7.

222 FATHER! in my life's young morning,
May thy word direct my way:
Let me heed each gracious warning,
Lest my feet should go astray;
Make me willing
All its precepts to obey.

2 Father! gentle is thy teaching;
Be a docile spirit mine:
Every day thy grace beseeching,
Let thy loving-kindness shine
Always on me,
And my heart be wholly thine.

3 Father! let me never covet
Things of vanity and pride:
Teach me truth, and may I love it
Better than all else beside:
Blessed Bible!
May it be my heavenward guide.
     Thos. MacKellar, 1841.

PRAYER.

"Our Guide unto death." M. 7.

223 GUIDE me, O thou great Jehovah,
　　Pilgrim through this barren land;
I am weak, but thou art mighty;
　　Hold me with thy powerful hand:
　　　Bread of heaven!
　　Feed me till I want no more.

2 Open thou the crystal fountain,
　　Whence the healing streams do flow;
Let the fiery, cloudy pillar
　　Lead me all my journey through:
　　　Strong Deliverer!
　　Be thou still my strength and shield.

3 When I tread the verge of Jordan,
　　Bid my anxious fears subside;
Death of death and hell's Destruction,
　　Land me safe on Canaan's side:
　　　Songs of praises
　　I will ever give to thee.
　　　　　　　　　　W. Williams.

The Lord is my Shepherd.   Psalm 23: 1. M. 7.

224 SAVIOUR, like a shepherd lead us,
　　Much we need thy tenderest care;
In thy pleasant pastures feed us,
　　For our use thy folds prepare:
　　　Blessèd Jesus,
　　Thou hast bought us, thine we are.

2 Thou hast promised to receive us,
　　Poor and sinful though we be;
Thou hast mercy to relieve us,
　　Grace to cleanse and power to free:
　　　Blessèd Jesus,
　　We will early turn to thee.

3 Early let us seek thy favor,
　　Early let us do thy will;
Blessed Lord and only Saviour,
　　With thy love our bosoms fill:
　　　Blessèd Jesus,
　　Thou hast loved us, love us still.
　　　　　　　　Dorothy Ann Thrupp.

GOLDEN HILL. S. M. ANANIAS DAVISSON, 1811.

The Lord is merciful and gracious. Ps. 103: 8.   S. M.

225 Teach me, my God and King,
   Thy will in all to see;
And what I do in any thing,
   To do it as for thee!

2 To scorn the senses' sway,
   While still to thee I tend;
In all I do, be thou the way,
   In all, be thou the end.

3 All may of thee partake;
   Nothing so small can be
But draws, when acted for thy sake,
   Greatness and worth from thee.

4 If done beneath thy laws
   E'en servile labors shine;
Hallow'd is toil, if this the cause;
   The meanest work, divine.

Pray without ceasing. 1 Thess. 5: 17.   S. M.

226 The Lord, who truly knows
   The heart of ev'ry saint,
Invites us by His holy word
   To pray and never faint.

2 He bows His gracious ear;
   We never plead in vain;
Yet we must wait till He appear,
   And pray, and pray again.

PRAYER.   159

3 'Twas thus a widow poor,
    Without support or friend,
  Beset the unjust judge's door,
    And gain'd at last her end.

4 And shall not Jesus hear
    His children when they cry?
  Yes, though He may awhile forbear,
    He'll not their suit deny.

5 Then let us earnest be,
    And never faint in prayer;
  He loves our importunity,
    And makes our cause His care.

After this manner therefore pray ye. Matt. 6: 9.   S. M.

227 OUR heavenly Father, hear
    The prayer we offer now:—
  Thy name be hallowed far and near,
    To thee all nations bow.

2 Thy kingdom come; thy will
    On earth be done in love,
  As saints and seraphim fulfill
    Thy perfect law above.

3 Our daily bread supply,
    While by thy word we live;
  The guilt of our iniquity
    Forgive, as we forgive.

4 From dark temptation's power,
    From Satan's wiles, defend;
  Deliver in the evil hour,
    And guide us to the end.

5 Thine, then, forever be
    Glory and power divine;
  The sceptre, throne, and majesty,
    Of heaven and earth are thine.
                    James Montgomery, ab. 1825.

LAKE ENON.   No. 190.

SWEET HOUR OF PRAYER. L. M.

W. B. Bradbury.
By per. of Biglow & Main, owners of copyright.

The sweet Hour. L. M.

228 Sweet hour of prayer! sweet hour of prayer!
That calls me from a world of care,
And bids me at my Father's throne
Make all my wants and wishes known;
In seasons of distress and grief,
My soul has often found relief,
And oft escaped the tempter's snare
By thy return, sweet hour of prayer.

2 Sweet hour of prayer! sweet hour of prayer!
Thy wings shall my petition bear,
To him whose truth and faithfulness
Engage the waiting soul to bless;
And, since he bids me seek his face,
Believe his word, and trust his grace,
I'll cast on him my every care,
And wait for thee, sweet hour of prayer.

PRAYER. 161

3 Sweet hour of prayer! sweet hour of prayer!
May I thy consolation share;
Till from Mount Pisgah's lofty height,
I view my home and take my flight;
This robe of flesh I'll drop, and rise
To seize the everlasting prize;
And shout, while passing through the air,
Farewell, farewell, sweet hour of prayer!
Walford.

Brethren, pray for us. 2 Thess. 3: 1.   L. M.

229 FATHER of mercies, bow thine ear,
Attentive to our earnest prayer;
We plead for those who plead for thee;
Successful pleaders may they be.
Clothe Thou their words with power divine,
And let those words be ever thine;
To them thy sacred truth reveal;
Suppress their fear, inflame their zeal.

2 Teach them to sow the precious seed;
Teach them thy chosen flock to feed;
Teach them thy wandering sheep to gain,
Nor let them labor, Lord, in vain.
Let thronging multitudes around
Hear from their lips the joyful sound;
In humble strains thy grace adore,
And feel thy new creating power.
Benjamin Beddome. ab. 1787.

God giveth the increase. 1 Cor. 3: 7.   L. M.

230 FATHER in heaven, upon Thy word,
Which thine assembled flock have heard;
Cause thou the Spirit's dew to fall,—
In bounteous blessing on us all.

2 May the good seed now sown take root,
And grow, and bear abundant fruit;
And may the souls assembled here,
In peace before thy throne appear.

HEBRON.   No. 95.

PRAYER.

I AM PRAYING FOR YOU. 11s & 12s. Used by per. of Ira. D Sankey.

Evening, and morning, and at noon, will I pray. Ps. 55: 17.   11s & 12s.

231
 1. I HAVE a Saviour, He's pleading in glory,
    A dear, loving Saviour tho earth-friends be few;
    And now He is watching in tenderness o'er me,
    And oh that my Saviour were your Saviour too!

 2. I have a Father: to me He has given
    A hope for eternity, blesséd and true;
    And soon will He call me to meet Him in heaven,
    But oh that He'd let me bring you with me too!

 3. I have a robe: 'tis resplendent in whiteness,
    Awaiting in glory my wandering view;
    Oh, when I receive it all shining in brightness,
    Dear friend, could I see you receiving it too!

4 I have a peace, it is calm as a river—
 A peace that the friends of this world never knew;
 My Saviour alone is its Author and Giver,
 And oh, could I know it was given to you!

5 When Jesus has found you, tell others the story,
 That my loving Saviour is your Saviour too,
 Then pray that your Saviour may bring them to glory,
 And prayer will be answered—'twas answered for you.
S. O'Maley Cluff.

SWEET HOME. M 11.   Sir H. R. Bishop.

Pre-pare me, dear Sav-iour, for glo-ry my home. Home, home, sweet, sweet, home,

They desire a better country. Heb. 11: 16.   M. 11.

232 'MID scenes of confusion and creature complaints,
 How sweet to my soul is communion with saints:
 To find at the banquet of mercy there's room,
 And feel in the presence of Jesus at home.

2 Sweet bonds that unite all the children of peace!
 And thrice, precious Jesus, whose love cannot cease!
 Though oft from thy presence in sadness I roam,
 I long to behold thee, in glory at home.

3 While here in the valley of conflict I stay,
 Oh, give me submission and strength as my day,
 In all my afflictions to thee would I come,
 Rejoicing in hope of my glorious home.

4 I long, dearest Lord! in thy beauty to shine,
 No more as an exile in sorrow to pine,
 And in thy dear image arise from the tomb,
 With glorified millions to praise thee at home.
David Dedham, 1826.

PRAYER.

NEW HAVEN. M 26. L. MASON, 1830.

"*Looking unto Jesus.*"   M. 26.

233   My faith looks up to thee,
Thou Lamb of Calvary,
   Saviour Divine!
Now hear me while I pray;
Take all my guilt away;
Oh, let me from this day,
   Be wholly thine!

2 May thy rich grace impart
Strength to my fainting heart,—
   My zeal inspire!
As thou hast died for me,
Oh, may my love to thee
Pure, warm and changeless be—
   A living fire!

3 While life's dark maze I tread,
And griefs around me spread,
   Be thou my guide;
Bid darkness turn to day,
Wipe sorrow's tears away,
Nor let me ever stray
   From thee aside.

4 When ends life's transient dream,
When death's cold sullen stream
   Shall o'er me roll,
Blest Saviour! then, in love,
Fear and distrust remove;
Oh, bear me safe above—
   A ransomed soul.

Ray Palmer.

PRAYER.

EVEN ME. M. 4.   W. B. BRADBURY.
Used by per. of Biglow and Main, owners of copyright.

E - ven me, E - ven me, Let thy bless-ing fall on me.

Bless me, even me also. Gen. 27: 34.   M. 4.

234   LORD, I hear of showers of blessing
Thou art scattering, full and free;
Showers the thirsty land refreshing;
Let some droppings fall on me. Even me.

2 Pass me not, O gracious Father!
Sinful though my heart may be;
Thou might'st leave me, but the rather
Let thy mercy light on me.

3 Pass me not, O tender Saviour!
Let me love and cling to thee;
I am longing for thy favor;
When thou comest, call for me.

4 Pass me not, O mighty Spirit!
Thou canst make the blind to see;
Witnesser of Jesus' merit,
Speak the word of power to me.

5 Love of God, so pure and changeless,
Blood of Christ, so rich and free,
Grace of God, so strong and boundless,
Magnify them all in me.

6 Pass me not! Thy lost one bringing,
Bind my heart, O Lord, to Thee;
While the streams of life are springing,
Blessing others, oh, bless me.
                                  Elizabeth Codner, 1860.

PRAYER.

JOSIE. M. 5.   A. S. KIEFFER, by per.

And he laid his hands on them, and departed thence.   *Matt. 19: 15.*   M. 5.

235   HEAR me, Saviour, while I pray
     On this holy Sabbath day;
   Bless me as Thou didst of old
   Bless the lambs of Israel's fold.

   2 Hold my hand within Thine own,
     That I may not walk alone;
     Guide my footsteps lest they stray
     Into sin's dark desert way.

God is present every-where.   M. 5.

236   THEY who seek the throne of grace,
     Find that throne in ev'ry place;
   If we live a life of pray'r,
   God is present ev'ry-where.

   2 In our sickness and our health,
     In our want, or in our wealth,
     If we look to God in pray'r,
     God is present ev'ry-where.

   3 When our earthly comforts fail,
     When the woes of life prevail,
     'Tis the time for earnest pray'r;
     God is present ev'ry-where.

   4 Then, my soul, in ev'ry strait,
     To thy Father come, and wait,
     He will answer ev'ry pray'r:
     God is present ev'ry-where.

SYKES. L. M.   J. H. HALL, by per.

He shall testify of me. John 15: 26.   L. M.

237 COME, Holy Spirit, calm my mind,
And fit me to approach my God;
Remove each vain, each worldly thought,
And lead me to thy blest abode.

2 Hast thou imparted to my soul
A living spark of holy fire?
Oh, kindle now the sacred flame,
And make me burn with pure desire.

3 A brighter faith and hope impart,
And let me now my Saviour see;
Oh, soothe and cheer my burdened heart,
And bid my spirit rest in thee.
John Stewart, 1803.

Gathered together in my name. Matt. 18: 20.   L. M.

238 "WHERE two or three, with sweet accord,
Obedient to their Sovereign Lord,
Meet to recount his acts of grace,
And offer solemn prayer and praise:

2 "There," says the Saviour, "will I be,
Amid this little company;—
To them unveil my smiling face,
And shed my glories round the place."

3 We meet at thy command, dear Lord,
Relying on thy faithful word:
Now send thy Spirit from above;
Now fill our hearts with heavenly love.
Samuel Stennett, 1787.

OLIVET. L. M.   Used by per. of O. Ditson & Co., owners of copyright.

I will sing and give praise. Psalm 108: 1.   L. M.

239
Awake my soul, awake my tongue;
My God demands the grateful song;
Let all my inmost powers record
The wondrous mercy of the Lord.

2 Divinely free his mercy flows,
Forgives my sins, allays my woes,
And bids approaching death remove,
And crowns me with indulgent love.

3 His mercy, with unchanging rays,
Forever shines, while time decays;
And children's children shall record
The truth and goodness of the Lord.

4 While all his works his praise proclaim,
And men and angels bless his name,
Oh, let my heart, my life, my tongue
Attend, and join the blissful song.

Anne Stelle, 1778.

Let us worship and bow down. Psalm 95: 6.   L. M.

240
OH, come, loud anthems let us sing,
Loud thanks to our almighty King!
For we our voices high should raise,
When our salvation's Rock we praise.

2 Into his presence let us haste,
To thank him for his favors past;
To him address in joyful songs
The praise that to his name belongs.

3 Oh, let us to his courts repair,
And bow with adoration there!
Down on our knees, devoutly, all
Before the Lord, our Maker, fall.
                               Tate and Brady, ab. 1696.

Praise waiteth for thee O God, in Zion. Psalm 65: 1.   L. M.

241
MY soul, with humble fervor raise
To God the voice of grateful praise,
And all my ransomed powers combine,
To bless his attributes divine.

2 Deep on my heart let memory trace
His acts of mercy and of grace,
Who, with a Father's tender care,
Saved me when sinking in despair;

3 Gave my repentant soul to prove
The joy of his forgiving love:
Poured balm into my bleeding breast,
And led my weary feet to rest.
                               Livingston, 1789.

Give unto the Lord glory and strength. Psalm 29: 1.   L. M.

242
THEE we adore, eternal Lord!
We praise thy name with one accord;
Thy saints, who here Thy goodness see,
Through all the world do worship Thee.

2 To Thee aloud all angels cry,
And ceaseless raise their songs on high,
Both cherubim and seraphim,
The heavens and all the powers therein.

3 The apostles join the glorious throng;
The prophets swell the immortal song;
The martyrs' noble army raise
Eternal anthems to Thy praise.

DUKE STREET. L. M.   J. HATTON.

How excellent is Thy loving kindness. Psalm 36: 7.   L. M.

243
1. AWAKE, my soul, in joyful lays,
And sing thy great Redeemer's praise:
He justly claims a song from me:
His loving-kindness, Oh, how free!

2. He saw me ruined in the fall,
Yet loved me notwithstanding all;
And saved me from my lost estate:
His loving-kindness is so great!

3. Through mighty hosts of cruel foes,
Where earth and hell my way oppose;
He safely leads my soul along:
His loving-kindness, Oh, how strong!

4. When trouble, like a gloomy cloud,
Has gathered thick and thundered loud,
He near my soul has always stood:
His loving-kindness, Oh, how good!

5. So when I pass death's gloomy vale,
And life and mortal powers shall fail;
Oh, may my last, expiring breath
His loving-kindness sing in death.

6. When conquered death shall yield its prey,
When Christ shall call us hence away;
Then shall I sing, with sweet surprise
His loving-kindness in the skies.

   Medley.

Bless the Lord, O my soul. Psalm 103: 1. L. M.

244
Bless, O my soul! the living God;
Call home thy thoughts that rove abroad:
Let all the powers within me join
In work and worship so divine.

2 Bless, O my soul! the God of grace;
His favors claim thy highest praise;
Why should the wonders he hath wrought
Be lost in silence, and forgot?

3 'Tis he, my soul, that sent his Son
To die for crimes which thou hast done;
He owns the ransom, and forgives
The hourly follies of our lives.

4 Let every land his power confess;
Let all the earth adore his grace:
My heart and tongue with rapture join
In work and worship so divine.
               Isaac Watts, ab. 1719.

Praise ye the Lord: it is good to sing praises unto our God. Psalm 147: 1.
L. M.

245
Come, O my soul! in sacred lays,
Attempt thy great Creator's praise:
But, oh, what tongue can speak his fame!
What mortal verse can reach the theme!

2 Enthroned amid the radiant spheres,
He glory, like a garment, wears;
To form a robe of light divine,
Ten thousand suns around him shine.

3 In all our Maker's grand designs,
Almighty power, with wisdom, shines;
His works, through all this wondrous frame,
Declare the glory of his name.

4 Raised on devotion's lofty wing,
Do thou, my soul, his glories sing:
And let his praise employ thy tongue,
Till listening worlds shall join the song!
               Blacklock.

WARD. No. 135.

OLD HUNDRED. L. M.
GUILLAUME FRANCK, 1543.

Serve the Lord with gladness. Psalm 100: 2.   L. M.

246 PRAISE God, from whom all blessings flow;
Praise him, all creatures here below;
Praise him above, ye heavenly host;
Praise Father, Son, and Holy Ghost.

2 Ye nations round the earth rejoice
Before the Lord your Sovereign King;
Serve him with cheerful heart and voice;
With all your tongues his glory sing.

3 The Lord is God: 'Tis he alone
Doth life, and breath, and being give:
We are his work, and not our own;
The sheep that on his pasture live.

4 Enter his gates with songs of joy,
With praises to his courts repair;
And make it your divine employ
To pay your thanks and honors there.

5 The Lord is good, the Lord is kind;
Great is his grace, his mercy sure;
And the whole race of man shall find
His truth from age to age endure.
Isaac Watts, 1719.

All thy works shall praise thee, O Lord. Psalm 145. 10.   L. M

247 ALL praise to Thee, the triune One,
The Holy Father, Holy Son,
And Holy Spirit! Thou alone
Art King on the eternal throne.
Thos. MacKellar.

O give thanks unto the Lord, for he is good: for his mercy endureth forever.
Psalm 107: 1. L. M.

248 O RENDER thanks to God above,
  The Fountain of eternal love,
Whose mercy firm through ages past
Has stood, and shall for ever last.

2 Who can his mighty deeds express,
  Not only vast, but numberless!
What mortal eloquence can raise
A tribute equal to his praise!

Surely his salvation is nigh them that fear him. Psalm 85: 9. L. M.

249 O LOVE, beyond conception great,
  That form'd the vast, stupendous plan,
Where all divine perfections meet
  To reconcile rebellious man.

2 There wisdom shines in fullest blaze,
  And justice all her right maintains—
Astonish'd angels stoop to gaze,
  While mercy o'er the guilty reigns.

3 Yes, mercy reigns, and justice too;
  In Christ they both harmonious meet;
He paid to justice all her due;
  And now he fills the mercy-seat.

God incomprehensible. Job 11: 7. L. M.

250 GREAT God, in vain man's narrow view
  Attempts to look thy nature through:
Our lab'ring pow'rs with rev'rence own
Thy glories never can be known.

2 Not the high seraph's mighty thought,
Who countless years his God has sought,
Such wondrous height or depth can find,
Or fully trace thy boundless mind.

3 Yet, Lord, thy kindness deigns to show
All that we mortals need to know;
While wisdom, goodness, pow'r divine,
Through all thy works and conduct shine.

4 O, may our souls with rapture trace
Thy works of nature and of grace;
Adore thy sacred name, and still
Press on to know and do thy will.

PRAISE.

WESTON. L. M.   L. O. Emerson, 1847.

Every thing that hath breath praise the Lord. Psalm 150: 6.   L. M.

251   From all that dwell below the skies,
Let the Creator's praise arise;
Let the Redeemer's name be sung,
Through every land, by every tongue.

2 Eternal are thy mercies, Lord,
Eternal truth attends thy word;
Thy praise shall sound from shore to shore,
Till suns shall rise and set no more.

3 Your lofty themes, ye mortals, bring,
In songs of praise divinely sing;
The great salvation loud proclaim,
And shout for joy the Saviour's name.

4 In every land begin the song,
To every land the strains belong;
In cheerful sound all voices raise,
And fill the world with loudest praise.

                                                                   I. Watts.

It is good to sing praises. Psalm 147: 1.   L. M.

252   O praise the Lord, 'tis sweet to raise
The grateful heart to God in praise:
When fallen raised, when lost restored,
Oh! it is sweet to praise the Lord!

2 Great is his power, divine his skill,
His love diviner, greater still;
The sinner's friend, the mourner's stay,
He sends no suppliant sad away.

O the depth of the riches both of the wisdom and knowledge of God.
Rom. 11: 33. L. M.

253 AWAKE, my tongue, the tribute bring
To him, who gave thee power to sing;
Praise him, who is all praise above,
The source of wisdom and of love.

2 How vast his knowledge! how profound!
A depth where all our thoughts are drowned!
The stars he numbers, and their names
He gives to all those heavenly flames.

3 Through each bright world above, behold
Ten thousand thousand charms unfold:
Earth, air, and mighty seas combine,
To speak his wisdom all divine.

4 But in redemption, O what grace!
Its wonders, O what thought can trace!
Here wisdom shines for ever bright:
Praise him, my soul, with sweet delight.
John Needham, 1768.

O give thanks unto the Lord; for he is good. *Psalm 118: 1.* L. M.

254 ALMIGHTY Sov'reign of the skies,
To Thee let songs of gladness rise,
Each grateful heart its tribute bring,
And ev'ry voice Thy goodness sing.

2 From Thee our choicest blessings flow;
Life, health and strength Thy hands bestow;
The daily good Thy creatures share,
Springs from Thy providential care.

3 The rich profusion nature yields,
The harvest waving o'er the fields,
The cheering light, refreshing shower,
Are gifts from Thy exhaustless store.

4 At Thy command the vernal bloom
Revives the world from winter's gloom;
The summer's heat the fruit matures,
And autumn all her treasures pours.

5 Let ev'ry power of heart and tongue
Unite to swell the grateful song;
While age and youth in chorus join,
And praise the Majesty Divine.
Watts.

CORONATION. C. M.   OLIVER HOLDEN, 1793.

On his head were many crowns. Rev. 19: 12.   C. M.

255 ALL hail the power of Jesus' name,
    Let angels prostrate fall!
Bring forth the royal diadem,
    And crown him Lord of all. Bring, etc.

2 Ye seed of Israel's chosen race,
    Ye ransomed from the fall;
Hail him who saves you by his grace,
    And crown him Lord of all. Hail, etc.

3 Let every kindred, every tribe,
    On this terrestrial ball,
To him all majesty ascribe,
    And crown him Lord of all. To him, **etc.**

4 Oh, that with yonder sacred throng,
    We at his feet may fall!
We'll join the everlasting song,
    And crown him Lord of all. We'll etc.
                          Edward Perronet, ab. 1779.

PRAISE.

Who his own self bare our sins. 1 Pet. 2: 24.   C. M.

256
1 AWAKE, awake the sacred song,
   To our incarnate Lord;
Let every heart and every tongue
   Adore th' Eternal Word.

2 That mighty Word, that sovereign Power,
   By whom the worlds were made,—
O happy morn! illustrious hour!—
   Was once in flesh arrayed.

3 To dwell with misery below,
   The Saviour left the skies,
And sunk to wretchedness and woe,
   That sinful man might rise.

4 Adoring angels tune their songs,
   To hail the joyful day;
With rapture then let mortal tongues,
   Their grateful worship pay.

"Unto Him be glory."   C. M.

257
1 O FOR a thousand tongues to sing
   My dear Redeemer's praise,
The glories of my God and King,
   The triumphs of his grace!

2 My gracious Master and my God,
   Assist me to proclaim,
To spread through all the earth abroad
   The honors of thy name.

3 Jesus! the name that calms our fears,
   That bids our sorrows cease—
'Tis music to my ravished ears,
   'Tis life, and health, and peace.

4 He breaks the power of reigning sin,
   He sets the prisoner free;
His blood can make the foulest clean:
   His blood availed for me!

5 Look unto him, ye nations; own
   Your God, ye fallen race!
Look and be saved through faith alone;
   Be justified by grace.

                                C. Wesley.

ST. MARTIN'S. C. M.   W. TANSUR.

A new song before the throne. Rev. 14: 3.   C. M.

258
BEHOLD the glories of the Lamb,
  Amid the Father's throne;
Prepare new honors for his name,
  And songs before unknown.

2 Let elders worship at His feet,
  The church adore around,
With vials full of odors sweet,
  And harps of sweeter sound.

3 Those are the prayers of all the saints,
  And these the hymns they raise;
Jesus is kind to our complaints,
  He loves to hear our praise.

4 Now, to the Lamb that once was slain
  Be endless blessings paid;
Salvation, glory, joy, remain
  Forever on thy head.

5 Thou hast redeemed our souls with blood,
  Hast set the prisoners free;
Hast made us kings and priests to God,
  And we shall reign with thee.
                  Isaac Watts, 1706.

PRAISE.

Gratitude.   C. M.

259 When all thy mercies, O my God,
    My rising soul surveys,
Transported with the view, I'm lost
    In wonder, love, and praise.

2 Unnumber'd comforts on my soul
    Thy tender care bestow'd,
Before my infant heart conceiv'd
    From whom those comforts flow'd.

3 When in the slippery paths of youth,
    With heedless steps I ran,
Thine arm, unseen, convey'd me safe,
    And led me up to man.

4 Ten thousand thousand precious gifts
    My daily thanks employ;
Nor is the least a cheerful heart,
    That tastes those gifts with joy.

5 Through every period of my life,
    Thy goodness I'll pursue;
And after death, in distant worlds,
    The glorious theme renew.

Addison.

God's goodness universal. Matt. 5: 45.   C. M.

260 Sweet is the mem'ry of thy grace,
    My God, my heav'nly King!
Let age to age thy righteousness
    In sounds of glory sing.

2 God reigns on high, but not confines
    His goodness to the skies:
Thro' the whole earth his goodness shines,
    And ev'ry want supplies.

3 How kind are thy compassions, Lord,
    How slow thine anger moves;
But soon he sends his pard'ning word,
    To cheer the soul he loves.

4 Creatures with all their endless race,
    Thy pow'r and praise proclaim;
But we who taste thy richer grace,
    Delight to bless thy name.

Watts.

ORTONVILLE. C. M.   Thomas Hastings, 1837.

The chiefest among ten thousand. Cant: 5: 10.   C. M.

261   MAJESTIC sweetness sits enthroned
        Upon the Saviour's brow;
    His head with radiant glories crowned,
        His lips with grace o'erflow.

2 No mortal can with him compare,
    Among the sons of men;
Fairer is he than all the fair
    That fill the heavenly train.

3 He saw me plunged in deep distress,
    He flew to my relief;
For me he bore the shameful cross,
    And carried all my grief.

4 His hand a thousand blessings pours
    Upon my guilty head;
His presence gilds my darkest hours,
    And guards my sleeping bed.

5 Since from his bounty I receive
    Such proofs of love divine,
Had I a thousand hearts to give,
    Lord, they should all be thine.
                        Samuel Stennett, ab. 1787.

Thy name is as ointment poured fourth. Canticles 1: 3.   C. M.

262   HOW sweet the name of Jesus sounds
        In a believer's ear!
    It soothes his sorrows, heals his wounds,
        And drives away his fear.

2 It makes the wounded spirit whole,
    And calms the troubled breast;
  'Tis manna to the hungry soul,
    And to the weary rest.

3 Dear Name! the rock on which I build,
    My shield and hiding-place;
  My never-failing treasury, filled
    With boundless stores of grace.

4 Jesus! my shepherd, Husband, Friend,
    My Prophet, Priest, and King;
  My Lord, my Life, my Way, my End,
    Accept the praise I bring.

5 Weak is the effort of my heart,
    And cold my warmest thought
  But when I see Thee as thou art,
    I'll praise thee as I ought.

6 Till then I would thy love proclaim
    With every fleeting breath;
  And may the music of thy name
    Refresh my soul in death!
                        John Newton, 1779.

Under the shadow of the Almighty. Psalm 91: 1.   C. M.

283 WHAT glory gilds the sacred page!
      Majestic like the sun;
    It gives a light to every age,
      It gives, but borrows none.

2 His hand that gave it, still supplies
    The gracious light and heat;
  His truths upon the nations rise;
    They rise, but never set.

3 Let everlasting thanks be thine,
    For such a bright display,
  As makes a world of darkness shine,
    With beams of heavenly day.

4 My soul rejoices to pursue
    The path of truth and love;
  Till glory breaks upon my view
    In brighter worlds above.

JOYFUL SOUND. C. M.

Salvation to our God. Rev. 7: 10. C. M.

264
SALVATION! oh, the joyful sound,
   What pleasure to our ears!
A sovereign balm for every wound,
   A cordial for our fears.

2 Buried in sorrow and in sin,
   On death's dark way we stray;
But we arise by grace divine,
   To see a heavenly day.

3 Salvation! let the echo fly
   The spacious earth around:
While all the armies of the sky
   Conspire to raise the sound!

4 Salvation! O thou bleeding Lamb,
   To thee the praise belongs;
Salvation shall inspire our hearts,
   And dwell upon our tongues.
Vs 1-3 Isaac Watts, 1709. Vs. 4 W. Shirley, 1725-1786.

Unto thee, O God, do we give thanks. Psalm 75: 1. C. M.

265
COME let us all unite to praise
   The Saviour of mankind;
Our thankful hearts in solemn lays
   Be with our voices joined.

2 O Lord, we cannot silent be;
   By love we are constrained
To offer our best thanks to thee,
   Our Saviour, and our Friend.

3 Though feeble are our best essays,
　　Thy love will not despise
　Our grateful songs of humble praise,
　　Our well-meant sacrifice.

4 Let every tongue thy goodness show,
　　And spread abroad thy fame;
　Let every heart with praise o'erflow,
　　And bless thy sacred name!

Unto him that loved us.   Rev. 1: 5.　　　C. M.

266　There is a name I love to hear;
　　I love to sing its worth;
　It sounds like music in mine ear,
　　The sweetest name on earth.

2 It tells me of a Saviour's love,
　　Who died to set me free;
　It tells me of his precious blood
　　The sinner's perfect plea.

3 It tells of One whose loving heart
　　Can feel my smallest woe:
　Who in each sorrow bears a part
　　That none can bear below.

4 Jesus! the name I love so well,
　　The name I love to hear!
　No saint on earth its worth can tell,
　　No heart conceive how dear.

Gathered together in my name.   Matt. 18: 20.　　C. M.

267　In thy great name, O Lord, we come,
　　To worship at thy feet;
　O, pour thy Holy Spirit down
　　On all that now shall meet.

2 We come to hear Jehovah speak,
　　To hear the Saviour's voice;
　Thy face and favor, Lord, we seek;
　　Now make our hearts rejoice.

3 Teach us to pray and praise, and hear,
　　And understand thy word;
　To feel thy blissful presence near,
　　And trust our living Lord.

NETTLETON. M. 4.   JOHN WYETH, 1812.

Hitherto hath the Lord helped us. 1 Sam. 7: 12.   M. 4.

268 COME thou Fount of every blessing,
    Tune my heart to sing thy grace;
Streams of mercy, never ceasing,
    Call for songs of loudest praise.
Teach me some melodious sonnet,
    Sung by flaming tongues above;
Praise the mount—oh, fix me on it,
    Mount of God's unchanging love.

2 Here I raise my Ebenezer,
    Hither by thine help I'm come;
And I hope, by thy good pleasure,
    Safely to arrive at home.
Jesus sought me when a stranger,
    Wandering from the fold of God,
He, to rescue me from danger,
    Interposed his precious blood.

3 Oh, to grace how great a debtor
    Daily I'm constrain'd to be!
Let that grace, now, like a fetter,
    Bind my wandering heart to thee.
Prone to wander, Lord, I feel it;
    Prone to leave the God I love—
Here's my heart, oh, take and seal it,
    Seal it from thy courts above.
                    Robert Robinson, 1758.

PRAISE.

Worthy the Lamb that was slain.. Rev. 5: 12.   M. 4.

269
   Hail! my ever blessèd Jesus,
     Only Thee I wish to sing;
   To my soul Thy name is precious,
     Thou my Prophet, Priest, and King.
   Oh, what mercy flows from heaven,
     Oh, what joy and happiness!
   Love I much? I've much forgiven;
     I'm a miracle of grace.

2 Once with Adam's race in ruin,
    Unconcern'd in sin I lay;
  Swift destruction still pursuing,
    Till my Saviour pass'd this way.
  Witness, all ye hosts of heaven,
    My Redeemer's tenderness;
  Love I much? I've much forgiven;
    I'm a miracle of grace.

3 Sing, ye bright angelic choir,
    Praise the Lamb enthroned above;
  Whilst astonish'd, I admire
    God's free grace and boundless love.
  That blest moment I received Him,
    Fill'd my soul with joy and peace;
  Love I much? I've much forgiven;
    I'm a miracle of grace.

Walk as children of light. Eph. 5: 8.   M. 4.

270
   Lord, a little band, and lowly,
     We are come to sing to thee;
   Thou art great, and high, and holy—
     O how solemn should we be!
   Fill our hearts with thoughts of Jesus,
     And of heav'n, where he is gone;
   And let nothing ever please us
     He would grieve to look upon.

2 For we know the Lord of glory
    Always sees what children do,
  And is writing now the story
    Of our thoughts and actions, too.
  Let our sins be all forgiven;
    Make us fear whate'er is wrong;
  Lead us on our way to heaven,
    There to sing a nobler song.

DIVINE COMPASSION. M. 4.

Looking unto Jesus, the author and finisher of our faith. Heb. 12: 2. M. 4.

271 Sweet the moments, rich in blessing,
   Which before the cross I spend,
Life and health and peace possessing
   From the sinner's dying Friend;
Here I'll sit forever viewing,
   Mercy's streams in streams of blood,
Precious drops my soul bedewing,
   Plead and claim my peace with God.

2 Truly blessèd is this station,
   Low before his cross to lie;
While I see divine compassion
   Floating in his languid eye;
Here it is I find my heaven,
   While upon the Lamb I gaze,
Love I much—I've much forgiven;
   I'm a miracle of grace.

3 Love and grief my heart dividing,
   With my tears his feet I'll bathe,
Constant still in faith abiding,
   Life deriving from his death;
May I still enjoy this feeling,
   In all need to Jesus go;
Prove his wounds each day more healing,
   And himself more deeply known.

James Allen.

Seeing he ever liveth to make intercession for them. Heb. 7: 25. M. 4.

272
Jesus, hail! enthroned in glory,
  There forever to abide;
All the heavenly hosts adore thee,
  Seated at thy Father's side:
There for sinners thou art pleading,
  There thou dost our place prepare,
Ever for us interceding,
  Till in glory we appear.

2 Worship, honor, power, and blessing,
  Thou art worthy to receive;
Loudest praises, without ceasing,
  Meet it is for us to give.
Help, ye bright angelic spirits!
  Bring your sweetest, noblest lays:
Help to sing our Saviour's merits;
  Help to chant Immanuel's praise.
                                        Bakewell.

Praise ye the Lord. Psalm 148. M. 4.

273
Praise the Lord; ye heavens, adore him;
  Praise him, angels, in the height;
Sun and moon, rejoice before him;
  Praise him, all ye stars of light.
Praise the Lord, for he hath spoken;
  Worlds his mighty voice obeyed;
Laws, which never can be broken,
  For their guidance he hath made.

2 Praise the Lord, for he is glorious;
  Never shall his promise fail;
God hath made his saints victorious;
  Sin and death shall not prevail.
Praise the God of our salvation;
  Hosts on high, his power proclaim;
Heaven, and earth, and all creation,
  Praise and magnify his name.

GREENVILLE.   No. 151.

WEBB. M. 14. GEORGE JAMES WEBB, 1830.

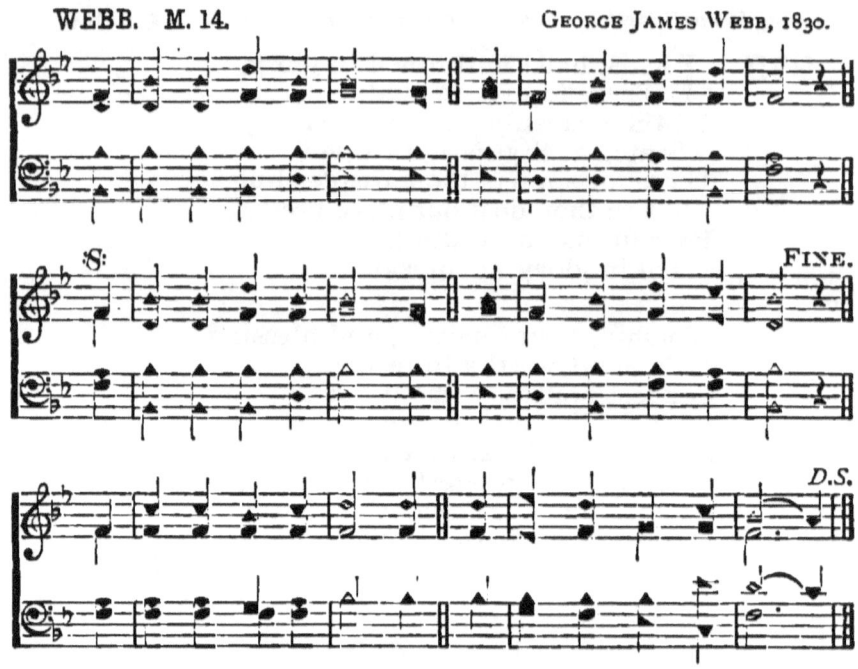

Our years are as a tale that is told. Ps. 90: 9.   M. 14.

274
O GOD, the Rock of Ages,
　Who evermore hast been,
What time the tempest rages,
　Our dwelling-place serene:
Before thy first creations,
　O Lord, the same as now,
To endless generations,
　The Everlasting thou!

2 Our years are like the shadows
　On sunny hills that lie,
Or grasses in the meadows
　That blossom but to die:
A sleep, a dream, a story,
　By strangers quickly told,
An unremaining glory
　Of things that soon are old.

Bickersteth.

Thou hast made the Lord thy habitation; There shall no evil befall thee.
Psalm 91: 9, 10. M. 14.

275
In heavenly love abiding,
  No change my heart shall fear,
And safe is such confiding,
  For nothing changes here:
The storm may roar without me;
  My heart may low be laid,
But God is round about me,
  And can I be dismayed?

2 Wherever he may guide me,
  No want shall turn me back;
My Shepherd is beside me,
  And nothing can I lack;
His wisdom ever waketh,
  His sight is never dim:
He knows the way he taketh,
  And I will walk with him.

3 Green pastures are before me,
  Which yet I have not seen;
Bright skies will soon be o'er me,
  Where darkest clouds have been:
My hope I can not measure;
  My path to life is free:
My Saviour has my treasure,
  And he will walk with me.
Anna L. Waring.

To Him be glory both now and forever. *2 Pet. 3: 18.* M. 14.

276
Thy love, O Holy Father,
  Thy grace, O Holy Son,
Thy peace, O Holy Spirit,
  Thy church abide upon:
While she her voice upraises
  To thy eternal throne,
And chants in endless praises
  Glory to God alone.
Thos. MacKellar.

I NEED THEE PRECIOUS JESUS. No. 189.

BOYLSTON. S. M.   L. Mason.

Bless the Lord O my soul, and forget not all his benefits. Ps. 103: 2.   S. M.

277
    OH, BLESS the Lord, my soul!
       Let all within me join,
   And aid my tongue to bless His name
       Whose favors are divine.

2 Oh, bless the Lord, my soul!
    Nor let his mercies lie
Forgotten in unthankfulness,
    And without praises die.

3 'Tis He forgives thy sins;
    'Tis He relieves thy pain;
'Tis He that heals thy sicknesses,
    And gives thee strength again.

4 He crowns thy life with love,
    When rescued from the grave,
He, that redeem'd our souls from death,
    Hath boundless power to save.

5 He fills the poor with good;
    He gives the suff'rers rest,
The Lord hath justice for the proud,
    And mercy for the oppress'd.

6 His wondrous works and ways
    He made by Moses known;
But sent the world His truth and grace
    By His beloved Son.

PRAISE.

I will sing a new song unto Thee. Psalm 144: 9.   S. M.

278 Raise your triumphant songs
   To an immortal tune;
Let the wide earth resound the deeds
   Celestial grace has done.

2 Sing how eternal love
   Its chief Beloved chose,
And bade Him raise our wretched race
   From their abyss of woes.

3 'Twas mercy filled the throne,
   And wrath stood silent by,
When Christ was sent with pardons down
   To rebels doomed to die.

4 Now, sinners, dry your tears,
   Let hopeless sorrows cease;
Bow to the sceptre of His love,
   And take the offered peace.

5 Lord, we obey thy call:
   We lay an humble claim
To the salvation thou hast brought,
   And love and praise thy name.
                              Isaac Watts, 1709.

*For as the heaven is high above the earth, so great is his mercy toward
them that fear him. Ps. 103: 11.*   S. M.

279 My soul, repeat his praise,
   Whose mercies are so great:
Whose anger is so slow to rise,
   So ready to abate.

2 God will not ever chide;
   And when his strokes are felt,
They're always fewer than our crimes,
   And lighter than our guilt.

3 His power subdues our sins,
   And his forgiving love,
Far as the east is from the west,
   Doth all our guilt remove.

4 High as the heavens are raised
   Above the ground we tread,
So far the riches of his grace,
   Our highest thoughts exceed.
                              Watts.

SALEM. S. M.   T. HASTINGS.

By grace are ye saved. Eph. 2: 5.   S. M.

280 GRACE! 'tis a charming sound,
Harmonious to the ear:
Heaven with the echo shall resound,
And all the earth shall hear.

2 Grace first contrived a way
To save rebellious man;
And all the steps that grace display,
Which drew the wondrous plan.

3 Grace taught my wandering feet
To tread the heavenly road;
And new supplies each hour I meet
While pressing on to God.

                         Doddridge.

How amiable are Thy tabernacles. Ps. 84: 1.   S. M.

281 HOW charming is the place
Where my Redeemer, God,
Unvails the beauties of his face,
And sheds his love abroad!

2 To him our prayers and cries
Our humble souls present;
He listens to our broken sighs,
And grants us every want.

PRAISE.

3 Give me, O Lord, a place
  Within thy blest abode,
Among the children of thy grace,
  The servants of my God.

S. Stennett.

For ye know the grace of our Lord. 2 Cor. 8: 9. S. M.

282 To God the only wise,
  Our Saviour and our King,
Let all the saints below the skies
  Their humble praises bring.

2 'Tis His almighty love,
  His counsel and His care,
Preserves us safe from sin and death,
  And ev'ry hurtful snare.

3 He will present our souls
  Unblemish'd and complete,
Before the glory of His face,
  With joys divinely great.

4 To our Redeemer, God,
  Wisdom and pow'r belongs,
Immortal crowns of majesty,
  And everlasting songs.

Watts.

His delight is in the law of the Lord. Ps. 1: 2. S. M.

283 Thy laws O God, are right,
  Thy throne shall ever stand,
And thy victorious gospel prove
  A sceptre in thy hand.

2 Oh, let thy God and King
  Thy sweetest thoughts employ;
Thy children shall his honors sing
  In palaces of joy.

3 Beside Thee, there is none:
  Eternal God and King,
The Father, Son, and Holy Ghost,
  Thy glorious praise we sing.

LAKE ENON.   No. 190.

CANA. C. M. By Com.

My soul shall make her boast in the Lord. Ps. 34: 2. C. M.

284 Long as I live I'll bless thy name,
My King, my God, my love;
My work and joy shall be the same
In the bright world above.

2 Great is the Lord; his power unknown;
And let his praise be great;
I'll sing the honors of thy throne,
Thy works of grace repeat.

3 Thy grace shall dwell upon my tongue,
And while my lips rejoice,
The men who hear my sacred song
Shall join their cheerful voice.

4 Fathers to sons, shall teach thy name,
And children learn thy ways;
Ages to come thy truth proclaim,
And nations sound thy praise.

5 The world is governed by thy hand;
Thy saints are ruled by love;
And thine eternal kingdom stand,
Though rocks, and hills remove.

And Jesus was called to the marriage. John 2: 2. C. M.

285 Since Jesus freely did appear
To grace a marriage feast;
O Lord, we ask thy presence here,
To be a wedding guest.

2 Upon the bridal pair look down,
  Who now have plighted hands;
Their union with thy favor crown,
  And bless the nuptial bands.

3 In purest love these souls unite,
  That they with Christian care,
May make domestic burdens light
  By taking mutual share.

4 And when that solemn hour shall come,
  And life's short space be o'er,
May they in triumph reach that home,
  Where they shall part no more.

Marriage is honorable. Heb. 13: 4.   C. M.

286 WE join to pray, with wishes kind,
  A blessing, Lord, from Thee,
On those who now the bands have twined
  Which ne'er may broken be.

2 We know that scenes not always bright
  Must unto them be given;
But over all give Thou the light
  Of love, and truth, and heaven.

3 Still hand in hand, their journey through
  Joint pilgrims may they go;
Mingling their joys as helpers true,
  And sharing every woe.

4 May each in each still feed the flame
  Of pure and holy love;
In faith, and trust, and heart the same,
  The same their home above.

I will bless the Lord at all times. Psalm 34: 1.   C. M.

287 THRO' all the changing scenes of life,
  In trouble and in joy,
The praises of my God shall still
  My heart and tongue employ.

2 The hosts of God encamp around
  The dwellings of the just;
Deliverance he affords to all
  Who on his succor trust.

Tate and Brady, 1696.

FREEDOM. L. M.

R. K. Higgins.
By per. of A. S. Kieffer.

Know ye that the Lord he is God. Psalm 100: 3.   L. M.

288
SING to the Lord with joyful voice;
Let every land his name adore;
Let distant isles in him rejoice,
And sound his praise from shore to shore.

2 Nations attend before his throne
With solemn fear, with sacred joy;
Know that the Lord is God alone,
He can create, and he destroy.

3 His sovereign power, without our aid,
Made us of clay and formed us men;
And when, like wand'ring sheep we strayed,
He brought us to his fold again.

4 We are his people; we his care;
Our souls, and all our mortal frame:
What lasting honors shall we rear,
Almighty Maker, to thy name?

5 We'll crowd thy gates with thankful songs,
High as the heavens our voices raise;
And earth, with her ten thousand tongues,
Shall fill thy courts with sounding praise.
Isaac Watts, 1719.

Praise waiteth for thee, O God, in Zion. Psalm 65: 1.   L. M.

289
PRAISE waits in Zion, Lord, for thee;
Thy saints adore thy holy name,
Thy creatures bend th' obedient knee,
And humbly thy protection claim.

2 Thy hand has raised us from the dust;
  The breath of life thy spirit gave;
Where, but in thee, can mortals trust?
  Who, but our God, has power to save?

3 Eternal source of truth and light,
  To thee we look, on thee we call;
Lord, we are nothing in thy sight,
  But thou to us art all in all.

4 Still may thy children in thy word
  Their common trust and refuge see;
Oh, bind us to each other, Lord,
  By one great tie—the love of thee.

5 So shall our sun of hope arise,
  With brighter still and brighter ray,
Till thou shalt bless our longing eyes
  With beams of everlasting day.
            Sir James Edward Smith, 1814.

The heavens declare the glory of God.   Psalm 19: 1.   L. M.

THE heavens declare thy glory, Lord,
  In every star thy wisdom shines;
But when our eyes behold thy word,
  We read thy name in fairer lines.

2 The rolling sun, the changing light,
  And nights and days, thy power confess;
But the blest volume thou hast writ,
  Reveals thy justice and thy grace.

3 Sun, moon, and stars, convey thy praise
  Round the whole earth, and never stand;
So when thy truth began its race,
  It touched and glanced on every land.

4 Nor shall thy spreading gospel rest,
  Till through the world thy truth has run,
Till Christ has all the nations blessed
  That see the light, or feel the sun.

5 Great Sun of Righteousness, arise!
  Bless the dark world with heavenly light;
Thy gospel makes the simple wise,
  Thy laws are pure, thy judgments right.
            I. Watts, 1719, ab.

BRIDGEWATER. C. M.   J. H. HALL, by per.

Daily shall he be praised. Psalm 72: 15.   C. M.

291
1. Come, ye that love the Saviour's name,
  And joy to make it known;
  The Sovereign of your heart proclaim,
  And bow before his throne.

2. Behold your King, your Saviour, crown'd
  With glories all divine;
  And tell the wondering nations round
  How bright those glories shine.

3. Infinite power and boundless grace
  In him unite their rays:
  You that have e'er beheld his face,
  Can you forbear his praise?

4. When in his earthly courts we view
  The glories of our King,
  We long to love as angels do,
  And wish like them to sing.

5. And shall we long and wish in vain?
  Lord, teach our songs to rise!
  Thy love can animate the strain,
  And bid it reach the skies.

6. Oh, happy period! glorious day!
  When heaven and earth shall raise,
  With all their powers, the raptured lay
  To celebrate thy praise.

                               Anne Steele, 1760.

Sing unto the Lord . . with the voice of a psalm. Psalm 98: 5.   C. M.

292
I'LL bless the Lord from day to day;
    How good are all his ways!
Ye humble souls that love to pray,
    Come help my lips to praise.

2 Sing to the honor of his name,
    How a poor suff'rer cried;
Nor was his hope exposed to shame,
    Nor was his suit denied.

3 When threat'ning sorrows round me stood,
    And endless fears arose
Like the loud billows of a flood,
    Redoubling all my woes;

4 I told the Lord my sore distress,
    With heavy groans and tears;
He gave my sharpest torments ease,
    And silenced all my fears.

5 O sinners, come and taste his love;
    Come, learn his pleasant ways;
And let your own experience prove
    The sweetness of his grace.
Watts.

Let us go into the house of the Lord. Psalm 122: 1.   C. M.

293
How did my heart rejoice to hear
    My friends devoutly say,
"In Zion let us all appear,
    And keep the solemn day."

2 I love her gates, I love the road;
    The church, adorned with grace,
Stands like a palace built for God,
    To show his milder face.

3 Peace be within this sacred place,
    And joy a constant guest;
With holy gifts and heavenly grace
    Be her attendants blessed!

4 My soul shall pray for Zion still,
    While life or breath remains;
There my best friends, my kindred, dwell,
    There God, my Saviour, reigns.
W.

CHATHAM. M. 5.

I laid me down and slept; I awaked: for the Lord sustained me.
Psalm 3: 5. M. 5.

294 Day is breaking in the sky;
  Restful night has passed away:
Now I lift my early cry,
  Lead thy servant, Lord, to-day.

2 Jesus, Master! forth I go,
  Taking up my 'customed task:
Teach me what I need to know,—
  Give me what I ought to ask.

3 I see not the way before,
  But I go at thy command,
Entering gladly duty's door,
  Led by thy directing hand.

4 Take away my sin and guilt,
  Make me whiter than the snow:
Be my will just what Thou wilt,
  Asking not, why is it so?

5 May my soul, impell'd by love,
  Do whate'er thy Spirit saith,
That my life this day may prove,
  Through thy grace, the power of faith.

6 Glory to Thee evermore!
  Glory to the uttermost!
Heaven and earth thy name adore,
  Father, Son, and Holy Ghost.

MacKellar, 1881.

PARTING HAND. L. M. D.

He that loveth his brother abideth in the light. 1 John 2: 10.   L. M. D.

295 My dearest friends, in bonds of love,
Our hearts in sweetest union prove,
Your friendship's like a drawing band,
Yet we must take the parting hand.
Your presence sweet, your union dear,
Your words delightful to my ear;
And when I see that we must part,
You draw like cords around my heart.

2 How sweet the hours have passed away,
Since we have met to sing and pray,
How loth I've been to leave the place
Where Jesus shows his smiling face!
O could I stay with friends so kind,
How would it cheer my struggling mind!
But duty makes me understand,
That we must take the parting hand.

3 And since it is God's holy will,
We must be parted for a while,
In sweet submission all as one,
We'll say our Father's will be done.
Dear fellow youth, in Christian ties,
Who seek for mansions in the skies,
Fight on you'll win the happy shore,
Where parting hands are known no more,

PARTING HYMNS.

SWEET DAY. S. M.

Salvation belongeth to the Lord: thy blessing is upon thy people.   Psalm 3: 8.
S. M.

296
    ONCE more, before we part,
      Oh, bless the Saviour's name!
    Let every tongue and every heart
      Adore and praise the same.

2 Lord, in thy grace we came,
    That blessing still impart,
  We met in Jesus' sacred name,
    In Jesus' name we part.

3 Still on thy holy word
    We'll live, and feed, and grow;
  And still go on to know the Lord,
    And practice what we know.

4 Now, Lord, before we part,
    Help us to bless thy name;
  Let every tongue and every heart,
    Adore and praise the same.

That their hearts might be comforted, being knit together in love.   Col. 2: 2.
S. M.

297
    NOW, brethren, though we part,
      And to our homes repair—
    May we be true, and join'd in heart,
      Like friends of Jesus are.

2 Oh, let us still proceed
    In Jesus' work below,
  And following our triumphant Head,
    To further conquests go.

PARTING. 203

3 Oh, let our hearts and mind
    With ev'ry day ascend,
  That haven of repose to find,
    Where all our labors end.

4 When all our toils are o'er,
    Our suff'ring and our pain :
  We'll meet on that celestial shore,
    And never part again.

EXPOSTULATION. 11. M.   Josiah Hopkins, 1830.

Pray for one another. James 5: 16.   M. 11.

298 FAREWELL, my dear brethren, the time is at hand,
  That we must be parted from this social band;
Our sev'ral engagements now call us away;
Our parting is needful, and we must obey.

2 Farewell my dear breathren, farewell for a while,
  We'll soon meet again, if kind Providence smile;
  And while we are parted and scattered abroad,
  We'll pray for each other, and trust in the Lord.

3 Farewell, faithful soldiers you'll soon be discharged,
  The war will be ended, your bounty enlarged;
  With shouting and singing, though Jordan may roar,
  We'll enter fair Canaan, and rest on the shore.

4 Farewell, younger brethren, just listed for war,
  Sore trials await you, but Jesus is near:
  Although you must travel the dark wilderness,
  Your Captain's before you, he'll lead you in peace.

PARTING.

GOD BE WITH YOU.
W. G. Tomer, By per.

The grace of our Lord Jesus Christ be with you. Rom. 16: 20.

299 God be with you till we meet again,
By his counsels guide, uphold you,
With his sheep securely fold you,
God be with you till we meet again.

2 God be with you till we meet again,
'Neath his wings protecting hide you,
Daily manna still provide you,
God be with you till we meet again.

3 God be with you till we meet again,
When life's perils thick confound you,
Put his arms unfailing round you,
God be with you till we meet again.

PARTING. 205

4 God be with you till we meet again,
  Keep love's banner floating o'er you,
  Smite death's threat'ning wave before you,
  God be with you till we meet again.

        J. E. Rankin, D. D.

HICK'S FAREWELL. C. M.   WM. WALKER.

Who shall seperate us from the love of Christ. Rom. 8: 35. C. M.

300 BLEST be the dear uniting love,
  That will not let us part:
 Our bodies may far off remove;
  We still are one in heart.

 2 Joined in one spirit to our Head,
  Where he appoints we go;
 And still in Jesus' footsteps tread,
  And show his praise below.

 3 Partakers of the Saviour's grace,
  The same in mind and heart,
 Not joy, nor grief, nor time, nor place,
  Nor life, nor death can part.

        C. Wesley.

It is good to be here. Matt. 17: 4. C. M.

301 LORD, when together here we meet,
  And taste thy heav'nly grace,
 Thy smiles are so divinely sweet,
  We're loth to leave the place.

 2 But, Father, since it is thy will
  That we must part again,
 Oh, may thy special presence still
  With ev'ry one remain.

42 PSALM. M. 55.   H. S. Rupp.

God is our refuge and strength, a very present help in trouble. Psalm 46. 1.

M. 55.

302 "As pants the wearied hart for cooling springs,"
That sinks exhausted in the summer's chase;
So pants my soul for thee, great King of kings!
So thirsts to reach thy sacred resting-place.

2 On briny tears my famished soul has fed,
While taunting foes deride my deep despair;
"Say, where is now thy great Deliverer fled?
Thy mighty God—Deserted wanderer, where?"

3 Oft dwell my thoughts on those thrice happy days,
When to thy fane I lead the jocund throng;
Our mirth was worship, all our pleasure praise,
And festal joys still closed with sacred song.

4 Why throb, my heart? Why sink, my saddening soul?
Why droop to earth with various woes oppressed?
My years shall yet in blissful circles roll,
And joy be yet an inmate of this breast.

5 By Jordan's banks with devious steps I stray,
O'er Hermon's rugged rocks, and deserts drear;
E'en there thy hand shall guide my lonely way,
There, thy remembrance shall my spirit cheer.

REFUGE. 207

6 In rapid floods the vernal torrents roll,
  Harsh-sounding cataracts responsive roar;
Thine angry billows overwhelm my soul,
  And dash my shattered bark from shore to shore.

7 Yet thy soft mercies, ever in my sight,
  My heart shall gladden through the tedious day;
And midst the dark and gloomy shades of night,
  To thee I'll fondly tune the grateful lay.
                    Hebrew Elegy. From Cottage Bible.

CLINTON. S. M.   J. H. Hall, by per.

Ye are not your own, for ye were bought with a price. 1 Cor. 6: 19, 20.
S. M.

303 I GIVE myself to God,
     My life, my soul, my all;
  He knows the devious paths I've trod,
     In mercy's hand I fall.

  2 My sins I cannot count,
       Nor sum his favours up:
    I humbly kneel at mercy's fount
       And take salvation's cup.

  3 I proffer but his own;
       And may the Master take
    The gift I lay before his throne,
       For my Redeemer's sake.

  4 I give myself to God,
       For evermore to hold:
    I pass beneath the Shepherd's rod
       To bide within his fold.
                    Thos. MacKellar, 1882.

REFUGE.

ALLEN. M. 5. A. L. LANDIS.

The Lord is my refuge. Psalm 91: 2.   M. 5.

304 JESUS, lover of my soul,
    Let me to thy bosom fly,
While the raging billows roll,
    While the tempest still is high!
Hide me, O my Saviour, hide,
    Till the storm of life be past;
Safe into the haven guide,
    Oh, receive my soul at last!

2 Other refuge have I none;
    Hangs my helpless soul on Thee;
Leave, oh, leave me not alone!
    Still support and comfort me:
All my TRUST on Thee is stayed,
    All my HELP from Thee I bring;
Cover my defenseless head
    With the shadow of thy wing.

3 Thou, O Christ, art all I want;
    All I need in Thee I find;
Raise the fallen, cheer the faint,
    Heal the sick, and lead the blind.

Just and holy is thy name,
  I am all unrighteousness;
False and full of sin I am,
  Thou art full of truth and grace.

4 Plenteous grace with thee is found,
    Grace to pardon all my sins:
  Let the healing streams abound;
    Make and keep me pure within.
  Thou of life the Fountain art,
    Freely let me take of thee;
  Spring thou up within my heart,
    Rise to all eternity.

C. Wesley, 1740.

TOPLADY. M. 17.   T. HASTINGS.

That Rock was Christ. 1 Cor. 10: 4.   M. 17.

305 Rock of Ages, cleft for me,
      Let me hide myself in thee,
    Let the water and the blood,
    From thy riven side that flowed,
    Be of sin the double cure;
    Cleanse me from its guilt and power.

  2 Could my zeal no respite know,
    Could my tears forever flow—
    All for sin could not atone:
    Thou must save, and thou alone!
    Nothing in my hand I bring;
    Simply to thy cross I cling.

  3 While I draw this fleeting breath,
    When my eyelids close in death,
    When I soar to worlds unknown,
    See thee on thy judgment throne,—
    Rock of Ages, cleft for me,
    Let me hide myself in thee.

Toplady.

REFUGE.

ARTHUR. M. 7.   H. S. Rupp, 1888.

Fear not—I will give unto him that is athirst of the water of life freely.
Rev. 21: 6.   M. 7.

306 JESUS! when my soul is parting
From this body frail and weak,
And the deathly dew is starting
Down this pale and wasted cheek,—
Thine, my Saviour,
Be the name I last shall speak.

2 Jesus! when my memory wanders
Far from loved ones at my side,
And in fitful dreaming ponders
Who are they that near me glide,—
Last, my Saviour,
Let my thoughts on thee abide.

3 When the morn in all its glory
Charms no more mine ear nor eye,
And the shadows closing o'er me
Warn me of the time to die,—
Last, my Saviour,
Let me see thee standing by.

4 When my feet shall pass the river,
    And upon the further shore
I shall walk, redeem'd forever,
    Ne'er to sin—to die no more,—
        First, Lord Jesus!
Let me see thee, and adore.
Thos. MacKellar, 1848.

God the defense of the church.   Psalm 125: 2.   M. 7.

307 ZION stands with hills surrounded—
    Zion, kept by pow'r divine;
All her foes shall be confounded,
    Though the world in arms combine:
        Happy Zion,
What a favor'd lot is thine!

2 Every human tie may perish;
    Friend to friend unfaithful prove;
Mothers cease their own to cherish;
    Heaven and earth at last remove;
        But no changes
Can attend Jehovah's love.

3 In the furnace God may prove thee,
    Thence to bring thee forth more bright,
But can never cease to love thee;
    Thou art precious in his sight;
        God is with thee—
God, thine everlasting light.

Son, go work to-day in my vineyard.   Matt. 21: 28.   M. 7.

308 IN the vineyard of our Father
    Daily work we find to do;
Scatter'd fruit our hands may gather,
    Though we are but weak and few:
        Little clusters
Help to fill the basket too.

2 Toiling early in the morning,
    Catching moments through the day,
Nothing small or lowly scorning,—
    So we work, and watch and pray;
        Gathering gladly
Free-will offerings by the way.
Thos. MacKellar, 1845.

MAGRUDER. L. M. J. H. HALL.

God is our refuge and strength. Ps. 46: 1. L. M.

309
G OD is our refuge and defense;
In trouble our unfailing aid:
Secure in his omnipotence,
What foe can make our souls afraid?

2 Yea, though the earth's foundations rock,
And mountains down the gulf be hurled,
His people shine amid the shock;
They look beyond this transient world.

3 There is a river pure and bright,
Whose streams make glad the heavenly plains;
Where, in eternity of light,
The City of our God remains.

4 Built by the word of his command,
With his unclouded presence blest,
Firm as his throne the bulwarks stand:
There is our home, our hope, our rest.
James Montgomery, 1771—1854.

The winds and the sea obey Him. Matt. 8: 27. L. M.

310
T HE billows swell, the winds are high,
Clouds overcast my wintry sky;
Out of the depths to Thee I call,
My fears are great, my strength is small.

2 O Lord, the pilot's part perform,
And guide and guard me through the storm;
Defend me from each threatening ill,
Control the waves, say, "Peace, be still!"

3 Amidst the roaring of the sea
My soul still hangs her hopes on Thee;
Thy constant love, Thy faithful care
Is all that saves me from despair.

4 Dangers of every shape and name
Attend the followers of the Lamb,
Who leave the world's deceitful shore,
And leave it to return no more.

5 Though tempest-tost and half a wreck,
My Saviour through the floods I seek:
Let neither winds nor stormy main
Force back my shattered bark again!
Wm. Cowper, 1779.

Thou art my hiding-place. Psalm 32: 7.   L. M.

311 HAIL, sovereign Love! that formed the plan
To save rebellious, ruined man;
Hail! matchless, free, eternal Grace,
That gave my soul a hiding-place.

2 Against the God who rules the sky
I fought, with hand uplifted high;
I madly ran the sinful race,
Regardless of a hiding-place.

3 Indignant Justice stood in view;
To Sinai's burning mount I flew:
But Justice cried, with frowning face,
"This mountain is no hiding-place."

4 Ere long a heavenly voice I heard;
A bleeding Saviour then appeared;
Led by the Spirit of his grace,
I found in him a hiding-place.
J. Brewer.

To Him be glory, both now and forever. 2 Pet. 3: 18.   L. M.

312 GLORY and thanks to God in heaven!
Praise to his blessed Son be given:—
Thee, Holy Spirit, we implore,
Be with us now and evermore.

OLD HUNDRED.   No. 246.

REFUGE.

TAMPICO. C. M.

He laid his hands on them. Matt. 19: 15.   C. M.

313 Dear Jesus, ever at my side,
How loving must thou be,
To leave thy home in heaven to guard
A little child like me!

2 I cannot feel thee touch my hand
With pressure light and mild,
To check me as my mother did,
When I was but a child.

3 But I have felt thee in my thoughts,
Rebuking sin for me;
And, when my heart loves God, I know
The sweetness is from thee.

4 And when, dear Saviour, I kneel down,
Morning and night, to prayer,
Something there is within my heart
Which tells me thou art there.

5 Yes! when I pray, thou prayest too—
Thy prayer is all for me;
But when I sleep, thou sleepest not,
But watchest patiently.

                              Faber.

Fear not, little flock. Luke 12: 32.   C. M.

314 There is a little lonely fold,
Whose flock One Shepherd keeps,
Through summer's heat and winter's cold,
With eye that never sleeps.

2 By evil beast, or burning sky,
　　Or damp of midnight air,
　Not one in all that flock shall die
　　Beneath that Shepherd's care.

3 For if, unheeding or beguiled,
　　In danger's path they roam,
　His pity follows through the wild,
　　And guards them safely home.

4 O gentle Shepherd, still behold
　　Thy helpless charge in me,
　And take a wanderer to Thy fold,
　　That trembling turns to Thee.
　　　　　　　　Maria Grace Saffery, 1834.

The good Shepherd giveth his life for the sheep. John 10: 11.　C. M.

315　Ye little flock whom Jesus feeds,
　　　Dismiss your anxious cares;
　　Look to the Shepherd of your souls,
　　　And smile away your fears.

2 Though wolves and lions prowl around,
　　His staff is your defense;
　'Midst sands and rocks, your Shepherd's voice
　　Calls streams and pastures thence.

3 Your Father will a kingdom give,
　　And give it with delight;
　His feeblest child his love shall call
　　To triumph in his sight.

4 Ten thousand praises, Lord, we bring
　　For sure supports like these;
　And o'er the pious dead we sing
　　Thy living promises.

5 For all we hope, and they enjoy,
　　We bless a Saviour's name;
　Nor shall that stroke disturb the song
　　Which breaks this mortal frame.

DUNDEE　　　　　　　　　No. 84.

REFUGE.

BROADWAY. C. M. H. S. Rupp.

Jesus said therefore unto the twelve, Will ye also go away? John 6: 67. C. M.

316 WHERE could I go but unto thee,
O man of Nazareth?
Thy blood was shed on Calvary
To give me life for death!

2 To whom, my Lord, but unto thee,
O Son of God most high,
When angels bend with reverent **knee**
Before thy Majesty?

3 Where could I go but unto thee,
The only refuge-tower
Impregnable, where I can flee
In sore temptation's hour?

4 To whom need I go but to thee?
Thou art the utmost sum
Of every Soul's necessity ;—
And therefore, Lord, I come.

5 O Lamb of God, who cam'st to take
The sin of man away,
Fast hold me for thy mercy's sake,
And I shall never stray.

Thos. MacKellar, 1882.

Lord, to whom shall we go? John 6: 68. C. M.

317 TO WHOM, my Saviour, shall I go,
If I depart from thee?
My guide through all this vale of woe,
And more than all to me.

REFUGE.

2 The world reject thy gentle reign,
    And pay thy death with scorn;
  Oh, they could plait thy crown again,
    And sharpen every thorn!

3 But I have felt thy dying love
    Breathe gently through my heart,
  To whisper hope of joys above—
    And can we ever part?

4 Ah, no! with thee I'll walk below,
    Through conflict, toil, and strife;
  To whom, my Saviour, shall I go?
    Thy words are endless life.
                          "Carus," 1815.

The full assurance of hope. Heb. 6: 11.   C. M.

318 WHEN floating on life's troubled sea,
    By storms and tempests driv'n,
  Hope, with her radiant finger, points
    To brighter scenes in heav'n.

2 She bids the storms of life to cease,
    The troubled breast be calm;
  And in the wounded heart she pours
    Religion's healing balm.

3 Her hallow'd influence cheers life's hours
    Of sadness and of gloom;
  She guides us through this vale of tears
    To joys beyond the tomb.

4 And when our fleeting days are o'er,
    And life's last hour draws near,
  With still unweari'd wing she hastes
    To wipe the falling tear.

5 She bids the anguish'd heart rejoice:
    Though earthly ties are riv'n,
  We still may hope to meet again
    In yonder peaceful heav'n.

SOLON.   No. 49.

REFUGE.

EVENING TWILIGHT. C. M.

The sure foundation. Isaiah 28: 16.   C. M.

319 BEHOLD the sure foundation stone,
Which God in Zion lays,
To build our heav'nly hopes upon,
And his eternal praise.

2 Chosen of God, to sinners dear,
Let saints adore the name;
They trust their whole salvation here,
Nor shall they suffer shame.

3 The foolish builders, scribe and priest,
Reject it with disdain;
Yet on this rock the church shall rest,
And envy rage in vain.

4 What though the gates of hell withstood,
Yet must this building rise;
'Tis thine own work, almighty God,
And wondrous in our eyes.

Watts.

Looking for that blessed hope. Titus 2: 13.   C. M.

320 OH, HAPPY soul that lives on high,
While men live grov'ling here,
His hopes are fix'd above the sky,
And faith forbids his fear.

2 His conscience knows no secret stings,
While grace and joy combine
To form a life whose holy springs
Are hidden, and divine.

3 He waits in secret on his God;
   His God in secret sees:
   Let earth be all in arms abroad,
   He dwells in heavenly peace.

4 His pleasures rise from things unseen,
   Beyond this world and time,
   Where neither eyes nor ears have been,
   Nor thoughts of mortals climb.

Her ways are ways of pleasantness. Prov. 3: 17.   C. M.

321
O HAPPY is the man who hears
   Religion's warning voice,
And who celestial wisdom makes
   His early, only choice.

2 For she hath treasures greater far
   Than east and west unfold;
And her rewards more precious are
   Than all their stores of gold.

3 In her right hand is length of days
   For those who heed her voice;
Her left hand offers wealth and praise
   To make her sons rejoice.

4 She guides the young with innocence
   In pleasure's paths to tread;
A crown of glory she bestows
   Upon the hoary head.

5 According as her labors rise,
   So her rewards increase;
Her ways are ways of pleasantness,
   And all her paths are peace.
        Michael Bruce, ab. 1746. v. 3, Hastings, 1883.

What is the chaff to the wheat? Jer. 23: 28.   C. M.

322
WHAT is the chaff, the word of man,
   When set against the wheat?
Can it a dying soul sustain,
   Like that immortal meat?

2 Thy word, O God, with heavenly bread
   Thy children doth supply;
And those who by thy word are fed
   Their souls shall never die.
        Charles Wesley, 1762.

REFUGE.

SHIRLAND. S. M.   SAMUEL STANLEY, 1800.

The Lord is my Shepherd, I shall not want. Ps. 23: 1   S. M.

323 THE Lord my Shepherd is;
  I shall be well suppli'd;
Since he is mine, and I am his,
  What can I want beside?

2 He leads me to the place
  Where heav'nly pasture grows,
Where living waters gently pass,
  And full salvation flows.

3 If e'er I go astray,
  He doth my soul reclaim,
And guides me in his own right way,
  For his most holy name.

4 While he affords his aid,
  I can not yield to fear;
Tho' I should walk thro' death's dark shade,
  My Shepherd's with me there.

5 In spite of all my foes,
  Thou dost my table spread;
My cup with blessings overflows,
  And joy exalts my head.

6 The bounties of thy love
  Shall crown my future days;
Nor from thy house will I remove,
  Nor cease to speak thy praise.
        Watts.

REFUGE.

THE SOLID ROCK. L. M. W. B. Bradbury.
Used by per. of Biglow & Main, Owners of Copyright.

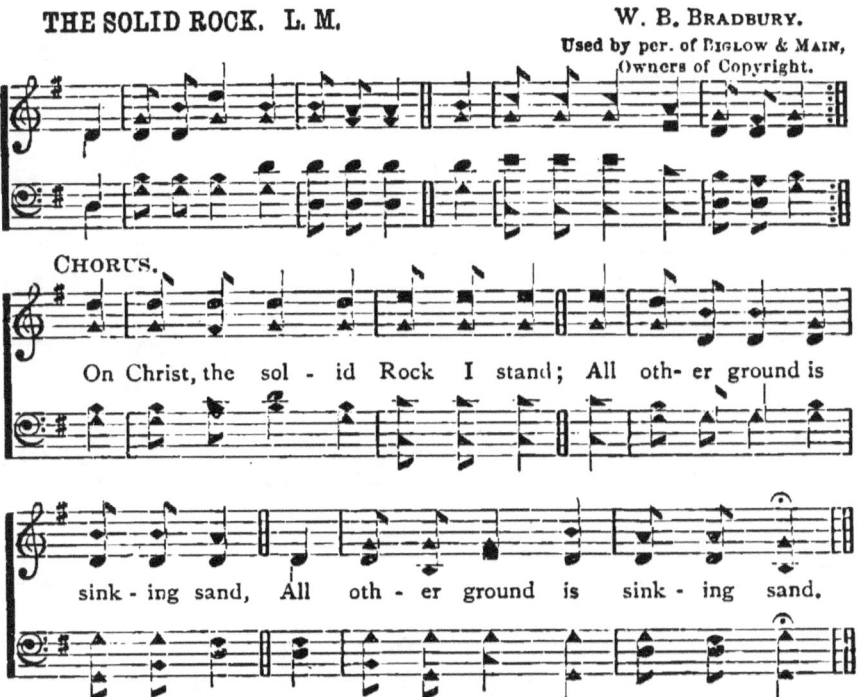

The Lord is my defense, and rock of my refuge. Ps. 94: 22. L. M.

324 My hope is built on nothing less
Than Jesus' blood and righteousness;
I dare not trust the sweetest frame;
But wholly lean on Jesus' name.

2 When darkness veils his lovely face,
I rest on his unchanging grace;
In every high and stormy gale,
My anchor holds within the veil.

3 His oath, His covenant, His blood,
Support me in the whelming flood;
When all around my soul gives way,
He then is all my hope and stay.

4 When He shall come with trumpet's sound,
Oh, may I then in him be found,
Dressed in his righteousness alone,
Faultless to stand before the throne.

Edward Mote. ab. 1825

REFUGE.

LYTE. M. 11. From Temple Star.

Faint, yet pursuing. Judges 8: 4. M. 11.

325 Though faint, yet pursuing, we go on our way;
The Lord is our Leader, his word is our stay;
Though suffering, and sorrow, and trial be near,
The Lord is our refuge and whom can we fear?

2 He raiseth the fallen, he cheereth the faint;
The weak and oppress'd, he will hear their complaint;
The way may be weary, and thorny the road,
But how can we falter? our help is in God.

3 Into his green pastures our footsteps he leads;
His flock in the desert how kindly he feeds!
The lambs in his bosom he tenderly bears,
And brings back the wanderers safe from the snares.

4 Though clouds may surround us, our God is our light;
Though storms rage around us, our God is our might;
So faint, yet pursuing, still onward we come;
The Lord is our Leader, his kingdom our home.

5 And there all his people eternally dwell,
With him who hath led them so safely and well;
The toilsome way over, the wilderness past;
And Canaan, the blessed, is theirs at the last.
John N. Darby, 1861.

REFUGE.

ALASKA. 11s, 12s & 4. By Com.

The Rock higher than I. Psalm 61: 2.   11S, 12S & 4.

326 IN seasons of grief to my God I'll repair,
When my heart's overwhelmed with sorrow and care;
From the end of the earth unto thee will I cry,
Lead me to the Rock that is higher than I—
    Higher than I—higher than I—
    Lead me to the Rock that is higher than I.

2 When Satan, my foe, cometh in like a flood,
To direct my poor soul from the fountain of God,
I will pray to the Saviour who kindly did die,
Lead me to the Rock that is higher than I.
    Higher than I, etc.

3 O Saviour of sinners, when faint and depress'd,
With my manifold trials and sorrows oppress'd,
I will bow at thy feet, and with confidence cry
" Lead me to the Rock that is higher than I."
    Higher than I, etc.

                                              Wm. Hunter.

REFUGE.

WE ARE TRAVELING ON OUR WAY. M. 5.
C. E. Leslie, by per. owner of copyright.

I am a stranger and a sojourner. Psalm 39; 12. M. 5.

327 WE are traveling on our way,
Clouds and darkness fill the day,
Every path is rough and steep,
And the streams are wide and deep.

2 Though the path be rough and steep,
Though the streams be dark and deep,
Though the tempest cloud the sky,
Call on Him, He will be nigh.

3 He will guide your weary feet,
To the pastures green and sweet,
By the waters calm and still,
He will save from every ill.

Let not your hearts faint. Duet. 20: 3. M. 5.

328 FAINT not, Christian! though the road,
Leading to the blest abode,
Darksome be, and dangerous too:
Christ, thy guide, will bring thee through.

2 Faint not, Christian! though the world
Hath its hostile flag unfurled:
Hold the cross of Jesus fast;
Thou shalt overcome at last.

3 Faint not, Christian! though within
There's a heart so prone to sin;
Christ the Lord, is over all,
He'll not suffer thee to fall.

DELAWARE. M. 5.   By Com.

Casting all your anxiety upon him, because he careth for you. 1 Pet 5: 7.
M. 5.

329 CAST thy burden on the Lord!
   Is this message meant for me?
 May I take him at his word,
   And will he my helper be?

2 In my daily household care,
   In the business of the day,
 Will the Lord the burden bear
   Or his strength upon me lay?

3 When the evil one shall cast
   Tempting baits to snare my soul,
 Or shall taunt me with the past,
   Will the Lord his power control?

4 When the bitterness of grief
   Shall upon my bosom prey,
 Will he give me swift relief?
   Will he take the pain away?

5 When the parting hour is near,
   Will his everlasting love
 Conquer every doubt and fear
   And the sting of death remove?

6 'Tis the promise of the Lord,
   Meant for me on every day:
 Heaven and earth may fail,—his word
   Never once shall pass away.
                    Thos. MacKellar, 1882.

RESIGNATION.

AUTUMN. M. 4.   Spanish Melody

We have left all, and followed thee. Mark 10: 28.   M. 4.

330 Jesus, I my cross have taken,
   All to leave and follow thee;
Destitute, despised, forsaken,
   Thou from hence my all shalt be;
Perish every fond ambition,
   All I've sought, and hoped, and known,
Yet how rich is my condition!
   God and heaven are still my own.

2 Let the world despise and leave me;
   They have left my Saviour too;
Human hearts and looks deceive me;
   Thou art not, like men, untrue;
And while thou shalt smile upon me,
   God of wisdom, love, and might,
Foes may hate, and friends may shun me,
   Show thy face and all is bright.

3 Haste thee on from grace to glory,
   Armed by faith and winged by prayer;
Heaven's eternal day's before thee—
   God's own hand shall guide thee there.

Soon shall close thine earthly mission,
  Soon shall pass thy pilgrim days;
Hope shall change to glad fruition,
  Faith to sight, and prayer to praise.
                        Henry Francis Lyte, 1824.

New heavens and a new earth. 2 Pet. 3: 13.   M. 4.

331
WEARY pilgrim, why this sadness?
  Why 'mid sorrow's scenes decline?
Trials strange bring joy and gladness,
  For all things shall yet be thine.
Earth anew, with robe of glory,
  Shall rejoice in hill and vale;
There glad harps shall tell the story
  Of the love that could not fail.

2 Thou shalt range the fields of pleasure,
    Where joy's gushing songs arise;
  Thou shalt have thy well-stored treasure,
    In the New Earth's Paradise.
  Weary pilgrim, leave thy sadness,
    To Mount Zion thou art come!
  Swell thy songs of joy and gladness,
    And rejoice in thy blest home.
                  Emily Clemens Pearson, cir. 1844.

It is a good land. Deut. 1: 25.   M. 4.

332
SEE, above time's clouds and shadows,
  See, my soul, the land of light!
Where the breeze is ever balmy,
  Where the sky is ever bright.
In it spring life's crystal fountains,
  Through it peaceful rivers flow
And renew its glorious landscapes,
  Which with life eternal glow.

2 Storms that rage in death's dark valleys
    Die this side its golden strand;
  Sighs are lost in songs of triumph
    On its shining border land.
  Now at length a mighty rapture
    Thrills this troubled heart of mine,
  In the prospect of possessing
    This inheritance divine.
         Welsh of W. Thomas. Tr. W. Edwards, ab. cir. 1880.

FOUNT OF GLORY. M. 4.

A. L. LANDIS, 1889.

O how love I thy law! Psalm 119: 97. M. 4.

333 BLESSED Bible, how I love it!
  How it doth my bosom cheer!
What hath earth like this to covet?
  Oh, what stores of wealth are here!
Man was lost and doomed to sorrow,
  Not one ray of light or bliss
Could he from earth's treasures borrow,
  Till his way was cheered by this.

Yes, I'll to my bosom press thee,
  Precious word! I'll hide thee here!
Sure my very heart will bless thee,
  For thou ever say'st, "Good cheer!"
Speak, my heart, and tell thy pond'rings,
  Tell how far thy rovings led,
When this book bro't back thy wand'rings,
  Speaking life as from the dead.

3 Yes, sweet Bible! I will hide thee
  Deep, yes, deeper in this heart;
Thou through all my life wilt guide me,
  And in death we will not part!
Part in death! no, never, never!
  Thro' death's vale I'll lean on thee;
And in brighter worlds, forever,
  Sweeter far thy truths shall be.
                    Phœbe Palmer, cir. 1860.

There am I in the midst. Matt. 18: 20. M. 4.

334
Far from mortal cares retreating,
  Sordid hopes and vain desires,
Here, our willing footsteps meeting,
  Every heart to heaven aspires.
From the Fount of glory beaming,
  Light celestial cheers our eyes,
Mercy from above proclaiming
  Peace and pardon from the skies.

2 Who may share this great salvation?
  Every pure and humble mind,
Every kindred, tongue and nation,
  From the dross of guilt refined.
Blessings all around bestowing,
  God withholds his care from none,
Grace and mercy ever flowing
  From the fountain of his throne.

3 Every stain of guilt abhorring,
  Firm and bold in virtue's cause,
Still thy providence adoring,
  Faithful subjects to thy laws;
Lord, with favor still attend us,
  Bless us with thy wondrous love;
Thou our Sun and Shield defend us,
  All our hope is from above.
                    John Taylor, 1760.

WHAT A FRIEND.   No. 38.

SAFETY. C. M.   H. S. Rupp.

The way of man is not in himself; it is not in man that walketh to direct his steps. Jer. 10: 23.   C. M.

335 I WOULD I were content to be
    Just as my Lord shall will,
So I with cheerful constancy
    His purpose may fulfil.

2 O may I be content to lay
    My hourly griefs and cares
Upon His arm that every day
    His children's burden bears:

3 Nor proudly strive to carry part
    And leave to Him the rest,
So losing comfort of the heart
    And healing of the breast.

4 Though I should ask the Lord to show
    Some greater things to do,
May I be ever quick to go
    On humble errands too :

5 To run in haste, or waiting stand,
    Content to go or stay,
While watching for his guiding hand
    To point the fitting way.

6 Whatever work the day shall bring,
    May I set Thee before,
And give to Thee, O Christ, my King,
    The glory evermore.
                      Thos. MacKellar, 1881.

Blessed are the pure in heart; for they shall see God. Matt. 5: 8. C. M.

336
By cool Siloam's shady rill,
   How fair the lily grows!
How sweet the breath, beneath the hill,
   Of Sharon's dewy rose!

2 Lo! such the child, whose early feet
   The paths of peace have trod,
Whose secret heart with influence sweet,
   Is upward drawn to God.

3 By cool Siloam's shady rill
   The lily must decay;
The rose that blooms beneath the hill
   Must shortly fade away.

4 And soon, too soon the wintry hour
   Of man's maturer age
Will shake the soul with sorrow's pow'r,
   And stormy passion's rage.

5 O thou, who givest life and breath,
   We seek thy grace alone,
In childhood, manhood, age and death,
   To keep us still thine own.
Heber.

Increase our faith. Luke 17: 5. C. M.

337
Oh, for a faith that will not shrink,
   Though pressed by every foe,
That will not tremble on the brink
   Of any earthly woe!

2 That will not murmur nor complain
   Beneath the chastening rod,
But, in the hour of grief or pain,
   Will lean upon its God.

3 A faith that shines more bright and clear
   When tempests rage without;
That, when in danger, knows no fear,
   In darkness, feels no doubt.

4 Lord, give us such a faith as this,
   And then, whate'er may come,
We'll taste, ev'n here, the hallowed bliss
   Of an eternal home.
W. H. Bathurst, 1831.

LAWRENCE. C. M.   A. L. LANDIS, 1883.

As many as touched him were made whole. Mark 6: 56.   C. M.

338 AT JESUS' feet I take my place:
    I touch his garment's hem:
A helpless child in need of grace
    My Lord will not condemn.

2 I have no hope but in his love;
    His promise is my plea:
I give myself to Him who strove
    E'en unto death for me.

3 I only ask that I may know
    What he would have me do,
That my obedient life may show
    The grace that bears me through.

4 I've nothing, Lord, to offer thee
    But this weak heart of mine:
O take it, Lord, and let it be
    Thine own, for ever thine.
                        MacKellar, 1882.

Our dwelling-place in all generations. Ps. 90: 1.   C. M.

339 OUR God, our help in ages past,
    Our hope for years to come,
Our shelter from the stormy blast,
    And our eternal home!

2 Under the shadow of thy throne,
    Thy saints have dwelt secure;
Sufficient is thine arm alone,
    And our defense is sure.

3 Before the hills in order stood,
   Or earth received her frame,
From everlasting thou art God,
   To endless years the same.

4 Thy word commands our flesh to dust,
   "Return, ye sons of men;"
All nations rose from earth at first,
   And turn to earth again.

5 Time, like an ever-rolling stream,
   Bears all its sons away:
They fly, forgotten, as a dream
   Dies at the opening day.

6 Our God, our help in ages past,
   Our hope for years to come,
Be thou our guard while troubles last,
   And our eternal home.
Isaac Watts, ab. 1709.

"Thy will be done."   C. M.

340 My God, my Father, blissful name!
   Oh, may I call thee mine?
May I with sweet assurance claim
   A portion so divine?

2 This only can my fears control,
   And bid my sorrows fly;
What real harm can reach my soul
   Beneath my Father's eye?

3 Whate'er thy providence denies
   I calmly would resign;
For thou art good, and just, and wise:
   Oh, bend my will to thine!

4 Whate'er thy sacred will ordains,
   Oh, give me strength to bear!
And let me know my Father reigns,
   And trust his tender care.

5 Thy sovereign ways are all unknown
   To my weak, erring sight:
Yet let my soul adoring own
   That all thy ways are right.
Mrs. Steele.

RESIGNATION.

ROCKINGHAM. L. M.   L. Mason, 1832.

Ye have not yet resisted unto blood, striving against sin. Heb. 12: 4.   L. M.

341
    WHY should I murmur or repine,
      O Lamb of God, who bled for me?
    What are my griefs compared with thine,
      Thy tears, thy groans, thine agony!

2 If thou the furnace dost employ,
    Thou sittest as refiner near
To purge away the base alloy,
    Till thine own image bright appear.

3 Though oft thy way is in the sea,
    Thy footsteps in the wingéd storm;
Though crested billows threaten me,
    Love slumbers in their frowning foam.

4 Submissive would I kiss the rod,
    Needful each stroke, I humbly own;
Help me to trust thee, O my God,
    If now thy wisdom be unknown.

Which also sat at Jesus' feet, and heard his word. Luke 10: 39.   L. M.

342
    OH, that I could forever dwell,
      Delighted at the Saviour's feet;
    Behold the form I love so well,
      And all his tender words repeat!

2 The world shut out from all my soul,
    And heaven brought in with all its bliss,—
Oh! is there aught, from pole to pole,
    One moment to compare with this?

3 This is the hidden life I prize—
  A life of penitential love!
 When most my follies I despise,
  And raise my highest thoughts above.

4 Thus would I live till nature fail,
  And all my former sins forsake;
 Then rise to God within the vail,
  And of eternal joys partake.

The communion of the Holy Ghost. 2 Cor. 13: 14.   L. M.

343
 O THOU who camest from above,
  The pure celestial fire to impart,
 Kindle a flame of sacred love
  On the mean altar of my heart.

2 There let it for thy glory burn,
  With inextinguishable blaze;
 And trembling to its source return,
  In humble prayer and fervent praise.

3 Jesus, confirm my heart's desire,
  To work, and speak, and think for thee;
 Still let me guard the holy fire,
  And still stir up thy gift in me.

4 Ready for all thy perfect will,
  My acts of faith and love repeat,
 Till death thy endless mercies seal,
  And make the sacrifice complete.
                              C. Wesley.

As thy days, so shall thy strength be. Deut. 33: 25.   L. M.

344
 LET me but hear my Saviour say,
  "Strength shall be equal to thy day,"—
 Then I rejoice in deep distress,
  Upheld by all-sufficient grace.

2 I can do all things, or can bear
  All suffering, if my Lord be there;
 Sweet pleasures mingle with the pains,
  While he my sinking head sustains.

3 I glory in infirmity,
  That Christ's own power may rest on me;
 When I am weak, then am I strong;
  Grace is my shield, and Christ my song.
                       Isaac Watts, ab. 1709.

RUTH. S. M.

It is not of him that willeth, nor of him that runneth, but of God that showeth mercy. Rom. 9: 16. S. M.

345 "My times are in thy hand,"
My God, I wish them there;
My life, my friends, my soul I leave
Entirely to thy care.

2 "My times are in thy hand,"
Whatever they may be;
Pleasing or painful, dark or bright,
As best may seem to thee.

3 "My times are in thy hand,"
Why should I doubt or fear?
My Father's hand will never cause
His child a needless tear.

4 "My times are in thy hand,"
I'll always trust in thee;
And after death, at thy right hand
I shall forever be.

And we know that all things work together for good to them that love God. Rom. 8: 28. S M.

346 If through unruffled seas
Toward heaven we calmly sail,
With grateful hearts, O God, to thee,
We'll own the fostering gale.

2 But should the surges rise,
And rest delay to come,
Blest be the sorrow, kind the storm,
Which drives us nearer home.

3 Soon shall our doubts and fears
   All yield to thy control;
 Thy tender mercies shall illume
   The midnight of the soul.

4 Teach us, in every state,
   To make thy will our own;
 And, when the joys of sense depart,
   To live by faith alone.

He careth for you. 1 Pet. 5: 7.   S. M.

347 DEAR Saviour, we are thine
           By everlasting bonds;
         Our names, our hearts, we would resign,
           Our souls are in thy hands.

2 To thee we still would cleave,
   With ever growing zeal;
 If millions tempt us Christ to leave,
   Oh let them ne'er prevail.

3 Thy Spirit shall unite
   Our souls to thee our Head;
 Shall form us to thy image bright,
   That we thy paths may tread.

Thanks be to God, which causeth us to triumph in Christ. 2 Cor. 2: 14.
                                                      S. M.

348 WHEN on the brink of death
           My trembling soul shall stand,
         Waiting to pass that awful flood,
           Great God, at thy command!—

2 When every scene of life
   Stands ready to depart,
 And the last sigh that shakes the frame
   Shall rend this bursting heart.

3 Thou Source of joy supreme,
   Whose arm alone can save—
 Dispel the darkness that surrounds
   The entrance to the grave.

4 Leaning on Jesus' breast,
   May I resign my breath;
 And in his kind embraces lose
   The bitterness of death.

RESIGNATION.

ROLLING BILLOWS. C. M. D.
C. H. Brunk, 1889.

What time I am afraid, I will trust in thee. Ps. 56: 3. C. M. D.

349
The billows round me rise and roll,
  The storms of worldly care
Beat heavily upon my soul,
  And shroud me in despair:
Forsaken, comfortless, betray'd,
  With none to succour me,—
Father, what time I am afraid,
  Then will I trust in Thee!

2 As feeble as the bruised reed,
  Infirm to will or do;
Oft working out the ungrateful deed
  'Twere better to eschew;
How were the sinking soul dismay'd
  But for this refuge-plea,—
Father, what time I am afraid,
  Then will I trust in Thee!

3 When hope is faint, and faith is weak,
  And fears the bosom fill,
And I a strong assurance seek
  That thou art gracious still;
I rest upon thy promise-word,
  To thine own truth I flee:
Father, what time I am afraid,
  Then will I trust in Thee!

4 When saintly paleness marks my face,
    And dimness fills mine eye,
And, hoping only in thy grace,
    I bow my head to die;
If, entering in the vale of shade,
    Nor sun nor star I see,
Father, what time I am afraid,
    Then will I trust in Thee!
                    Thos. MacKellar, 1853.

How I love thy law. Psalm 119: 97.   C. M. 𝌂

350 OH, how I love Thy holy law!
        'Tis daily my delight:
    And thence my meditations draw
        Divine advice by night.
    My waking eyes prevent the day,
        To meditate Thy word;
    My soul with longing melts away,
        To hear Thy gospel, Lord.

2 How doth Thy word my heart engage,
    How well employ my tongue,
And in my tiresome pilgrimage
    Yields me a heavenly song.
Am I a stranger, or at home,
    'Tis my perpetual feast:
Not honey dropping from the comb
    So much allures the taste.

3 No treasures so enrich the mind,
    Nor shall Thy word be sold
For loads of silver, well refined,
    Nor heaps of choicest gold.
When nature sinks, and spirits droop,
    Thy promises of grace
Are pillars to support my hope,
    And there I write Thy praise.
                    Isaac Watts, 1719.

VARINA.   No. 105.

URBANA. C. M.   J. H. Hall, by per.

The God of all grace.   *1 Peter 5: 10.*   C. M.

351   THE God of love, the God of peace,
     On whom our souls depend,
Shall guide us through the wilderness,
     Until our journey's end:

2 The God of power shall still be near
     To strengthen and to save,
To bring us off victorious there,
     Triumphant o'er the grave.

3 The God of hope shall comfort us,
     Through troubles yet to come;
The God of truth shall be our trust,
     When lying lips are dumb.

4 The God of Abraham and his seed
     Shall be our guide and guard,
Our help in every time of need,
     Our shield and great reward.

It is I; be not afraid.   *Matt. 14: 27.*   C. M.

352   WHEN waves of trouble round me swell,
     My soul is not dismayed:
I hear a voice I know full well—
     "'Tis I—be not afraid."

2 When black the threatening clouds appear,
     And storms my path invade,
Those accents tranquilize each fear—
     "'Tis I—be not afraid."

RESIGNATION.

3 There is a gulf that must be crossed;
   Saviour, be near to aid!
Whisper when my frail bark is tossed,
   "'Tis I—be not afraid."

4 There is a dark and fearful vale,
   Death hides within its shade:
Oh, say, when flesh and heart shall fail,
   "'Tis I—be not afraid."
                          Charlotte Elliott, 1834.

That Christ may dwell in your hearts. Eph. 3: 17.   C. M.

353 O SAVIOUR, welcome to my heart;
   Possess thy humble throne;
Bid every rival hence depart,
   And claim me for thine own.

2 The world and Satan I forsake;
   To thee I all resign;
My longing heart, O Saviour, take,
   And fill with love divine.

3 Oh, may I never turn aside,
   Nor from thy bosom flee;
Let nothing here my heart divide;
   I give it all to thee.
                H. Bourne and W. Sanders, 1825.

Thou art with me. Psalm 23: 4.   C. M.

354 THAT solemn hour will come for me,
   When, though their charms I own,
All human ties resigned must be,
   For I must die alone.

2 All earthly pleasures will be o'er,
   All earthly labors done,
And I shall tread the eternal shore,
   And I must die alone.

3 But O, I will not view with dread
   That shadowy vale unknown;
I see a light within it shed;
   I shall not die alone!

4 One will be with me there, whose voice
   I long have loved and known;
In Him my spirit shall rejoice,
   I shall not die alone.

ALBION. S. M.

Wherein he had made us accepted in the Beloved. Eph. 1: 6. S. M.

355
My soul, with joy attend,
  While Jesus silence breaks;
No angel's harp such music yields,
  As what my Shepherd speaks.

2 "I know my sheep," he cries,
  "My soul approves them well:
Vain is the treach'rous world's disguise,
  And vain the rage of hell.

3 I freely feed them now
  With tokens of my love;
But richer pastures I prepare,
  And sweeter streams above.

4 Unnumbered years of bliss
  I to my sheep will give;
And while my throne unshaken stands,
  Shall all my chosen live.

5 This tried Almighty Hand,
  Is raised for their defense:
Where is the power shall reach them there?
  Or what shall force them thence "

6 Enough, my gracious Lord,
  Let faith triumphant cry;
My heart can on this promise live,
  Can on this promise die.

For the same cause also do ye joy. Phil. 2: 18.　　S. M.

356
Come, we that love the Lord,
　And let our joys be known;
Join in a song with sweet accord,
　And thus surround the throne.

2 The sorrows of the mind,
　Be banished from the place!
Religion never was designed
　To make our pleasures less.

3 Let those refuse to sing
　Who never knew their God,
But favorites of the heavenly King
　May speak their joys abroad.

4 The hill of Zion yields
　A thousand sacred sweets,
Before we reach the heavenly fields,
　Or walk the golden streets.

5 Then let our songs abound,
　And every tear be dry;
We're marching through Immanuel's ground
　To fairer worlds on high.
　　　　　　　　　　Watts.

To every man his work. Mark 13: 34.　　S. M.

357
Laborers of Christ, arise,
　And gird you for the toil!
The dew of promise from the skies,
　Already cheers the soil.

2 Go where the sick recline,
　Where mourning hearts deplore;
And where the sons of sorrow pine,
　Dispense your hallowed store.

3 Be faith, which looks above,
　With prayer, your constant guest;
And wrap the Saviour's changeless **love**
　A mantle round your breast.

4 So shall you share the wealth,
　That earth may ne'er despoil;
And the blest gospel's saving health
　Repay your arduous toil.
　　　　　Mrs. Lydia H. Sigourney, 1841.

REJOICING.

ELKHART. C. M.

Rejoice in the Lord always. Phil. 4: 4.   C. M.

358
JESUS! the very thought of thee
  With gladness fills my breast;
But dearer far thy face to see,
  And in thy presence rest.

2 Nor voice can sing, nor heart can frame,
  Nor can the memory find
A sweeter sound than thy blest name,
  O Saviour of mankind!

3 O Hope of every contrite heart,
  O Joy of all the meek!
To those who fall, how kind thou art,
  How good to those who seek!

4 And those who find thee, find a bliss
  Nor tongue nor pen can show:
The love of Jesus, what it is,
  None but his loved ones know!
                        E. Caswall, Tr.

Grateful acknowledgments. Psalm 116: 12.   C. M.

359
WHAT shall I render to my God
  For all his kindness shown?
My feet shall visit thine abode,
  My songs address thy throne.

2 Among the saints that fill thine house
  My off'ring shall be paid;
There shall my zeal perform the vows
  My soul in anguish made.

REJOICING.

3 How happy all thy servants are!
  How great thy grace to me!
My life, which thou hast made thy care,
  Lord, I devote to thee.

4 Now I am thine, for ever thine,
  Nor shall my purpose move;
Thy hand has loosed my bonds of pain,
  And bound me with thy love.

5 Here, in thy courts, I leave my vow,
  And thy rich grace record;
Witness, ye saints, who hear me now,
  If I forsake the Lord.
                                    Isaac Watts.

By the grace of God, I am what I am. 1 Cor. 15: 10.   C. M.

360 AMAZING grace! how sweet the sound,
  That saved a wretch like me;
I once was lost, but now am found;
  Was blind, but now I see.

2 'Twas grace that taught my heart to fear,
  And grace my fears relieved;
How precious did that grace appear,
  The hour I first believed.

3 Thro' many dangers, toils, and snares,
  I have already come;
'Tis grace has brought me safe thus far,
  And grace will lead me home.

4 The Lord has promised good to me,
  His word my hope secures;
He will my shield and comfort be,
  As long as life endures.

5 Yes, when this flesh and heart shall fail,
  And mortal life shall cease;
I shall possess, within the veil,
  A life of joy and peace.
                                    Newton.

NAOMI.   No. 196.

BROWN. C. M.   W. B. BRADBURY.

A High-Priest, that hath been in all points tempted like as we are, yet without sin. Heb. 4: 15.   C. M.

361 WAS Jesus tempted like as we,
    The Holy One of God?
Were paths of pain and poverty
    By him, our Master, trod?

2 Was there no place in all the earth
    To lay his head upon,
A King of more than royal birth,
    Yea, God's eternal Son?

3 If thus the sinless Saviour fared,
    Can I, dare I repine,
When sorrow, want, and death he shared
    To make salvation mine!

4 O child redeem'd by his own blood,
    Why yield to anxious care?
Thou canst not sink beneath the flood
    When Christ is walking there.

5 Think not thy Saviour does not see
    When Satan casts a dart:
No arrow ever wounded thee
    That did not pierce his heart.

6 The great High-Priest is touch'd by all
    Thy weaknesses and woes;
And He, when grievous sorrows fall,
    Sufficient grace bestows.
                    Thos. MacKellar, 1881.

REJOICING.

All my springs are in thee. Psalm 87: 7.   C. M.

362
My God, the spring of all my joys,
  The life of my delights,
The glory of my brightest days,
  The comfort of my nights!

2 In darkest shades, if thou appear,
  My dawning is begun;
Thou art my soul's bright morning star,
  And thou my rising sun.

3 The op'ning heav'ns around me shine
  With beams of sacred bliss,
While Jesus shows his mercy mine,
  And whispers I am his.

4 My soul would leave this heavy clay
  At that transporting word,
And run with joy the shining way
  To meet my dearest Lord.
                Watts.

My refuge and my fortress. Psalm 91: 2.   C. M.

363
Be strong, my soul, in God most High,
  And trust his mighty arm:
The hand that holds the starry sky
  Preserves thee safe from harm.

2 He who hath spread the heavens above,
  And earth's foundations laid,
Walks by thy side, a guide and God,
  And says, "Be not afraid."

3 O rest, my soul, in God most High,
  Beneath his sheltering wing;
While tempests wild go sweeping by
  Rejoice, my soul, and sing.

4 He is thy buckler and defense,
  Thy Rock, thy strength, and tower;
And he will be thy confidence,
  In each distressing hour.

5 Be strong, my soul, in God most High,
  Though helpless, poor, and low;
The gleaming worlds that stud the sky
  His power and glory show.
        Hastings. From Songs of Pilgrimage.

CHARLESTON. M. 4. STEPHEN JENKS, 1803.

We glory in tribulation. Rom. 5: 3.   M. 4.

364
1 IN the cross of Christ I glory,
    Tow'ring o'er the wrecks of time;
   All the light of sacred story
    Gathers round its head sublime.

2 When the woes of life o'ertake me,
    Hopes deceive, and fears annoy,
   Never shall the cross forsake me:
    Lo! it glows with peace and joy.

3 When the sun of bliss is beaming
    Light and love upon my way,
   From the cross the radiance streaming,
    Adds more luster to the day.

4 Bane and blessing, pain and pleasure,
    By the cross are sanctified;
   Peace is there, that knows no measure,
    Joys that through all time abide.

5 In the cross of Christ I glory,
    Tow'ring o'er the wrecks of time;
   All the light of sacred story
    Gathers round its head sublime.
                        John Bowring, 1825.

Bring ye all the tithes. Mal. 3: 10.   M. 4.

365
1 WITH my substance I will honor
    My Redeemer and my Lord;
   Were ten thousand worlds my manor,
    All were nothing to his word.

2 While the heralds of salvation
　　His unbounding grace proclaim,
　Let his friends in every station
　　Gladly join to spread his fame.

3 Be his kingdom now promoted;
　　Let the earth her Monarch know;
　Be my all to him devoted;
　　To my Lord my all I owe.

4 Praise the Saviour, all ye nations!
　　Praise him, all ye hosts above!
　Shout, with joyful acclamations,
　　His divine, victorious love.
　　　　　　　　　　Rev. B. Francis.

The salvation of the righteous is of the Lord. Psalm 37: 39. M. 4.

388 Call the Lord thy sure salvation,
　　Rest beneath th' Almighty's shade;
　In his secret habitation
　　Dwell, and never be dismayed!

2 There no tumult can alarm thee,
　　Thou shalt dread no hidden snare;
　Guile nor violence can harm thee,
　　In eternal safeguard there.

3 Thee, though winds and waves are swelling,
　　God, thy Hope, shall bear through all;
　Plague shall not come nigh thy dwelling,
　　Thee no evil shall befall.

4 He shall charge his angel legions,
　　Watch and ward o'er thee to keep,
　Though thou walk through hostile regions,
　　Though in desert wilds thou sleep.

5 Since, with firm and pure affection,
　　Thou on God hast set thy love,
　With the wings of his protection
　　He shall shield thee from above.
　　　　　　　　　　Montgomery.

NETTLETON.　　　　No. 268.

PEORIA. C. M. Wm. B. Bradbury.
Used by per. of Biglow and Main, owners of copyright.

I will be glad and rejoice in thy mercies. Ps. 31: 7. C. M.

367
Sweet was the time when first I felt
　The Saviour's pard'ning blood
Applied to cleanse my soul from guilt,
　And bring me home to God.

2 Soon as the morn the light reveal'd,
　　His praises tuned my tongue;
　And when the evening shades prevail'd,
　　His love was all my song.

3 In prayer, my soul drew near the Lord,
　　And saw His glory shine;
　And when I read His holy word,
　　I call'd each promise mine.

4 Now when the evening shade prevails,
　　My soul in darkness mourns;
　And when the morn the light reveals,
　　No light to me returns.

5 Now Satan threatens to prevail,
　　And make my soul his prey;
　Yet, Lord, Thy mercies cannot fail,
　　Oh, come without delay!

Whereby we cry, Abba, Father. Rom. 8: 15. C. M.

368
My Father, God! how sweet the sound!
　How tender, and how dear!
Not all the melody of heaven
　Could so delight the ear.

2 Come, sacred Spirit, seal the name
  On my expanding heart,
 And show, that in Jehovah's grace
  I share a filial part.

3 Cheered by a signal so divine,
  Unwavering I believe;
 My spirit, "Abba, Father," cries,
  Nor can the sign deceive.

4 On wings of everlasting love
  The Comforter is come;
 All terrors at his voice disperse,
  And endless pleasures bloom.
                    Philip Doddridge, d. 1751.

How precious also are Thy thoughts. Ps. 139: 17.   C. M.

369 LORD, when I count thy mercies o'er,
   They strike me with surprise;
 Not all the sands that spread the shore
  To equal numbers rise.

2 My flesh with fear and wonder stands,
  The product of thy skill;
 And hourly blessings from thy hands
  Thy thoughts of love reveal.

3 These on my heart by night I keep:
  How kind, how dear to me!
 Oh may the hour that ends my sleep
  Still find my thoughts with thee!
                         Isaac Watts, 1718.

God is love. 1 John 4: 8.   C. M.

370 AMID the splendors of thy state,
   My God, thy love appears,
 Soft as the radiance of the moon
  Among a thousand stars.

2 In all thy doctrines and commands,
  Thy counsels and designs,
 In every work thy hands have framed,
  Thy love supremely shines.

3 Angels and men the news proclaim
  Through earth and heaven above;
 And all with holy transport sing
  That God, the Lord, is love.
                    Rippon's Collection. ab. 1800.

LINCOLNSHIRE M. 5.

We are journeying. Numb. 10: 29. M 5.

871 CHILDREN of the heavenly King!
As ye journey, sweetly sing;
Sing your Saviour's worthy praise,
Glorious in his works and ways.

2 Ye are traveling home to God,
In the way your fathers trod;
They are blessed now; and we
Soon their blessedness shall see.

3 Glory be to Jesus' name,
Glory be to Christ, the Lamb,
Through thy blood were we redeemed,
When we justly were condemned.

4 O ye banished seed, be glad!
Christ our Advocate is made;
Us to save, our flesh assumes,
Brother to our soul becomes.

5 Shout, ye little flock, and blest!
You on Jesus' throne shall rest,
There your seat is now prepared,
There your kingdom and reward.

6 Lift your eyes, ye sons of light,
Zion's city is in sight;
There our endless home shall be;
There our Lord we soon shall see.

Rev. John Cennick, ab. 1717

Worship the Lord in the beauty of holiness. Psalm 29: 2.   M. 5.

372
To thy temple we repair;
Lord, we love to worship there;
There within the vail we meet
Christ upon the mercy seat.

2 While thy glorious name is sung,
Tune our lips, inspire our tongue;
Then our joyful souls shall bless
Christ, the Lord, our Righteousness.

3 While to thee our prayers ascend,
Let thine ear in love attend;
Hear us, for thy Spirit pleads;
Hear, for Jesus intercedes.

4 While thy word is heard with awe,
While we tremble at thy law,
Let thy gospel's wondrous love
Ev'ry doubt and fear remove.

5 From thy house when we return,
Let our hearts within us burn;
Then, at evening, we may say,
"We have walked with God to-day."
Montgomery.

The Lord shall reign forever. Psalm 146: 10.   M. 5.

373
WAKE the song of Jubilee;
Let it echo o'er the sea:
Now is come the promised hour,
Jesus reigns with glorious power.

2 All ye nations, join and sing,
Praise your Saviour, praise your King;
Let it sound form shore to shore,
"Jesus reigns for evermore!"

3 Hark! the desert lands rejoice;
And the islands join their voice:
Joy! the whole creation sings,
"Jesus is the King of kings!"
Leonard Bacon, 1873.

YARBROUGH.   No. 184.

RESURRECTION.

MARTYN. M. 5. SIMEON BUTLER MARSH, 1834.

Woman, why weepest thou? John 20: 13. M. 5.

374
Mary to the Saviour's tomb
  Hasted at the early dawn;
Spice she brought and rich perfume,
  But the Lord she loved was gone.
For a while she lingering stood,
  Filled with sorrow and surprise,
Trembling, while a crystal flood
  Issued from her weeping eyes.

2 But her sorrows quickly fled
  When she heard her Saviour's voice;
Christ has risen from the dead,
  Now he bids her heart rejoice.
What a change his word can make,
  Turning darkness into day!
You who weep for Jesus' sake,
  He will wipe your tears away.

3 He who came to comfort her,
  When she thought her all was lost,
Will for your relief appear,
  Though you now are tempest-tossed.
On his word your burden cast;
  On his love your thoughts employ;
Weeping for a night may last,
  But the morning brings the joy.
            John Newton, ab. 1779.

MONMOUTH. P. M.   JOSEPH KLUG's Gesangbuch.

When the Son of man shall come in his glory.   P. M.

375 GREAT God, what do I see and hear?—
    The end of things created;
Behold the Judge of man appear,
    On clouds of glory seated!
The trumpet sounds; the graves restore
The dead which they contained before;
    Prepare, my soul, to meet him.

2 The dead in Christ shall first arise,
    At the last trumpet's sounding,—
Caught up to meet him in the skies,
    With joy their Lord surrounding;
No gloomy fears their souls dismay;
His presence sheds eternal day
    On those prepared to meet him.

3 But sinners, filled with guilty fears,
    Behold his wrath prevailing;
For they shall rise, and find their tears
    And sighs are unavailing:
Beneath his cross I view the day,
When heaven and earth shall pass away,
    And thus prepare to meet him.
                                Collyer.

CROSS AND CROWN. C. M.

They desire a better country. Heb. 11: 16.   C. M.

376
How happy every child of grace,
  Who knows his sins forgiven!
This earth, he cries, is not my place,
  I seek my place in heaven.

2 A country far from mortal sight,
  Yet, oh! by faith I see
The land of rest, the saints' delight,
  The heaven prepared for me.

3 Its evils in a moment end,
  Its joys as soon are past;
But oh! the bliss to which I tend
  Eternally shall last.

4 To that Jerusalem above
  With singing I repair;
While in the flesh my hope and love,
  My heart and soul, are there.

5 We feel the resurrection near,
  Our life in Christ concealed,
And with his glorious presence here
  Our earthen vessels filled.

6 In rapturous awe on Him to gaze,
  Who bought the bliss for me,
And shout and wonder at his grace
  Through all eternity.

                    Charles Wesley, ab. 1759.

RESURRECTION.

The Lord is risen indeed. Luke 24: 34. C. M.

377 This is the day the Lord hath made,
　　He calls the hours his own:
Let heaven rejoice, let earth be glad,
　　And praise surround the throne.

2 To-day he rose and left the dead,
　　And Satan's empire fell;
To-day the saints his triumph spread,
　　And all his wonders tell.

3 Hosanna to th' anointed King,
　　To David's holy Son;
Help us, O Lord; descend and bring
　　Salvation from thy throne.

4 Bless'd is the Lord, who comes to men
　　With messages of grace;
Who comes in God his Father's name,
　　To save our sinful race.

5 Hosanna in the highest strains,
　　The church on earth can raise;
The highest heavens in which he reigns,
　　Shall give him nobler praise.

Them also which sleep in Jesus will God bring with him. 1 Thess. 4: 14.
　　　　　　　　　　　　　　　　　C. M.

378 As Jesus died, and rose again,
　　Victorious, from the dead;
So his disciples rise and reign
　　With their triumphant Head.

2 The saints of God, from death set free,
　　With joy shall mount on high;
The heavenly host with praises loud,
　　Shall meet them in the sky.

3 Together to their Father's house
　　With joyful hearts they go,
And dwell forever with the Lord,
　　Beyond the reach of woe.

4 A few short days of evil past,
　　We reach the happy shore,
Where death-divided friends, at last
　　Shall meet, to part no more.
　　　　　　　　Michael Bruce, 1744–1767.

WOODLAND. C. M.
N. D. GOULD, 1832.

There remaineth therefore a rest. Heb. 4:9.　　C. M.

379
There is an hour of peaceful rest,
　To mourning wanderers given;
There is a joy for souls distressed,
A balm for every wounded breast,
　'Tis found alone—in heaven.

2 There is a soft and downy bed,
　'Tis fair as breath of even,
A couch for weary mortals spread,
Where they may rest the aching head,
　And find repose in heaven.

3 There is a home for weary souls,
　By sin and sorrow driven,—
When toss'd on life's tempestuous shoals,
Where storms arise, and ocean rolls,
　And all is drear but heaven.

4 There faith lifts up her cheerful eye
　To brighter prospects given;
And views the tempest passing by,
The evening shadows quickly fly,
　And all serene in heaven.

5 There fragrant flowers immortal bloom,
　And joys supreme are given;
There rays divine disperse the gloom;
Beyond the confines of the tomb
　Appears the dawn of heaven.
　　　　　　William Bingham Tappan, 1822.

A little while. John 16: 16. S. M.

380
A FEW more years shall roll,
A few more seasons come;
And we shall lie with them that rest,
Asleep within the tomb.

2 A few more suns shall set
O'er these dark hills of time;
And we shall be where suns are not,
A far serener clime.

3 A few more storms shall beat
On this wild, rocky shore;
And we shall be where tempests cease,
And surges swell no more.

4 A few more struggles here,
A few more partings o'er,
A few more toils, a few more tears,
And we shall weep no more.

5 A few more meetings here
Shall cheer us on our way;
And we shall reach the endless **rest**,
Th' eternal Sabbath day.

Borar.

EUGENE. S. M. By Com.

There remaineth therefore a rest to the people of God. Heb. 4: 9. S. M.

381 OH, where shall rest be found,
Rest for the weary soul?
'Twere vain the ocean depths to sound,
Or pierce to either pole.

2 The world can never give
The bliss for which we sigh;
'Tis not the whole of life to live,
Nor all of death to die.

3 Beyond this vale of tears
There is a life above,
Unmeasur'd by the flight of years;
And all that life is love.

4 There is a death whose pang
Outlasts the fleeting breath:
Oh, what eternal horrors hang
Around the second death!

5 Lord God of truth and grace,
Teach us that death to shun,
Lest we be banish'd from thy face,
And evermore undone.

Let us labor therefore to enter into that rest. Heb. 4: 11. S. M.

382 OH cease, my wandering soul,
On restless wings to roam;
All the wide world, to either pole,
Has not for thee a home.

REST.

2 Behold the ark of God,
　　Behold the open door;
　Hasten to gain that dear abode,
　　And rove, my soul, no more.

3 There, safe thou shalt abide,
　　There, sweet shall be thy rest,
　And every longing satisfied,
　　With full salvation blessed.

4 And when the waves of ire
　　Again the earth shall fill,
　The ark shall ride the sea of fire;
　　Then rest on Zion's hill.
　　　　　William Augustus Muhlenberg, ab 1826.

My flesh also shall rest in hope. Ps. 16: 9.　　S. M.

383　Rest for the toiling hand,
　　Rest for the anxious brow,
　Rest for the weary, way-worn feet,
　　Rest from all labor now;—

2 Rest for the fevered brain,
　　Rest for the throbbing eye;
　Through these parched lips of thine no more
　　Shall pass the moan or sigh.

3 Soon shall the trump of God
　　Give out the welcome sound
　That shakes thy silent chamber-walls,
　　And breaks the turf-sealed ground.

4 Ye dwellers in the dust,
　　Awake! come forth and sing;
　Sharp has your frost of winter been,
　　But bright shall be your spring.

5 'Twas sown in weakness here;
　　'Twill then be raised in power:
　That which was sown an earthly seed,
　　Shall rise a heavenly flower.

SHIRLAND.　　　　No. 323.

EDEN. M. 4. Arr. by J. S. Coffman.

For we which have believed do enter into rest. Heb. 4: 3. M. 4.

384   Oh, **the bliss of loved ones, resting**
By **the crystal river bright**;
'Neath the shade of trees immortal,
Where no shadows dim the light;
Resting, resting, sweetly resting,
Where no shadows dim the light.

2 For this rest they longed and waited,
Heaven's glory was their song;
Living FAITH now bids us hear them
Singing with the blood-washed throng;
Resting, resting, sweetly resting,
Singing with the blood-washed throng.

3 May we not on earth sing with them,
Echoing back their notes of praise?
Yes, but blesséd HOPE inspires us
Heaven's eternal songs to raise;
Resting, resting, sweetly resting,
Heaven's eternal songs to raise.

4 Oh, the peace and rest in heaven!
Oh, the bliss of loved ones there!
LOVE divine now bears us upward
All their blessédness to share;
Resting, resting, sweetly resting,
All their blessedness to share.

J. S. Coffman.

BRINGING HOME OUR SHEAVES. 10s. & 6s.   H. S. Rupp, 1888.

He that goeth forth weeping, bearing precious seed, shall come again rejoicing, bringing his sheaves with him. Psalm 126: 6.   10s. & 6s.

385
THE time for toil is past, and night has come,
   The last and saddest of the harvest eves;
Worn out with labor long and wearisome,
   Drooping and faint, the reapers hasten home, :||
     Each laden with his sheaves. :||

2 Few, light, and worthless—yet their trifling weight
   Through all my frame a weary aching leaves;
For long I struggled with my hapless fate,
   And staid and toiled till it was dark and late, :||
     Yet these are all my sheaves. :||

3 Full well I know I have more tares than wheat,
   Brambles and flowers, dry stalks and withered leaves;
Wherefore I blush and weep, as at Thy feet
   I kneel down reverently, and repeat, :||
     Master, behold my sheaves. :||

4 So do I gather hope and strength anew;
   For well I know Thy patient love perceives
Not what I did, but what I strove to do—
   And though the full ripe ears be sadly few, :||
     Thou wilt accept my sheaves. :||

                            Elizabeth Akers.

HURSLEY. L. M.
FRANCIS JOSEPH HAYDN, 1798.
Arr. WILLIAM HENRY MONK, 1861.

For the Lord God is a sun and shield.   Psalm 84: 11.   L. M.

385   Sun of my soul, Thou Saviour dear,
It is not night if Thou be near;
Oh, may no earth-born cloud arise,
To hide Thee from Thy servant's eyes.

2 When the soft dews of kindly sleep
My wearied eye-lids gently steep,
Be my last thought, how sweet to rest
Forever on my Saviour's breast.

3 Abide with me from morn till eve,
For without Thee I cannot live;
Abide with me when night is nigh,
For without Thee I dare not die.

4 If some poor wandering child of Thine
Have spurned to-day the voice divine—
Now, Lord, the gracious work begin;
Let him no more lie down in sin.

5 Watch by the sick; enrich the poor
With blessings from Thy boundless store;
Be every mourner's sleep to-night,
Like infant's slumbers, pure and light.

6 Come near and bless us when we wake,
Ere through the world our way we take;
Till in the ocean of Thy love
We lose ourselves in heaven above.

John Keble, 1827.

REST.

Happy is the man that findeth wisdom. Prov. 3: 13. L. M.

387
1. Happy the man that finds the grace,
   The blessing of God's chosen race,
   The wisdom coming from above,
   The faith that sweetly works by love.

2. Happy, beyond description, he
   Who knows, "the Saviour died for me!"
   The gift unspeakable obtains,
   And heavenly understanding gains.

3. Wisdom divine! Who tells the price
   Of Wisdom's costly merchandise?
   Wisdom to silver we prefer,
   And gold is dross compared to her.

4. Her hands are filled with length of days,
   True riches, and immortal praise;
   Riches of Christ on all bestowed,
   And honor that descends from God.

5. To purest joys she all invites,
   Chaste, holy, spiritual delights;
   Her ways are ways of pleasantness,
   And all her flowery paths are peace.

6. Happy the man who Wisdom gains;
   Thrice happy, who his guest retains!
   He owns, and shall for ever own,
   Wisdom, and Christ, and Heaven are one.
   Wesley, 1747.

Blessed are they that mourn. Matt. 5: 4. L. M.

388
1. Deem not that they are blest alone
   Whose days a peaceful tenor keep;
   The anointed Son of God makes known
   A blessing for the eyes that weep.

2. The light of smiles shall fill again
   The lids that overflow with tears;
   And weary hours of woe and pain
   Are promises of happier years.

3. There is a day of sunny rest
   For every dark and troubled night;
   And grief may bide an evening guest,
   But joy shall come with early light.
   William Cullen Bryant, 1794-1879.

SHINING SHORE. Pec. 8, 7.

Geo. F. Root, 1856.

Used by per. of O. Ditson & Co., Owners of Copyright.

Thou art to pass over Jordan. Deut. 9: 1.   Pec. 8, 7.

389 My days are gliding swiftly by,
    And I, a pilgrim stranger,
Would not detain them as they fly,
    Those hours of toil and danger.

Cho.— For oh! we stand on Jordan's strand,
    And soon we'll all pass over,
And just before, the shining shore
    We may almost discover.

2 We'll gird our loins, my brethren dear,
    Our distant home discerning;
Our absent Lord has left us word,
    Let every lamp be burning.

3 Should coming days be cold and dark,
    We need not cease our singing;
That perfect rest nought can molest,
    Where golden harps are ringing.

4 Let sorrow's rudest tempest blow,
    Each chord on earth to sever;
Our King says Come, and there's our home
    Forever, oh, forever!

                  David Nelson, 1835.

HOLY SPIRIT, FAITHFUL GUIDE. M. 5.

M. M. Wells.

I will guide thee with mine eye. Ps. 32: 8.   M. 5.

390
Holy Spirit, faithful guide,
Ever near the Christian's side;
Gently lead us by the hand,
Pilgrims in a desert land;
Weary souls for e'er rejoice,
While they hear that sweetest voice
Whisp'ring softly, wanderer come!
Follow me, I'll guide thee home.

2 Ever present, truest Friend,
Ever near Thine aid to lend,
Leave us not to doubt and fear,
Groping on in darkness drear;
When the storms are raging sore,
Hearts grow faint, and hopes give o'er,
Whispering softly, wanderer come!
Follow me, I'll guide thee home.

3 When our days of toil shall cease,
Waiting still for sweet release,
Nothing left but heaven and prayer,
Wond'ring if our names were there;
Wading deep the dismal flood,
Pleading nought but Jesus' blood;
Whispering softly, wanderer come!
Follow me, I'll guide thee home.

M. M. Wells, 1858.

REPOSE. L. M.

To whom shall we go? John 6:68. L. M.

391 Thou only Soverign of my heart,
My refuge, my almighty friend,
And can my soul from thee depart,
On whom alone my hopes depend?

2 Whither, ah, whither shall I go,
A wretched wanderer from my Lord?
Could this dark world of sin and woe,
One glimpse of happiness afford?

3 Eternal life thy words impart,
On these my fainting spirit lives,
Here sweeter comforts cheer my heart,
Than all the round of nature gives.

4 Let earth's alluring joys combine,
While thou art near, in vain they call;
One smile, one blissful smile of thine,
My gracious Lord, outweighs them all.

5 Low at thy feet my soul would lie,
Here safety dwells, and peace divine;
Still let me live beneath thine eye,
For life, eternal life is thine.

Annè Steele, ab. 1760.

I count all things but loss. Phil. 3: 8. L. M.

392 No more, my God, I boast no more
Of all the duties I have done;
I quit the hopes I held before,
To trust the merits of Thy Son.

2 Now for the love I bear his name,
   What was my gain I count my loss;
   My former pride I call my shame,
   And nail my glory to his cross.

3 Yes, and I must and will esteem
   All things but loss for Jesus' sake;
   Oh, may my soul be found in him,
   And of his righteousness partake!

4 The best obedience of my hands
   Dares not appear before thy throne;
   But faith can answer thy demands,
   By pleading what my Lord has done.
                        Isaac Watts, 1709

His ways past finding out. Rom. 11: 33. L. M.

393 THY ways, O Lord, with wise design,
   Are framed upon Thy throne above,
   And every dark and bending line
   Meets in the centre of Thy love.

2 With feeble light and half obscure,
   Poor mortals Thy arrangements view;
   Not knowing that the least are sure,
   And the mysterious just and true.

3 Thy flock, thine own peculiar care,
   Though now they seem to roam uneyed,
   Are led or driven only where
   They best and safest may abide.

4 They neither know nor trace the way,
   But, trusting to thy piercing eye,
   None of their feet to ruin stray,
   Nor shall the weakest fail or die.

5 My favored soul shall meekly learn
   To lay her reason at thy throne;
   Too weak thy secrets to discern,
   I'll trust Thee for my guide alone.
                        Ambrose Serle, 1787.

HEBRON.   No. 95.

TRUST.

BACA. L. M.   WM. B. BRADBURY.

Consider the lilies, how they grow. Luke 12: 27.   L. M.

394
BEHOLD the lilies of the field
   That bloom around the Master's feet;
Their drooping leaves new fragrance yield,
   By Hermon's dew and grateful heat.

2 Behold the sparrows as they fly;
   They come at his command and call;
They seem but specks upon the sky;
   And yet he notes them when they fall.

3 Our very hairs he counts with care;
   He knows our daily hopes and fears;
When griefs assail and tempests scare,
   He notes the mourner's secret tears.

4 Oh, look upon the Lord so near!
   Repose beneath the sheltered rock;
The cross he lightens by his cheer,
   The wind he tempers to his flock.

God is our refuge and strength, a very present help in trouble. Ps. 46: 1.   L. M.

395
GOD is the refuge of his saints,
   When storms of sharp distress invade;
Ere we can offer our complaints,
   Behold him present with his aid.

2 There is a stream whose gentle flow
   Supplies the city of our God,—
Life, love, and joy, still gliding through,
   And watering our divine abode.

3 That sacred stream, thy holy word,
   Our grief allays, our fear controls;
Sweet peace thy promises afford,
   And give new strength to fainting souls.

4 Zion enjoys her Monarch's love,
   Secure against a threatening hour;
Nor can her firm foundations move,
   Built on his truth and armed with power.
Watts.

Ye are complete in Him. Col. 2: 10.   L. M.

396 Fountain of grace, rich, full, and free,
   What need I, that is not in thee?
Full pardon, strength to meet the day,
And peace which none can take away.

2 Doth sickness fill my heart with fear?
'Tis sweet to know that thou art near;
Am I with dread of justice tried?
'Tis sweet to know that Christ hath died.

3 In life, thy promises of aid
Forbid my heart to be afraid;
In death, peace gently veils the eyes;
Christ rose, and I shall surely rise.

4 O all-sufficient Saviour, be
This all-sufficiency to me;
Nor pain, nor sin, nor death can harm
The weakest, shielded by thine arm.
James Edmeston, 1844.

Behold, all things are become new. 2 Cor. 5: 17.   L. M.

397 Thou strong and loving Son of Man,
   Redeemer from the bonds of sin,
'Tis thou the living spark dost fan,
That sets my heart on fire within.

2 In thee I find a nobler birth;
A glory o'er the world I see;
And Paradise returns to earth,
And blooms again for us in thee.

3 Thou openest heaven once more to men,
The soul's true home, thy kingdom, Lord,
And I can trust and hope again,
And feel myself akin to God.
German, Fred. von Hardenberg, 1752.

HENDON. M. 5.   H. A. MALAN.

The Lord is my Shepherd, I shall not want. Ps. 23: 1.   M. 5.

398 To thy pastures fair and large,
Heavenly Shepherd, lead thy charge;
And my couch, with tenderest care,
'Mid the springing grass prepare.

2 When I faint with summer's heat,
Thou shalt guide my weary feet
To the streams that, still and slow,
Through the verdant meadows flow.

3 Safe the dreary vale I tread,
By the shades of death o'erspread,
With thy rod and staff supplied—
This my guard, and that my guide.

4 Constant to my latest end,
Thou my footsteps shalt attend;
Thou shalt bid thy hallowed dome
Yield me an eternal home.

James Merrick, 1765.

Even the sure mercies of David. Is. 55: 3.   M. 5.

399 As the sun doth daily rise,
Bright'ning all the morning skies,
So to thee with one accord,
Lift we up our hearts, O Lord.

2 Day by day provide us food,
For from thee come all things good;
Strength unto our souls afford
From thy living bread, O Lord.

TRUST.

3 Be our guide 'mid sin and strife,
   Be the leader of our life,
   Lest like sheep we go abroad;
   Stay our wayward feet, O Lord.

4 Quickened by thy Spirit's grace,
   All thy holy will to trace,
   While we daily search thy word,
   Wisdom true impart, O Lord.

5 When the hours are dark and drear,
   When the tempter lurketh near,
   By thy strengthening grace outpoured,
   Save the tempted ones, O Lord.
                King Alfred, 848-901. Tr. Earl Nelson, 1864.

Come unto me, all ye that labor. *Matt. 11: 28.*   M. 5.

400 Come, said Jesus' sacred voice,
   Come, and make my paths your choice;
   I will guide you to your home,
   Weary pilgrim, hither come!

2 Thou who, houseless, sole forlorn,
   Long hast borne the proud world's scorn,
   Long hast roamed the barren waste,
   Weary wanderer, hither haste.

3 Ye who tossed on beds of pain,
   Seek for ease, but seek in vain;
   Ye, by fiercer anguish torn,
   In remorse for guilt who mourn:

4 Hither come! for here is found
   Balm that flows for every wound;
   Peace that ever shall endure,
   Rest eternal, sacred, sure.
                          Anna Lætitia Barbauld, ab. 1825.

He sendeth out his word *Psalm 147: 18.*   M. 5.

401 Saviour, bless thy word to all;
   Quick and powerful let it prove;
   Oh, may sinners hear thy call;
   Let thy people grow in love.

2 Thine own gracious message bless;
   Follow it with power divine;
   Give the gospel great success;
   Thine the work, the glory thine.
                                              T. Kelly

DAYTON. C. M.   A. J. SHOWALTER.

O the depth of the riches both of the wisdom and knowledge of God.
Rom. 11:33.   C. M.

402   GOD moves in a mysterious way,
        His wonders to perform;
    He plants his footsteps in the sea,
        And rides upon the storm.

2 Deep in unfathomable mines
    Of never-failing skill,
He treasures up his bright designs,
    And works his sovereign will.

3 Ye fearful saints, fresh courage take;
    The clouds ye so much dread
Are big with mercy, and shall break
    In blessings on your head.

4 Judge not the Lord by feeble sense,
    But trust him for his grace;
Behind a frowning providence
    He hides a smiling face.

5 His purposes will ripen fast,
    Unfolding every hour;
The bud may have a bitter taste,
    But sweet will be the flower.

6 Blind unbelief is sure to err,
    And scan his work in vain;
God is his own interpreter,
    And he will make it plain.

                                            William Cowper, 1774.

TRUST.

God our portion. Psalm 119: 57. C. M.

403 Whom have we, Lord, in heav'n, but thee,
    And whom on earth beside?
Where else for succor can we flee,
    Or in whose strength confide?

2 Thou art our portion here below,
    Our promis'd bliss above;
Ne'er may our souls an object know
    So precious as thy love.

3 When heart and flesh, O Lord, shall fail,
    Thou wilt our spirits cheer,
Support us through life's thorny vale,
    And calm each anxious fear.

4 Yes, thou shalt be our guide through life,
    And help and strength supply;
Sustain us in death's fearful strife,
    And welcome us on high.

As an anchor of the soul. Heb. 6: 19. C. M

404 The Lord of glory is my light,
    And my salvation, too;
God is my strength, nor will I fear
    What all my foes can do.

2 One privilege my heart desires;
    Oh, grant me an abode
Among the churches of thy saints,
    The temples of my God.

3 There shall I offer my requests,
    And see thy beauty still,
Shall hear thy messages of love,
    And there inquire thy will.

4 When troubles rise, and storms appear,
    There may his children hide;
God has a strong pavilion, where
    He makes my soul abide.

5 Now shall my head be lifted high
    Above my foes around;
And songs of joy and victory
    Within thy temple sound.

                              Isaac Watts, 1719.

ROCHESTER. C. M. WATTS.

"They shall talk of thy power." C. M.

405 WHILE thee I seek, protecting Power!
Be my vain wishes stilled;
And may this consecrated hour
With better hopes be filled.

2 Thy love the power of thought bestowed;
To thee my thoughts would soar;
Thy mercy o'er my life has flown;
That mercy I adore.

3 In each event of life, how clear
Thy ruling hand I see!
Each blessing to my soul more dear,
Because conferred by thee.

4 In every joy that crowns my days,
In every pain I bear,
My heart shall find delight in praise,
Or seek relief in prayer.

5 When gladness wings my favored hour,
Thy love my thoughts shall fill;
Resigned, when storms of sorrow lower,
My soul shall meet thy will.

6 My lifted eye, without a tear,
The gathering storm shall see;
My steadfast heart shall know no fear;
That heart will rest on thee.
Miss Williams.

TRUST.

"Filled with all the fullness of God."   C. M.

406
O Lord, I would delight in thee,
   And on thy care depend;
To Thee in every trouble flee,
   My best, my only friend.

2 When all created streams are dried,
   Thy fullness is the same;
May I with this be satisfied,
   And glory in thy name!

3 He who has made my heaven secure,
   Will here all good provide:
While Christ is rich, can I be poor?
   What can I want beside?

4 O Lord, I cast my care on thee;
   I triumph and adore:
Henceforth my great concern shall be
   To love and please thee more.
                        Ryland.

When my spirit was overwhelmed within me, then thou knewest my path.
                      Psalm 142: 3.   C. M.

407
Though darkness turn the skies to night,
   Though sorrows fill the air,
Nor moon nor stars my pathway light,
   Yet thou art with me there.

2 I cannot see thee, but I know
   A stronger arm than mine
Upholds me in the time of woe,—
   Jesus! that arm is thine.

3 Though words may fail when I would pray,
   And mute I lift my hands,
Thou hearest what I cannot say,
   And Gabriel near me stands.

4 A just God and a Saviour, thou
   Art full of love and grace:
Before thy majesty I bow
   With glad and trustful face.

5 Thy sovereign grace gives sweet relief,
   Dispelling faithless gloom,
And the dark chamber of my grief
   Becomes a sunny room.
                     Thos. MacKellar, 1881.

Rejoice, because your names are written in heaven. Luke 10: 20. M. 14. Pec.

408 Lord, I care not for riches,
Neither silver nor gold;
I would make sure of heaven,
I would enter the fold.
In the book of thy kingdom,
With its pages so fair,
Tell me, Jesus, my Saviour,
Is my name written there?

2 Lord, my sins they are many,
Like the sands of the sea,
But thy blood, O my Saviour!
Is sufficient for me;

TRUST.   279

 For thy promise is written,
  In bright letters that glow,
 "Though your sins be as scarlet,
  I will make them like snow."

3 Oh! that beautiful city,
 With its mansions of light,
With its glorified beings,
 In pure garments of white;
Where no evil thing cometh,
 To despoil what is fair;
Where the angels are watching,—
 Is my name written there?
     Mrs. Mary A. Kidder.

I WOULD LOVE THEE. M. 4.

"I will love thee, O Lord, my strength."   M. 4.

409 I WOULD love thee, God and Father!
 My Redeemer, and my King!
I would love thee; for without thee
 Life is but a bitter thing.

2 I would love thee; every blessing
 Flows to me from out thy throne;
I would love thee—he who loves thee
 Never feels himself alone.

3 I would love thee; look upon me,
 Ever guide me with thine eye:
I would love thee; if not nourished
 By thy love, my soul would die.

4 I would love thee, I have vowed it;
 On thy love my heart is set;
While I love thee, I will never
 My Redeemer's blood forget.
     Madame Guyon.

OAKLAND. M. 4.

Be not therefore anxious for the morrow. Matt. 6: 28. M. 4.

410
BE not anxious for the morrow,
　Let the morrow have its cares:
Soul, be not forecasting sorrow;
　Grace is giv'n to him who bears
Crosses that he does not borrow:
　God controls the unawares.

2 Neither sowing, neither reaping,
　Gathering not to store away,
Birds are in the Father's keeping,—
　Cares he not when children pray?
Why then, faithless, sighing, weeping,
　Doubt him for the coming day?

3 Lilies, toiling not nor spinning,
　Gleam in robes beyond compare:
Never king from time's beginning
　Had such glorious dress to wear:
Souls that cost his life in winning
　Christ will keep with loving care.

　　　　　　　　　Thos. MacKellar, 1881.

Cast thy burden on the Lord, and he shall sustain thee. Ps. 55: 22. M. 4.

411
OH, the blessedness of leaning
　On a strength beyond thine own!
Oh, the fullness of the meaning—
　Oh, the sweetness of the tone—
Cast thy burden, cast thy burden
　On thy loving Lord alone.

TRUST. 281

2 Often weary, yet contending,—
    Beaten down, again to rise,—
  On his help alone depending,
    Looking up with trustful eyes,—
      Cast thy burden :‖
    On the arm that built the skies.

3 Take his easy yoke upon thee,
    Lowly be like him in heart :
  Child, it was his love that won thee,
    Will he bid thee now depart
      With thy burden, :‖
    When thy soul is full of smart?

4 Long ago the word was written,—
    Word to generations blest,—
  Hear it, children sorely smitten,
    Hear it, ye of troubled breast,—
      Cast thy burden :‖
    On the Lord : he'll give thee rest.
                    Thos. MacKellar, 1881.

      Of such is the kingdom. Matt. 19: 14.   M. 4.

412 JESUS Christ, our Lord and Saviour,
          Who hath bid us come to thee,
       Now extend to us thy favor,
         Little children though we be ;
       Low we humbly bend before thee,
         All unworthy of thy love ;
       Lord of life, and light, and glory,
         Hear us from thy throne above.

2 Thou who holdest high dominion
    Over air, and earth, and sea,
  Yet didst bless the little children
    That of old were brought to thee :
  Lord, this day we ask thy blessing,
    Send thy Holy Spirit down ;
  May we all, our sins confessing,
    Thee our Lord and Saviour own.

AUTUMN.   No. 330.

WAVERLY. L. M.
CHESTER G. ALLEN.
Used by per. of BIGLOW & MAIN, owners of copyright.

Faith looking into the future. Heb. 11:13. L. M.

413
'TIS by the faith of joys to come
  We walk through deserts dark as night;
Till we arrive at heav'n, our home,
  Faith is our guide, and faith our light.

2 The want of sight she well supplies;
  She makes the pearly gates appear;
Far into distant worlds she pries,
  And brings eternal glories near.

3 Cheerful we tread the desert through,
  While faith inspires a heav'nly ray;
Though lions roar, and tempests blow,
  And rocks and dangers fill the way.

4 So Abra'am, by divine command
  Left his own house to walk with God,
His faith beheld the promis'd land,
  And cheer'd him on his toilsome road.
                                  Watts.

My meditation of him shall be sweet. Ps. 104:34. L. M.

414
SWEET meditation on the Lord
  Brings purest joy and boundless bliss;
This world no comfort can afford,
  Compared with Jesus' love and peace.

TRUST.

2 No sweeter name my tongue shall sing,
    No other sound so sweet shall be,
My heart shall know no dearer thing
    Than Christ who bled and died for me.

3 O Christ, my peace, my joy, my bliss,
    The wellspring of my life, my sun;
Earth hath no blessedness like this,
    That I my Saviour's love have known.

4 O Christ, within my deepest soul
    Thy sacred flame of love I hide,
There streams of endless comfort roll,
    There thousand thousand joys abide.

5 On Thee my heart delights to rest,
    Thy faithfulness to me is known,
I glory in Thee, and am blessed,
    For Thou, O Christ, art Lord alone.
           Old German Hymn, Tr by Hastings, 1879.

Your sorrow shall be turned into joy. John 16: 20.   L. M.

415
OH, deem not they are blest alone,
    Whose lives a peaceful tenor keep;
For God, who pities man, hath shown
    A blessing for the eyes that weep.

2 The light of smiles shall fill again
    The lids that overflow with tears;
And weary hours of woe and pain
    Are promises of happier years.

3 There is a day of sunny rest
    For every dark and troubled night;
And grief may bide an evening guest,
    But joy shall come with early light.

4 Nor let the good man's trust depart,
    Though life its common gifts deny;
Though with a pierced and broken heart,
    And spurn'd of men he goes to die.

5 For God has mark'd each sorrowing day,
    And number'd every secret tear,
And heaven's long age of bliss shall pay
    For all His children suffer here.
           W. C. Bryant.

TRUST.

HOME. S. M.   By per. of O. Ditson & Co., owners of copyright.

"His commandments are not grievous."   S. M.

416 How gentle God's commands!
How kind his precepts are!
Come, cast your burdens on the Lord,
And trust his constant care.

2 Beneath his watchful eye
His saints securely dwell,
That hand which bears all nature up,
Shall guard his children well.

3 Why should this anxious load
Press down your weary mind?
Haste to your heavenly Father's throne,
And sweet refreshment find.

4 His goodness stands approved,
Unchanged from day to day:
Come, drop your burden at his feet,
And bear a song away.

Doddridge.

Commit thy way unto the Lord. Psalm 37: 5.   S. M.

417 Commit thou all thy griefs
And ways into His hands;
To His sure truth and tender care,
Who earth and heaven commands:

2 Who points the clouds their course,
Whom winds and seas obey;
He shall direct thy wand'ring feet;
He shall prepare thy way

3 Put thou thy trust in God;
   In duty's path go on;
Fix on His word thy steadfast eye;
   So shall thy work be done.

4 No profit canst thou gain
   By self-consuming care;
To Him commend thy cause; His ear
   Attends thy softest prayer.

5 Leave to his sovereign sway
   To choose and to command;
So shalt thou wondering own, His sway
   How wise, how strong His hand.
Gerhardt. Tr. J. Wesley.

If I forget thee, O Jerusalem! Psalm 137: 5.   S. M.

418 Far from my heavenly home,
   Far from my Father's breast,
Fainting, I cry, "Blest Spirit, come,
   And speed me to my rest!"

2 Upon the willows long
   My harp has silent hung;
How should I sing a cheerful song,
   'Till thou inspire my tongue?

3 My spirit homeward turns,
   And fain would thither flee;
My heart, O Zion, droops and yearns
   When I remember thee.

4 To thee, to thee I press—
   A dark and toilsome road:
When shall I pass the wilderness,
   And reach the saints' abode!

5 God of my life, be near!
   On Thee my hopes are cast;
Oh, guide me through the desert here,
   And bring me home at last!
Henry Francis Lyte, 1834.

BOYLSTON.   No. 277.

BETHANY. 6s & 4s.   L. MASON, 1856.
Used by per. of O. Ditson & Co., owners of copyright.

Draw nigh to God. James 4: 8.   6s & 4s.

419

Nearer, my God, to thee,
    Nearer to thee!
E'en tho' it be a cross
    That raiseth me;
Still all my song shall be,
||: Nearer, my God, to thee, :||
    Nearer to thee!

2 Tho' like a wanderer,
    The sun gone down,
Darkness comes over me,
    My rest a stone;
Yet in my dreams I'd be
||: Nearer, my God, to thee, :||
    Nearer to thee!

3 There let my way appear
    Steps unto heaven;
All that thou sendeth me
    In mercy given;
Angels to beckon me
||: Nearer, my God, to thee, :||
    Nearer to thee!

4 Then with my waking thoughts
    Bright with thy praise,
Out of my stony griefs
    Bethel I'll raise;
So by my woes to be
‖: Nearer, my God, to thee, :‖
    Nearer to thee!

5 Or if on joyful wing,
    Cleaving the sky,
Caught up to meet my King,
    Swiftly I fly;
Still all my song shall be—
‖: Nearer, my God, to thee, :‖
    Nearer to thee!

                      Sarah Flower Adams, 1840.

Wash me thoroughly from mine iniquity. *Psalm 51: 2.* 6s & 4s.

420 WASH me, O Lamb of God,
    Wash me from sin;
By thy atoning blood
    Oh, make me clean;
Purge me from every stain,
Let me thine image gain,
In love and mercy reign
    O'er all within.

2 Wash me, O Lamb of God,
    Wash me from sin;
By faith thy cleansing blood
    Now makes me clean.
So near Thou art to me,
So sweet my rest in thee,
O, blessèd purity,
    Saved, saved from sin.

3 Wash me, O Lamb of God,
    Wash me from sin;
Thou, while I trust in thee,
    Wilt keep me clean;
Each day to Thee I bring
Heart, life, yea, everything;
Saved, while to thee I cling,
    Saved from all sin.

                      H. B. Beegle, cir. 1882.

NUREMBURG. M. 5.   J. R. AHLE.

I will praise the Lord with my whole heart. Psalm III: 1.   M. 5.

421
PRAISE to God, immortal praise,
   For the love that crowns our days!
Bounteous source of every joy,
Let thy praise our tongues employ!

2 For the blessings of the field,
For the stores the gardens yield,
For the joy which harvests bring,
Grateful praises now we sing.

3 Clouds that drop refreshing dews;
Suns that genial heat diffuse;
Flocks that whiten all the plain;
Yellow sheaves of ripened grain;

4 All that Spring, with bounteous hand,
Scatters o'er the smiling land;
All that liberal Autumn pours
From her overflowing stores;

5 These, great God, to thee we owe,
Source whence all our blessings flow;
And, for these our souls shall raise
Grateful vows and solemn praise.
                      Mrs. Barbauld.

Give thanks unto the Lord, for he is good. Psalm 136: 1.   M. 5.

422
PRAISE, oh, praise our God and King;
   Hymns of adoration sing;
For his mercies still endure,
Ever faithful, ever sure.

2 Praise him for our harvest store,
   He hath filled the garner-floor;
   And for richer food than this,
   Pledge of everlasting bliss.

3 Glory to our bounteous King;
   Glory let Creation sing;
   Glory to the Father, Son,
   And blest Spirit, Three in One.
                        H. W. Baker, ab. 1821.

The field is the world. Matt. 13: 38   M. 5.

423 Come, ye thankful people, come,
        Raise the song of Harvest-home;
        All is safely gathered in,
        Ere the winter storms begin.

2 God, our Maker, doth provide
   For our wants to be supplied;
   Come to God's own temple, come,
   Raise the song of Harvest-home.

   All the world is God's own field,
   Fruit unto his praise to yield;
   Wheat and tares together sown,
   Unto joy or sorrow grown:

4 First the blade, and then the ear,
   Then the full corn shall appear;
   Lord of harvest, grant that we
   Wholesome grain and pure may be.

5 Soon the Lord our God shall come,
   And shall take his harvest home:
   From his field shall in that day
   All offences purge away;

6 Give his angels charge at last
   In the fire the tares to cast;
   But the fruitful ears to store
   In his garner evermore.
                        Henry Alford, ab. 18—

MARTYN.   No. 374.

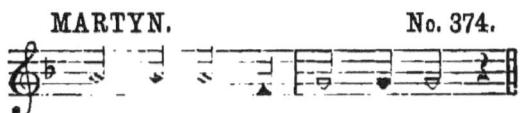

MIGDOL. L. M.   Lowell Mason, 1840.

The Lord reigneth; let the earth rejoice. Ps. 97: 1.   L M

424 OH, hallowed is the land and blest,
Where Christ, the Ruler, is confessed!
On, happy hearts and happy homes,
To whom the great Redeemer comes!

2 Lift up your heads, ye mighty gates!
Behold, the King of glory waits:
The King of kings is drawing near;
The Saviour of the world is here.

3 Fling wide the portals of your heart,
Make it a temple set apart
From earthly use for heaven's employ,
Adorned with prayer, and love, and joy.

4 Redeemer, come! I open wide
My soul to thee; here, Lord, abide!
Thankful and glad my song I raise,
And give to thee a life of praise.

Geo. Weissel.
Miss Winkworth. Tr.

Give thanks unto the Lord. Ps. 107: 1.   L. M.

425 GIVE thanks to God, He reigns above;
Kind are His thoughts, His name is love;
His mercy ages past have known,
And ages long to come shall own.

2 Let the redeemèd of the Lord
The wonders of His grace record;
How great His works! how kind His ways!
Let every tongue pronounce His praise.

Isaac Watts, ab. 1719.

SALVATION. M. 14.   Mozart.

Giving thanks always for all things. Eph. 5: 20.   M. 14.

426 I THANK the Lord my Maker
    For all his gifts to me:
For making me partaker
    Of bounties rich and free:
For father and for mother,
    Who give me clothes and food,
For sister and for brother,
    And all the kind and good.

2 I thank the Lord my Saviour
    Who came for me to die,
And bless me with his favor,
    And fit me for the sky,—
That, all my sins out-blotted,
    By Jesus wash'd away,
I may be found unspotted
    When comes the final day.

3 I thank the Lord for giving
    The Spirit of his grace,
That I may serve him living,
    And dying, reach the place
Where Jesus in his glory
    I shall forever see,
And tell the wondrous story
    Of all his love for me.

                     Thos. MacKellar, 1844.

THANKSGIVING.

LAND OF REST. C. M.

Thou crownest the year with thy goodness.   Psalm 65: 11.   C. M.

427 'TIS by thy strength the mountains stand,
  God of eternal power;
The sea grows calm at thy command,
  And tempests cease to roar.

2 Thy morning light, and evening shade,
  Successive comforts bring;
Thy plenteous fruits make harvest glad,
  Thy flowers adorn the spring.

3 Seasons, and times, and moons, and hours,
  Heaven, earth, and air are thine;
When clouds distil in fruitful showers,
  The Author is divine.

4 Thy showers the thirsty furrows fill,
  And ranks of corn appear;
Thy ways abound with blessings still,
  Thy goodness crowns the year.
            Isaac Watts, ab. 1719.

Seed-time and harvest.   Gen. 8. 22.   C. M.

428 FOUNTAIN of mercy, God of love,
  How rich thy bounties are!
The changing seasons as they move,
  Proclaim thy constant care.

2 When in the bosom of the earth
  The sower hid the grain,
Thy goodness marked its secret birth,
  And sent the early rain.

THANKSGIVING. 293

3 The Spring's sweet influence, Lord, was thine;
　The plants in beauty grew;
Thou gav'st refulgent suns to shine,
　And soft, refreshing dew.

4 These varied mercies, from above,
　Matur'd the swelling grain:
A kindly harvest crowns thy love,
　And plenty fills the plain.

5 We own and bless thy gracious sway,
　Thy hand all nature hails:
Seed-time nor harvest, night nor day,
　Summer nor winter fails.

Needham.

HARVEST. M. 26.

The valleys also are covered over with corn; they shout for joy, they also sing.
Psalm 65: 13. M. 26.

429　THE God of harvest praise;
　　In loud thanksgiving raise,
　　　Hand, heart, and voice;
　　The valleys smile and sing,
　　Forests and mountains ring,
　　The plains their tribute bring
　　　The streams rejoice.

2 The God of harvest praise;
　　Hearts, hands, and voices raise,
　　　With sweet accord;
　　From field to garner throng,
　　Bearing your sheaves along,
　　And in your harvest song,
　　　Praise ye the Lord.

TAMAR. C. M. Used by per. of O. Ditson & Co., owners of Copyright.

The saints but one family. Eph. 1: 10.   C. M.

430 Come let us join our friends above,
Who have obtained the prize,
And on the eagle wings of love
To joys celestial rise.

2 Let saints below in concert sing
With those to glory gone,
For all the servants of our King
In heaven and earth are one.

3 One family,—we dwell in him;
One church, above, beneath;
Though now divided by the stream,
The narrow stream of death.

4 The saints on earth, and those above,
But one communion make;
Join'd to their Lord, in bonds of love,
All of his grace partake.

5 One army of the living God,
To his commands we bow;
Part of the host have crossed the flood,
And part are crossing now.

6 Lo thousands to their endless home
Are swiftly born away;
And we are to the margin come,
And soon must launch as they.

UNITY.   295

Meeting for council. Acts 15: 6.   C. M.

431 Lord, in thy presence here we meet;
    May we in thee be found!
  Oh, make the place divinely sweet,
    And let thy grace abound.

  2 With harmony thy servants bless,
      That we may own to thee
    How good, how sweet, how pleasant 'tis
      When brethren all agree.

  3 May Zion's good be kept in view,
      And bless our feeble aim,
    That all we undertake to do,
      May glorify thy name.

Love as brethren. 1 Pet. 3: 8.   C. M.

432 How sweet, how heavenly is the sight,
    When those who love the Lord
  In one another's peace delight,
    And so fulfill his word.

  2 When each can feel his brother's sigh,
      And with him bear a part;
    When sorrow flows from eye to eye,
      And joy from heart to heart.

  3 When, free from envy, scorn, and pride,
      Our wishes all above,
    Each can his brother's failings hide,
      And show a brother's love.

  4 Let love, in one delightful stream,
      Through every bosom flow,
    And union sweet, and dear esteem,
      In every action glow.

  5 Love is the golden chain that binds
      The happy souls above;
    And he's an heir of heaven who finds
      His bosom glow with love.
                    J. Swain.

WOODLAND.   No. 379.

GERAR. S. M.

Being knit together in love. Col. 2: 2. S. M.

433 Blest be the tie that binds
Our hearts in Christian love;
The fellowship of kindred minds
Is like to that above.

2 Before our Father's throne
We pour our ardent prayers;
Our fears, our hopes, our aims are one,
Our comforts, and our cares.

3 We share our mutual woes,
Our mutual burdens bear;
And often for each other flows
The sympathizing tear.

4 When we asunder part,
It gives us inward pain;
But we shall still be joined in **heart**,
And hope to meet again.

5 This glorious hope revives
Our courage by the way;
While each in expectation lives,
And longs to see the day.

6 From sorrow, toil, and pain,
And sin, we shall be free;
And perfect love and friendship reign
Through all eternity.

John Fawcett, 1772.

UNITY.

How good, and how pleasant   Psalm 133: 1.   S. M.

434   BLEST are the sons of peace,
   Whose hearts and hopes are one,
Whose kind designs to serve and please
   Through all their actions run.

2 Blest is the pious house,
   Where zeal and friendship meet;
Their songs of praise, their mingled vows,
   Make their communion sweet.

3 Thus on the heavenly hills,
   The saints are blest above,
Where joy, like morning dew, distils,
   And all the air is love.

4 From those celestial springs
   Such streams of pleasure flow,
As no increase of riches brings,
   Nor honors can bestow.
                    Isaac Watts, ab. 1718.

One body in Christ.   Rom. 12: 5.   S. M.

435   AND let our bodies part,
   To different climes repair,—
Inseparably joined in heart
   The friends of Jesus are.

2 Jesus, the Corner-stone,
   Did first our hearts unite,
And still he keeps our spirits one,
   Who walk with him in white.

3 The vineyard of their Lord
   Before his laborers lies;
And lo! we see the vast reward
   Reserved in paradise.

4 There all our toils are o'er,
   Our suffering and our pain:—
Who meet on that eternal shore,
   Shall never part again.

5 To gather home his own
   God shall his angels send,
And bid our bliss on earth begun,
   In deathless triumph end.
                    Charles Wesley. 1749.

RETREAT. L. M.   T. Hastings.

A prayer for a church newly organized.   L. M.

436 Lord, bless thy saints assembled here,
In solemn cov'nant now to join;
Unite them in thy holy fear,
And in thy love their hearts combine.

2 Oh, give this church a large increase
Of such as thou wilt own and bless;
Lord, fill their hearts with joy and peace,
And clothe them with thy right'ousness.

3 Make her a garden wall'd with grace,
A temple built for God below,
Where thy blest saints may see thy face;
And fruits of thy bless'd Spirit grow.

The God of love and peace shall be with you. 2 Cor. 13: 11.   L. M.

437 Indulgent God of love and pow'r,
Be with us at this place and hour!
Smile on our souls; our plans approve,
By which we seek to spread thy love.

2 Let each discordant thought be gone,
And love unite our hearts in one:
Let all we have and all combine
To forward objects so divine.

3 Oh, may we feel the worth of souls,
Be men of God, whom grace controls,
Fight the good fight, and win the crown,
And by our Father's side sit down.

UNITY.

Heavenly places in Christ. Eph. 1: 3. L. M.

438
Lord, how delightful 'tis to see
A whole assembly worship thee!
At once they sing, at once they pray;
They hear of heav'n, and learn the way.

2 I have been there, and still would go;
'Tis like the dawn of heaven below;
Not all that careless sinners say
Shall tempt me to forget this day.

3 O write upon my mem'ry, Lord,
The truths and precepts of thy word,
That I may break thy laws no more,
But love thee better than before.
                                    Watts.

Thou shalt love thy neighbor as thyself. Matt. 22: 39. L. M.

439
Blessed Redeemer, how divine—
How righteous is this rule of thine,
"Never to deal with others worse
Than we would have them deal with us."

2 This golden lesson, short and plain,
Gives not the mind nor memory pain;
And every conscience must approve
This universal law of love.

3 Is reason ever at a loss?
Call in self-love to judge the cause;
Let our own fondest passions show
How we should treat our neighbor too.

4 How bless'd would every nation prove,
Thus ruled by equity and love!
All would be friends without a foe,
And form a paradise below.

Where two or three are gathered. Matt. 18: 20. L. M.

440
Where two or three with faithful heart
Unite to plead the promise given,
As truly in the midst thou art,
As with the countless hosts of heaven.

2 Can we believe this precious word,
And not assemble in thy name?
Sure if we meet to meet our Lord,
And catch thy whisper, "Here I am?"
                            Charles Wesley, 1762.

ENNIUS. M. 5.

Thy people shall be my people. Ruth 1: 16.   M. 5.

441
PEOPLE of the living God,
   I have sought the world around;
Paths of sin and sorrow trod,
   Peace and comfort nowhere found:
Now to you my spirit turns,—
   Turns a fugitive unblest;
Brethren, where your altar burns,
   Oh, receive me to your rest.

2 Lonely I no longer roam
   Like the cloud, the wind, the wave;
Where you dwell shall be my home,
   Where you die shall be my grave;
Mine the God whom you adore;
   Your Redeemer shall be mine;
Earth can fill my soul no more,—
   Every idol I resign.

3 Tell me not of gain and loss,
   Ease, enjoyment, pomp, and power;
Welcome poverty and cross,
   Shame, reproach, affliction's hour.
"Follow me"— I know thy voice;
   Jesus, Lord, thy steps I see;
Now I take thy yoke by choice;
   Light thy burden now to me.

James Montgomery. 1771—1854

UNITY.

DEAREST TIE. C. M.

It is the hope the blissful hope, Which Jesus grace has giv'n, The hope when days and years are past, We all shall meet in heav'n.

Which hope we have as an anchor of the soul, both sure and steadfast.
Heb. 6: 19. C. M.

442
Hail, sweetest, dearest tie, that binds
　Our glowing hearts in one ;
Hail, sacred hope, that tunes our minds
　To harmony divine.

2 What though the northern wintry blast
　Shall howl around our cot ;
What though beneath an eastern sun
　Be cast our distant lot.

3 From eastern shores, from northern lands,
　From western hill and plain,
From southern climes, the brother-bands
　May hope to meet again.

4 From Burmah's shores, from Afric's strand,
　From India's burning plain,
From Europe, from Columbia's land,
　We hope to meet again.

5 No ling'ring look, nor parting sigh ,
　Our future meeting knows ;
There friendship beams from every eye,
　And love immortal glows.

　　　　　　　　　　　　Sutton.

UNITY 6s & 5s. L. MASON.

In the unity of faith. Eph. 4: 13. 6s & 5s.

443
WHEN shall we meet again?—
 Meet ne'er to sever?
When will peace wreathe her chain
 Round us forever?
Our hearts will ne'er repose
Safe from each blast that blows,
In this dark vale of woes—
 Never—no, never!

2 When shall love freely flow
 Pure as life's river?
When shall sweet friendship glow
 Changeless forever?
Where joys celestial thrill,
Where bliss each heart shall fill,
And fears of parting chill—
 Never—no, never!

UNITY. 303

3 Up to that world of light,
  Take us, dear Saviour;
May we all there unite,
  Happy forever;
Where kindred spirits dwell,
There may our music swell,
And time our joys dispel
  Never—no, never!

NINETY-THIRD. S. M. WATTS.

Peace be unto you.   Luke 24: 36. S. M.

444 LORD, at this closing hour,
       Establish every heart
    Upon thy word of truth and power,
       To keep us when we part.

2 Peace to our brethren give;
    Fill all our hearts with grace;
  In faith and patience may we live,
    Till we shall see thy face.

3 Through changes bright or drear,
    We would thy will pursue;
  And toil to spread thy gospel here
    Till we thy glory view.

4 To God, the only Wise,
    In every age adored,
  Let glory from the church arise
    Through Jesus Christ our Lord!
                Eleazar T. Finch, 1846.

UNITY.

ST. THOMAS. S. M. WILLIAM TANSUR, 1743.

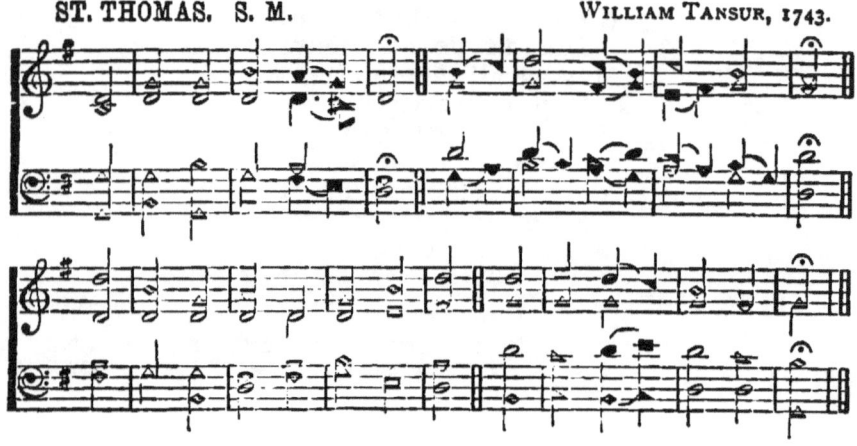

Be at peace among yourselves. *1 Thess. 5: 13.*   S. M.

445 Lo, what a pleasing sight
   Are brethren that agree!
How blest are all whose hearts **unite**
   In bonds of piety.

   2 From those celestial springs,
      Such streams of comfort flow,
   As no increase of riches brings
      Nor honors can bestow.

   3 All in their stations move,
      And each performs his part,
   In all the cares of life and love,
      With sympathizing heart.

   4 Form'd for the purest joys,
      By one desire possessed,
   One aim the zeal of all employs,
      To make each other blessed.

   5 No bliss can equal theirs,
      Where such affections meet;
   While praise devout, and mingled prayers
      Make their communion sweet.

   6 'Tis the same pleasure fills
      The breast in worlds above,
   Where joy, like morning-dew, distils,
      And all the air is love.

UNITY.

Your redemption draweth nigh. Luke 21: 28.   S. M.

446
What cheering words are these!
    Their sweetness who can tell?
In time, and to eternity,
    'Tis with the righteous well.

2 In ev'ry state secure,
    Kept by Jehovah's eye,
'Tis well with them while life endures,
    And well when call'd to die.

3 'Tis well when on the mount
    They feast on dying love;
And 'tis as well, in God's account,
    When they the furnace prove.

4 'Tis well when Jesus calls:
    "From earth and sin arise;
Join with the hosts of virgin souls
    Made to salvation wise!"
                                            Kent.

Thou hast delivered my soul from death. Psalm 116: 8.   S. M.

447
It is not death to die,—
    To leave this weary road,
And, 'mid the brotherhood on high,
    To be at home with God.

2 It is not death to close
    The eye long dimm'd by tears,
And wake in glorious repose
    To spend eternal years.

3 It is not death to bear
    The key that sets us free
From dungeon chain, to breathe the air
    Of boundless liberty.

4 It is not death to fling
    Aside the sinful dust,
And rise, on strong, exulting wing,
    To live among the just.

5 Jesus, thou Prince of life!
    Thy chosen cannot die;
Like Thee, they conquer in the strife,
    To reign with Thee on high.
                                    G. W. Bechune

MENDOTA. C. M.   Arr.

Admonish him as a brother. 2 Thess. 3: 15.   C. M.

448
1 SPEAK gently to the erring ones:—
   Ye know not all the pow'r
With which the dark temptation came,
   In some unguarded hour.

2 Ye may not know how earnestly
   They struggled, or how well,
Until the hour of weakness came,
   And sadly thus they fell.

3 Speak gently to the erring one:—
   Oh, do not thou forget,
However darkly stain'd by sin,
   He is thy brother yet.

4 Heir of the self-same heritage,
   Child of the self-same God,
He hath but stumbled in the path
   Thou hast in weakness trod.

5 Speak gently to the erring one:
   For is it not enough
That innocence and peace are gone,
   Without our censure rough?

6 It surely is a weary lot
   That sin crushed heart to bear;
And they who share a happier fate
   Their chidings well may spare.

                                   I. G. Lee.

TALMAR. M. 4.   I. B. Woodbury, 1850.
Used by per. of O. Ditson & Co., owners of copyright.

Now is the day of salvation. 2 Cor. 6: 2.   M. 4.

449 Listen to the gentle promptings
  Of the Spirit's warning voice;
Will ye heed his solemn warnings?
  Can ye slight his wondrous love?

2 Sweetly calling on the erring,
  Pardons offered without price;
Come, accept the invitation,
  And receive the offered grace.

3 Joy and hope the troubled conscience
  Will allay with soothing peace;
Press ye then to realms of glory,
  Run with joy the offered race.

4 Hesitate no longer, sinner,
  Lest the Spirit, sad and grieved,
Should forsake thee, now and ever,
  Nevermore to be deceived.

5 Broken hearts and contrite spirits,
  These the Lord will not despise:
Trust in Christ's atoning merits,
  In his precious sacrifice.

6 Time is short, and life is flying;
  You must perish if you stay:
Christ is coming, men are dying,
  Halt no longer, come to-day.

WARNING.

WINDHAM. L. M.   DANIEL READ, 1785.

Broad is the way that leadeth to destruction. Matt. 7: 13.   L. M.

450   BROAD is the road that leads to death,
        And many walk together there;
    But wisdom shows a narrow path,
        With here and there a traveler.

2 "Deny thyself, and take thy cross,"
    Is the Redeemer's great command;
Nature must count her gold but dross,
    If she would gain this heavenly land.

3 The fearful soul that tires and faints,
    And walks the ways of God no more,
Is but esteemed almost a saint,
    And makes his own destruction sure.

4 Lord, let not all my hopes be vain,
    Create my heart entirely new;
Which hypocrites could ne'er attain;
    Which false apostates never knew.
                                            Watts !

Behold, I stand at the door, and knock. Rev. 3: 20.   L. M.

451   BEHOLD a stranger at the door!
        He gently knocks, has knocked before,
    Has waited long, is waiting still;
    You treat no other friend so ill.

2 Oh, lovely attitude! he stands
    With melting heart and loaded hands!
Oh matchless kindness! and he shows
This matchless kindness to his foes!

WARNING.

3 But will he prove a friend indeed?
   He will; the very friend you need;
   The Friend of sinners—yes, 'tis He,
   With garments dyed on Calvary.

4 Rise, touched with gratitude divine;
   Turn out his enemy and thine,
   That soul-destroying monster, sin,
   And let the heavenly Stranger in.
                              Joseph Grigg.

HUGER. M. 11.

It is high time to awake. Rom. 13: 11.   M 11.

452
  WHY sleep ye, my brethern? come, let us arise;
     Oh, why should we slumber in sight of the prize?
  Salvation is nearer, our day is far spent,
  Oh, let us be active, awake, and repent!

2 Oh, how can we slumber? the Master will come;
   He's calling on sinners to seek them a home;
   The Spirit and bride now in concert unite,
   The weary they welcome, the careless invite.

3 Oh, how can we slumber? our foes are awake;
   To ruin poor souls every effort they make;
   T' accomplish their object no means are untried,
   The careless they comfort, the wakeful misguide.

4 Oh, how can we slumber? ye sinners look round,
   Before the last trumpet your hearts shall confound;
   Oh, fly to the Saviour! he calls you to-day;
   While mercy is waiting, oh, make no delay!
                              Josiah Hopkins, 1831.

WARNING.

BUTLER. S. M.

Turn ye from your evil ways; for why will ye die. Ez. 33: 11. S. M.

453   Destruction's dang'rous road,
  What multitudes pursue!
While that which leads the soul to God
  Is known or sought by few.

2 Believers enter in
  By Christ, the living door;
But they, who will not leave their sin,
  Must perish evermore.

3 If self must be denied,
  And sin forsaken quite;
They rather choose the way that's wide,
  And strive to think it right.

4 Encompass'd by a throng,
  On numbers they depend;
They think so many can't be wrong,
  And miss a happy end.

5 But numbers are no mark
  That men will right be found;
A few were sav'd in Noah's ark,
  For many millions drown'd.

6 Obey the gospel call,
  And enter while you may;
The flock of Christ remains still small,
  And none are safe but they.

                              Newton.

WARNING.

Do not frustrate the grace of God.   Gal. 2: 21.   S. M.

454
Let sinners take their course,
  And choose the road to death;
But in the worship of my God
  I'll spend my daily breath.

2 My thoughts address his throne
    When morning brings the light;
  I seek his blessings every noon,
    And pay my vows at night.

3 Thou wilt regard my cries,
    O my eternal God,
  While sinners perish in surprise,
    Beneath thine angry rod.

4 Because they dwell at ease,
    And no sad changes feel,
  They neither fear nor trust thy **name**,
    Nor learn to do thy will.

5 But I, with all my cares,
    Will lean upon the Lord;
  I'll cast my burdens on his arm,
    And rest upon his word.

The Judge standeth before the door.   Jas. 5: 9.   S. M.

455
Make haste, O man, to live,
  For thou so soon must die;
Time hurries past thee like the breeze,—
  How swift its moments fly!

2 Make haste, O man, to do
    Whatever must be done;
  Thou hast no time to lose in sloth,
    Thy day will soon be gone.

3 Up then with speed, and work;
    Fling ease and self away;
  This is no time for thee to sleep,
    Up, watch and work and pray.

4 Make haste, O man, to live,
    Thy time is almost o'er;
  Oh, sleep not, dream not, but **arise**,
    The Judge is at the door.

Bonar.

BEAUFORT. L. M. D.

L. C. Everett.

Used by per. of R. M. McIntosh, Owner of Copyright.

Jesus died and rose again. 1 Thess. 4: 14.   L. M. D.

456
1. He dies! the Friend of sinners dies!
   Lo! Salem's daughters weep around;
A solemn darkness veils the skies;
   A sudden trembling shakes the ground:
Come, saints, and drop a tear or two,
   For Him who groaned beneath your load;
He shed a thousand drops for you,
   A thousand drops of richest blood.

2 Here's love and grief beyond degree,
   The Lord of glory dies for men;
But lo! what sudden joys we see!
   Jesus, the dead, revives again:
The rising God forsakes the tomb,
   Up to His Father's court he flies;
Cherubic legions guard Him home,
   And shout Him welcome to the skies.

BOAZ. P. M.   By Com.

The harvest is past. Jer. 8: 20.   P. M.

457 WHEN the harvest is past, and the summer is gone,
    And sermons and pray'rs shall be o'er;
When the beams cease to break of the blest Sabbath-
And Jesus invites thee no more.—   [morn,

2 When the rich gales of mercy no longer shall blow,
    The gospel no message declare—
Sinner, how canst thou bear the deep wailing of wo,
    How suffer the night of despair!

3 When the holy have gone to the regions of peace,
    To dwell in the mansion above;
When their harmony wakes, in the fullness of bliss,
    Their song to the Saviour of love.—

4 Say, O sinner, that livest at rest and secure,
    Who fearest no trouble to come,
Can thy spirit the swellings of sorrow endure,
    Or bear the impenitent's doom?

                      Samuel Francis Smith, b. 1808.

INDEX OF SCRIPTURE TEXTS.

Hymn No

Gen.	32.26	A blessing humbly and earnestly sought	217
"	27.34	Bless me, even me also	234
"	5.22	Enoch walked with God	193
"	32.26	I will not let thee go exept thou bless me	221
"	8.22	Seed time and harvest	428
"	24.63	To meditate in the field in the evening	101
Lev.	8.35	Keep the charge of the Lord	2
Num.	10.29	We are journeying	371
Deut.	33.25	As thy days, so shall thy strength be	344
"	1.25	It is a good land	332
"	20.3	Let not your hearts faint	328
"	28.8	The Lord shall command the blessing	214
"	9.1	Thou art to pass over Jordan	389
Josh.	24.15	Choose you this day whom ye will serve	134
"	24.14	Fear the Lord, serve him in sincerity	107
Judges	8.4	Faint, yet pursuing	325
Ruth.	1.16	Thy people shall be my people	441
I Sam.	20.21	Come thou, for there is peace	152
"	7.12	Hitherto hath the Lord helped us	268
"	3.10	Speak, Lord, thy servant heareth	183
Esther	4.16	So will I go in unto the king	138
Job	1.21	Blessed be the name of the Lord	79
"	11.7	God is incomprehensible	250
Psalm	51.17	A broken heart God's sacrifice	182
"	145.10	All thy works shall praise thee	247
"	87.7	All my springs are in thee	362
"	119.2	Blessed are they that keep his testimonies	28
"	128.1	Blessed is every one that feareth the Lord	74
"	103.2	Bless the Lord, O my soul, and forget not all his benefits	277
"	103.1	Bless the Lord, O my soul	244
"	55.22	Cast thy burden upon the Lord	43
"	55.2	Cast thy burden on the Lord, he will sustain thee	411
"	37.5	Commit thy way unto the Lord	417
"	51.10	Create in me a clean heart	202
"	19.2	Day unto day uttereth speech	163
"	3.6	Divine protection acknowledged	164
"	56.13	Deliver my feet from falling	194
"	72.15	Daily shall he be praised	291
"	100.4	Enter into his gates with thanksgiving	157
"	55.17	Evening and morning and at noon	231
"	150.6	Everything that hath breath, praise the Lord	251
"	31.23	For the Lord preserveth the faithful	165

INDEX OF SCRIPTURE TEXTS.

			Hymn No.
Psa.	103.11	For as the heaven is high above the earth	279
"	84.11	For the Lord God is a sun and a shield	386
"	46.1	God is our refuge and strength	302, 309
"	125.2	God the defense of the Church	307
"	116.12	Grateful acknowledgment	359
"	49.1	God is our refuge and strength	395
"	119.57	God our portion	403
"	136.1	Give thanks unto the Lord, for he is good	422
"	107.1	Give thanks unto the Lord	425
"	29.1	Give unto the Lord glory and strength	242
"	45.11	He is thy Lord, worship thou him	6
"	27.5	He shall hide me	204
"	23.2	He leadeth me	220
"	36.7	How excellent is thy loving kindness	243
"	1.2	His delight is in the law of the Lord	283
"	84.1	How amiable are thy tabernacles	281
"	119.97	How I love thy law	350
"	139.17	How precious also are thy thoughts	369
"	126.6	He that goeth forth weeping, bearing precious	385
"	147.18	He sendeth out his word	401
"	133.1	How good and how pleasant	434
"	38.8	I am feeble and sore broken	65
"	4.8	I will lay me down in peace and sleep	95
"	32.8	I will instruct thee in the way	168
"	59.16	I will sing aloud of thy mercy in the morning	169
"	88.9	I have stretched out my hands unto thee	199
"	23.4	I will fear no evil	218
"	108.1	I will sing, and give praise	239
"	147.1	It is good to sing praises	252
"	144.9	I will sing a new song unto thee	278
"	34.1	I will bless the Lord at all times	289
"	3.5	I laid me down and slept	294
"	39.12	I am a stranger and sojourner	327
"	31.7	I will be glad and rejoice in thy mercies	367
"	32.8	I will guide thee with mine eye	390
"	137.5	If I forget thee, O Jerusalem	418
"	111.1	I will praise the Lord with my whole heart	421
"	100.3	Know ye that the Lord he is God	288
"	84.9	Look upon the face of thine anointed	18
"	127.3	Lo, children are a heritage of the Lord	76
"	39.4	Lord, make me to know mine end	86
"	122.1	Let us go into the house of the Lord	293
"	95.6	Let us worship and bow down	8, 240
"	84.2	My soul longeth,—even fainteth for the courts of the Lord	14

INDEX OF SCRIPTURE TEXTS.

			Hymn No.
Psa.	34.2	My soul shall make her boast in the Lord	31, 284
"	55.4	My heart is sore pained within me	71
"	35.9	My soul shall be joyful in the Lord	108
"	91.2	My refuge and my fortress	363
"	16.9	My flesh also shall rest in hope	383
"	104.34	My meditation of him shall be sweet	414
"	5.3	My voice shalt thou hear in the morning	166
"	55.6	Oh, that I had wings like a dove	124, 131
"	119.133	Order my steps in thy word	197
"	107.1	O give thanks unto the Lord	248
"	118.1	O give thanks unto the Lord	254
"	90.9	Our years are as a tale that is told	274
"	119.97	O how love I thy law	333
"	90.1	Our dwelling place in all generations	339
"	147.1	Praise ye the Lord, it is good to sing praise unto our God	245
"	148.1	Praise ye the Lord	273
"	65.1	Praise waiteth for thee, O God, in Zion	241, 289
"	25.6	Remember, O Lord, thy tender mercies	175
"	116.7	Return unto thy rest, O my soul	161
"	100.2	Serve the Lord with gladness	246
"	98.5	Sing unto the Lord with the voice of a psalm	292
"	85.9	Surely his salvation is nigh them that fear him	249
"	3.8	Salvation belongeth to the Lord	296
"	36.9	The fountain of life	24
"	119.105	Thy word is a lamp unto my feet	36
"	23.4	Thou art with me, thy rod and thy staff	118
"	111.10	The fear of the Lord is the beginning of wisdom	143
"	95.7, 8	To-day if ye will hear his voice, harden not your hearts	148
"	27.1	The Lord is my light and my salvation	156
"	118.24	The day which the Lord hath made	160
"	3.5	The Lord sustained me	167, 170
"	65.11	Thou crownest the year	172
"	23.1	The Lord is my Shepherd	195, 224
"	36.5	Thy mercy, O Lord, is in the heavens	198
"	103.8	The Lord is merciful and gracious	225
"	141.2	The evening sacrifice	94
"	4.8	Thou, Lord, makest me dwell in safety	93
"	91.9, 10	Thou hast made the Lord thy habitation	275
"	19.1	The heavens declare the glory of God	290
"	91.2	The Lord is my refuge	304
"	32.7	Thou art my hiding place	311
"	94.22	The Lord is my defence and Rock	324
"	61.2	The Rock higher than I	326
"	23.4	Thou art with me	354

INDEX OF SCRIPTURE TEXTS.

Hymn No.

Psa.	37.39	The salvation of the righteous is of the Lord	366
"	146.10	The Lord shall reign forever	373
"	23.1	The Lord is my shepherd	323, 398
"	97.1	The Lord reigneth; let the earth rejoice	424
"	4.8	Thou Lord makest me to dwell in safety	93
"	65.11	Thou crownest the year with thy goodness	427
"	65.13	The valleys are also covered over with corn	429
"	116.8	Thou hast delivered my soul from death	447
"	91.1	Under the shadow of the Almighty	263
"	75.1	Unto thee, O God, do we give thanks	265
"	90.9	We spend our years as a tale that is told	174, 171
"	56.3	What time I am afraid, I will trust in thee	349
"	142.3	When my spirit was overwhelmed within me	407
"	51.2	Wash me thoroughly from mine iniquity	420
"	29.2	Worship the Lord in the beauty of holiness	372
Prov.	23.23	Buy the truth and sell it not	145
"	18.24	Christ our friend	27
"	3.17	Her ways are ways of pleasantness	321
"	3.13	Happy is the man that findeth wisdom	387
"	23.26	My son, give me thine heart	150
"	3.24	Yea, thou shalt lie down and thy sleep shall be sweet	100
Eccl.	9.10	Do it with thy might	154
"	12.1	Remember thy Creator in the days of thy youth	144
Cant.	5.10	The chiefest among ten thousand	261
"	1.3	Thy name is an ointment poured forth	262
Isaiah	40.1	Comfort ye my people	46
"	55.3	Even the sure mercies of David	399
"	53.7	He is brought as a lamb to the slaughter	50
"	55.7	Let him return unto the Lord	139
"	1.16	Put away the evil of your doings	21
"	40.7	The flower fadeth	70
"	26.3	Thou wilt keep him in perfect peace	96
"	35.10	The Ransomed of the Lord shall come	111
"	28.16	The sure foundation	319
"	26.9	With my soul have I desired thee in the night	98
Jer.	3.4	Thou art the guide of my youth	192
"	8.20	The harvest is past	457
"	10.23	The way of man is not in himself	335
"	3.4	Wilt thou not from this time cry unto me	222
"	23.28	What is the chaff to the wheat	322
Ezek.	18.31	Why will ye die	155
"	33.11	Turn ye from your evil ways for why will ye die	453
Amos	4.12	Prepare to meet thy God	186
Zech.	13.1	A fountain opened	22

INDEX OF SCRIPTURE TEXTS.

			Hymn No.
Zech.	1.5	Your fathers, where are they	87
Mal.	3.10	Bring ye all the tithes	365
Matt.	27.35	And they crucified him	60
"	28.11	As it began to dawn	158
"	7.7	Ask, and it shall be given you	216
"	6.9	After this manner therefore pray ye	227
"	19.15	And he laid his hands on them and departed	235
"	5.4	Blessed are they that mourn	176
"	5.5	Blessed are the meek	219
"	5.8	Blessed are the pure in heart	336
"	5.4	Blessed are they that mourn	388
"	26.34	Be not, therefore, anxious for the morrow	410
"	7.13	Broad is the way that leadeth to destruction	450
"	25.34	Come, ye blessed of my Father	91
"	11.28	Come unto me, and I will give you rest	132, 140
"	11.28	Come unto me all ye that labor	179, 400
"	21.28	Go, work in my vineyard	16
"	18.20	Gathered together in my name	267, 213
"	5.45	God's goodness universal	260
"	19.15	He laid his hands on them	313
"	17.4	It is good to be here	301
"	14.27	It is I, be not afraid	352
"	6.20	Lay up treasures for yourselves in heaven	5
"	26.20	Lo, I am with you alway	189
"	19.14	Of such is the Kingdom	412
"	19.14	Suffer the little children to come unto me	65
"	21.28	Son, go work to-day in my vineyard	308
"	22.39	Thou shalt love thy neighbor as thyself	439
"	8.27	The winds and the sea obey him	310
"	13.38	The field is the world	423
"	18.20	There am I in the midst	334
"	26.38	Then saith he unto them, My soul is exceeding sorrowful	61
"	26.39	Thy will be done	340
"	25.21	Well done, thou good and faithful servant	11
"	18.20	Where two or three are gathered	238, 440
Mark	6.56	As many as touched him were made whole	338
"	16.16	He that believeth and is baptized	29
"	10.47	Thou Son of David, have mercy on me	188
"	13.34	To every man his work	357
"	14.38	Watch and pray	3
"	10.28	We have left all, and followed thee	330
Luke	22.44	And being in an agony he prayed more earnestly	62
"	24.29	Abide with us, for it is toward evening	97, 159

INDEX OF SCRIPTURE TEXTS.

			Hymn No.
Luke	23.26	Bear the cross after Jesus	17
"	2.10	Behold, I bring you good tidings	33
"	12.27	Consider the lilies, how they grow	394
"	22.19	Do this in remembrance of me	52, 56
"	12.32	Fear not, little flock	44, 314
"	23.46	Father, into thy hands I commend my spirit	59
"	2.14	Glory to God in the highest	32
"	19.41	He beheld the city and wept over it	187
"	15.18	I will arise and go to my Father	142
"	17.5	Increase our faith	337
"	23.42	Lord, remember me	207
"	24.36	Peace be unto you	444
"	10.20	Rejoice because your names are written in heaven	408
"	4.18	To heal the broken-hearted	47
"	23.43	To-day shalt thou be with me in paradise	58
"	19.10	To seek and to save	190
"	8.18	Take heed therefore, how ye hear	208
"	24.34	The Lord is risen indeed	377
"	2.11	Unto you is born this day a Savior	34
"	10.39	Which also sat at Jesus' feet, and heard his word	342
"	14.22	Yet there is room	153
"	21.28	Your redemption draweth nigh	446
John	16.24	Ask, and ye shall receive	38
"	8.32	And the truth shall make you free	82
"	2.2	And Jesus was called to the marriage	285
"	16.16	A little while	380
"	1.29	Behold the Lamb of God	181
"	13.9	Desiring an entire cleansing	54
"	1.32	Descending from heaven like a dove	200
"	10.11	The good shepherd giveth his life for the sheep	315
"	6.37	Him that cometh unto me I will in no wise cast out	19, 137
"	16.13	He will guide you into all truth	211
"	15.26	He shall testify of me	237
"	14.2	In my Father's house are many mansions	4, 120, 122
"	7.37	If any man thirst, let him come unto me and drink	1
"	6.35	I am the bread of life	55
"	13.15	I have given you an example	53
"	7.37	If any man thirst, let him come unto me	141
"	4.23	In spirit and in truth	203
"	6.67	Jesus said therefore, will ye also go away	316
"	6.68	Lord, to whom shall we go	317, 391
"	21.17	Thou knowest that I love thee	180
"	4.23	The Father seeketh such to worship him	201
"	14.3	Where I am, there ye may be also	117

INDEX OF SCRIPTURE TEXTS.

			Hymn No.
John	20.13	Woman, why weepest thou	374
"	16.20	Your sorrow shall be turned into joy	130, 415
Acts	16.31	Believe on the Lord Jesus Christ	41
"	8.39	He went on his way rejoicing	30
"	15.6	Meeting for counsel	431
"	19.20	So mightily grew the word of the Lord	23
"	20.24	So that I might finish my course with joy	99
Rom.	8.28	And we know that all things work for good	346
"	11.33	His ways past finding out	393
"	8.31	If God be for us, who can be against us	92
"	9.16	It is not of him that willeth, but of God	345
"	13.11	It is high time to awake	452
"	8.37	More than conquerors	9
"	13.11	Now is our salvation nearer	126
"	11.33	O the depth of the riches, both of the wisdom, etc.	253, 402
"	12.5	One body in Christ,	435
"	16.20	The grace of our Lord Jesus Christ be with you	299
"	8.35	Who shall separate us from the love of Christ	48, 300
"	5.3	We glory in tribulation	364
"	8.15	Whereby we cry, Abba, Father	368
1 Cor.	10.4	And that Rock was Christ	206, 305
"	15.10	By the grace of God I am what I am	360
"	15.3	Christ died for our sins	57, 261
"	11.26	For as often as ye eat this bread	51
"	13.12	For now we see through a glass darkly	128
"	3.7	God giveth the increase	230
"	15.43	It is sown in weakness	88
"	11.26	Ye show forth the Lord's death	49
"	6.19,20	Ye are not your own	84, 303
2 Cor.	5.1	A house not made with hands	109, 112
"	6.2	Behold, now is the accepted time	133, 149
"	5.17	Behold, all things are become new	397
"	5.15	He died that we should live unto him	184
"	8.9	For ye know the grace of our Lord	282
"	6.2	Now is the day of salvation	146, 449
"	4.18	The things which are not seen	129
"	13.14	The communion of the Holy Ghost	343
"	2.14	Thanks be to God which causeth us to triumph	348
"	13.11	The God of love and peace shall be with you	437
"	5.7	We walk by faith and not by sight	40
Gal.	2.21	Do not frustrate the grace of God	454
"	6.14	God forbid that I should glory save in the cross	63, 177
"	3.27	Ye have put on Christ	20

21

INDEX OF SCRIPTURE TEXTS.

			Hymn No.
Eph.	4.23	Be renewed in the spirit of your mind	205
"	2.5	By grace are ye saved	280
"	4.32	Be kind to one another	209
"	3.19	Filled with all the fullness of God	406
"	2.4	God, who is rich in mercy	45
"	4.30	Grieve not the Holy Spirit	147
"	5.20	Give thanks always for all things	426
"	1.3	Heavenly places in Christ	438
"	4.13	In the unity of faith	443
"	1.7	Jesus in whom you have redemption	83
"	3.17	That Christ may dwell in your hearts	353
"	1.10	The saints but one family	430
"	5.8	Walk as children of light	270
"	1.6	Wherein he had made us accepted	355
Phil.	2.18	For the same cause also do ye joy	356
"	3.8	I count all things but loss	392
"	4.4	Rejoice in the Lord always	358
"	4.7	The peace of God	102
"	3.21	Who shall change our vile bodies	67
Col.	2.2	Being knit together in love	433
"	3.15	Let the peace of God rule in your hearts	196
"	3.1	Seek those things which are above	106
"	3.4	Then shall we also appear with him in glory	121
"	2.2	That their hearts might be comforted	297
"	2.10	Ye are complete in him	396
1 Thess.	5.13	Be at peace among yourselves	445
"	4.18	Comfort ye one another	89
"	4.14	For if we believe that Jesus died and rose again	126, 456
"	5.17	Pray without ceasing	226
"	4.14	Them also which sleep in Jesus	72, 378
2 Thess.	3.15	Admonish him as a brother	448
"	3.1	Brethren, pray for us	229
1 Tim.	1.15	Christ came into the world to save sinners	151, 185
"	2.1	First of all, supplications	210
"	1.2	Grace, mercy and peace	162
"	2.6	Who gave himself a ransom for all	64
2 Tim.	2.3	Endure hardness as a good soldier	7
Titus	2.12	Denying ungodliness	212
"	2.13	Looking for that blessed hope	320
"	2.14	Zealous of good works	12
Heb.	4.15	A high priest that hath been in all points tempted	361
"	6.19	As an anchor to the soul	404
"	7.27	Christ the great sacrifice	25

		Hymn No.
Heb.	4.3 ....For we which have believed do enter into rest..........384	
"	11.13....Faith looking into the future.......................413	
"	12.1 ....Let us run with patience the race before us............116	
"	12.2 ....Looking unto Jesus..........................233, 271	
"	4 11....Let us labor therefore, to enter into that rest..........382	
"	13.4 ....Marriage is honorable..............................286	
"	11.16....Now they desire a better country...................123, 376	
"	2.10....Perfect through suffering............................ 37	
"	11.13....Strangers and pilgrims...............................104	
"	7 25....Seeing he ever liveth to make intercession.............272	
"	4.9 ....There remaineth therefore a rest..............105, 379, 381	
"	3.7 ....To day if ye hear his voice...........................136	
"	11.16....They desire a better country........................232	
"	6 11....The full assurance of faith............................318	
"	6 19....Which hope we have as an anchor of the soul.......85, 442	
"	11.10....Whose builder and maker is God.......................115	
"	12.4 ....Ye have not yet resisted unto blood....................341	
James	4.8 ....Draw nigh to God 419	
"	4.14....It is even a vapor...................................119	
"	5.16....Pray for one another................................298	
"	5.9 ....The Judge standeth before the door...................455	
1 Peter	2.21....An example that ye should follow..................... 13	
"	5.7 ....Casting our cares upon him......................191, 329	
"	2.21....Follow his steps..................................... 15	
"	5.7 ....He careth for you...................................347	
"	2.21....Leaving us an example............................. 35	
"	3.8 ....Love as brethren....................................432	
"	5.10....The God of all grace.................................351	
"	2.24....Who his own self bore our sins.......................256	
2 Peter	1 4 ....Great and precious promises......................... 39	
"	3.13....New heavens and a new earth.........................331	
"	3.18....To him be glory both now and forever............276, 312	
1 John	1.7 ....And the blood of Christ cleanseth us.................135	
"	3.1 ....Behold, what manner of love..........................178	
"	4.8 ....God is love...370	
"	1,5 ....God is light, and in him is no darkness................ 42	
"	2.10....He that loveth his brother abideth in the light........295	
"	5.3 ....His commandments are not grievous..,.................416	
"	4.19....We love him because he first loved us..................215	
Rev.	21.23....And the city had no need of the sun....................114	
"	14.3 ....A new song before the throne.........................258	
"	2.10....Be thou faithful unto death...........................113	
"	3.20....Behold, I stand at the door and knock.................451	

INDEX OF SCRIPTURE TEXTS.

			Hymn No.
Rev.	21.6	Fear not—I will give unto him that is athirst	306
"	19.12	On his head were many crowns	255
"	7.10	Salvation to our God	264
"	21.2	The holy city, New Jerusalem	127
"	1.5	Unto Him that loved us	266
"	14.13	Which die in the Lord	73
"	5.12	Worthy the Lamb that was slain	269

A funeral thought... 75
A prayer for a church newly organized................436
Death of a mother... 68
Death of a brother.. 80
Death of a youth.. 81
Gratitude..259
God is present everywhere................................236
Hebrews—eleven... 10
Hope in prospect of eternity............................... 77
I will love thee, O Lord, my strength..................409
Mag auch die Liebe weinen................................ 90
Our guide unto death.......................................223
Prospect of heaven...110
Reflection at the end of the year.........................173
Sister, thou wast mild and lovely........................ 78
The widow's God... 69
The night cometh..103
The sweet hour...228
They shall talk of thy power..............................405
Unto Him be glory...257
When the Son of man shall come in his glory........375

METRICAL INDEX OF HYMNS AND TUNES.

L. M.

| | | Hymn No. |

A broken heart, my God, my King.....182
All praise to Thee, the Triune God.....247
Almighty Sov'reign of the skies.....254
Another day has passed along.....159
Another year, another year.....171
Asleep in Jesus! blessed sleep.....*Rest*.....72
Awake my soul, awake my tongue.....*Olivet*.....239
Awake my soul, in joyful lays.....*Duke Street*.....243
Awake my tongue, thy tribute bring.....253

Before thy face with lifted hands.....*My Helplessness*.....18
Behold a stranger at the door.....451
Behold the lilies of the field.....*Baca*.....394
Blessed Redeemer, how divine.....439
Bless, O my soul, the living God.....244
Broad is the road that leads to death.....*Windham*.....450

Christ in the night he was betrayed.....*Federal Street*.....53
Come gracious Spirit, heavenly Dove.....*Sharon*.....211
Come hither all ye weary souls.....*Herald*.....132
Come, Holy Spirit, calm my mind.....*Sykes*.....237
Come, O my soul, in sacred lays.....245

Deem not that they are blest alone.....388
Deep are the wounds which sin has made.....19
Dismiss us with thy blessing Lord.....214

Father in heaven, upon thy word.....230
Father of mercies, bow thine ear.....229
Fountain of grace, rich, full and free.....396
From all that dwell below the skies.....*Weston*.....251

Give thanks to God, He reigns above.....425
Glory and thanks to God in heaven.....312
Glory to thee, my God, this night.....96
God is our refuge and defense.....*Magruder*.....309
God is the refuge of his saints.....395
Great God, in vain man's narrow view.....250
Great God! we sing that mighty hand.....172

Hail, sovereign love that formed the plan.....311
Happy the man that finds the grace.....387
He dies, the Friend of sinners dies.....*Beaufort*.....456
How blest the righteous when he dies.....73
How vain is all beneath the sky.....*Uxbridge*.....119

                                                              Hymn No.
Indulgent God of love and power..437
In this lone hour of deep distress... 69

Jesus, be endless praise to thee... 64
Jesus, dear name, how sweet it sounds...... *Ward*...................135
Jesus, my Savior, let me be..209
Jesus, thy blood and righteousness... 20
Jesus, the spring of joys divine.. 41
Just as I am, without one plea................. *Woodworth*..........181

Let me but hear my Saviour say..344
Life is the time to serve the Lord .... *Wells*...................154
Lord, bless thy saints assembled here....... *Retreat*. 436
Lord, how delightful t'is to see..438

My dearest friends, in bonds of love.......... *Parting Hand*......295
My dear Redeemer and my Lord... 13
My God, permit me not to be...212
My heav'nly home is bright and fair....... *Going Home*.........115
My hope is built on nothing less.............. *The Solid Rock*.....324
My op'ning eyes with rapture see............ *Hamburg* 158
My soul, with humble fervor raise..241

No more, my God, I boast no more...392

Oh, come, loud anthems let us sing..240
Oh, deem not they are blest alone..415
Oh, do not let the word depart 134
Oh, hallowed is the land and blest..424
Oh, that I could forever dwell..342
O happy day, that fixed my choice.......... *Happy Day* 30
O love, beyond conception great 249
O praise the Lord, 'tis sweet to raise. 252
O render thanks to God above.. 248
O thou who camest from above..343

Praise God, from whom all blessings flow .*Old Hundred*........246
Praise waits in Zion, Lord, for thee..289

Say, sinner, hath a voice within 133
Sing to the Lord with joyful voice........... *Freedom*..............288
So fades the lovely blooming flower.. 76
Soft be the turf on thy dear breast........... *Juniata*................ 88
So let our lives and lips express... 12
Some day the word will come................. *Elm Street*.......... 11
Sun of my soul thou Saviour dear .... *Hursley*................386
Sweet hour of prayer .... *Sweet Hour of P*....228
Sweet meditation on the Lord..414

	Hymn No.
The billows swell, the winds are high......................................	310
The bosom where I oft have lain ....*Hattie*..................	68
Thee we adore, eternal Lord..	242
The heavens declare thy glory, Lord.....................................	290
There is a calm for those who weep.........*Star of Day*...........	125
There is a glorious world on high...	89
The time is short ere all that live...	91
Thou only Sovereign of my heart..............*Repose*	391
Though love may weep, with breaking heart......................	90
Thou strong and loving Son of Man.....................................	397
Thus far the Lord has led me on ....*Hebron*................	95
Thy presence, gracious Lord, afford........*Urvilla*.................	208
Thy ways, O Lord, with wise design.....................................	393
'Tis by the faith of joys to come.............*Waverly*...............	413
'Tis midnight; and on Olive's brow ....*Missionary Chant.*	62
We've no abiding city here ....*Welton*...............	40
We now have met to worship thee..........*Whiteside*	6
We pray for those who do not pray...	210
When I survey the wondrous cross	63
Where two or three with faithful heart................................	440
Where two or three, with sweet accord................................	238
While life prolongs its precious light...................................	136
While now thy throne of grace we seek................................	183
Why should I murmur or repine............*Rockingham*.........	341
Why should we start and fear to die.....................................	71
With tearful eyes I look around..	137
With thankful hearts we meet, O Lord	213

C. M.

Above the trembling elements...	198
Alas! and did my Savior bleed...............*Balerma*...............	57
Alas! what hourly dangers rise...	194
All hail the power of Jesus' name............*Coronation*	255
Amazing grace, how sweet the sound...................................	360
Am I a soldier of the cross....................*Arlington*.............	7
Amid the splendors of thy state...	370
And let this feeble body fail...	77
And now my soul, another year............*Elida*	173
A pilgrim through this lonely world........*Pilgrim*...............	35
As children dwelling in their home.....................................	51
As Jesus died and rose again...	378
As on the cross the Savior hung...	58
At Jesus' feet I take my place.................*Lawrence*	338

	Hymn No.
Awake, awake the sacred song	256
Awake my soul, stretch every nerve	9
Awake, ye saints, and raise your eyes	131
Behold the glories of the Lamb......*St. Martins*	258
Behold the Savior of mankind	59
Behold the sure foundation stone......*Evening Twilight*	319
Be strong, my soul, in God most high	363
Blest be the dear uniting love......*Hick's Farewell*	300
By cool Siloam's shady rill	336
Come, children, learn to fear the Lord	143
Come, Holy Spirit, heavenly Dove	200
Come, humble sinner, in whose breast......*Dunlap's Creek*	138
Come in ye blessed of the Lord......*Howard*	28
Come, let us all unite to praise	265
Come, let us join our friends above	430
Come let us join our souls to God	8
Come let us now forget our mirth	107
Come, ye that love the Savior's name......*Bridgewater*	291
Dear Father, to thy mercy seat	204
Dear Jesus, ever at thy side......*Tampico*	313
Far from affliction, toil and care	82
Father, I stretch my hands to thee......*Memphis*	199
Father, whate'er of earthly bliss......*Naomi*	196
Fond parents, calm the heaving breast	85
Forever here my rest shall be......*Azmon*	54
Fountain of mercy, God of love	428
From thee, my God, my joy shall rise......*Heber*	108
Give me a foothold on the rock......*Give me a Footh'ld*	206
Give me to know thy will, O God	197
God moves in a mysterious way......*Dayton*	402
God of my life, my morning song	165
Great God, preserved by thine arm	167
Hail, sweetest, dearest tie that binds......*Dearest Tie*	442
Hark, from the tomb a doleful sound......*Mear*	75
How condescending and how kind	50
How did my heart rejoice to hear	293
How happy are these little ones	83
How happy every child of grace......*Cross and Crown*	376
How precious is the book divine	36
How sweet, how heavenly is the sight	432
How sweet the name of Jesus sounds	262

METRICAL INDEX OF HYMNS AND TUNES.

Hymn No.

I heard the voice of Jesus say	*Athens*	141
I'll bless the Lord from day to day		292
I long for God the living God	*Bethlehem*	1
I love to steal awhile away		101
Indulgent Father, by whose care		99
In evil long I took delight	*Downs*	21
In memory of the Savior's love		56
In mercy Lord, remember me	*Evan*	98
In Thy great name, O Lord, we come		267
I owe the Lord a morning song	*Gratitude*	169
I would I were content to be	*Safety*	335
Jerusalem my happy home	*Canaan*	127
Jesus, the very thought of thee	*Elkhart*	358
Jesus, thou art the sinner's friend	*Prayer*	207
Let us adore th' eternal Word		55
Long as I live, I'll bless thy name	*Cana*	284
Lord, for the mercies of the night		170
Lord, in the morning thou shalt hear	*Warwick*	166
Lord, in thy presence here we meet		431
Lord, when I count thy mercies o'er		369
Lord, when together here we meet		301
Majestic sweetness sits enthroned	*Ortonville*	261
Must Jesus bear the cross alone	*Maitland*	17
My Father, God! how sweet the sound		368
My God, my Father, blissful name		340
My God, the spring of all my joys		362
My God was with me all the night		164
My latest sun is sinking fast	*Angel Band*	116
Now, gracious Lord, thine arm reveal		175
O for a closer walk with God	*Elizabethtown*	193
O for a thousand tongues to sing		257
O happy is the man who hears		321
O land of rest for thee I sigh	*Varina*	105
O Lord, I would delight in thee		406
O Savior, welcome to my heart		353
O weary wanderer, come home	*Barr*	142
Oh, could I find from day to day		205
Oh, could our thoughts and wishes fly		129
Oh, for a faith that will not shrink		337
Oh, for a heart to praise my God	*Solitude*	202
Oh, happy soul that lives on high		320
Oh, how I love thy law		350

	Hymn No.
Oh, what amazing words of grace	140
Once more my soul, the rising day ....*Peterboro*	163
Once more we come before our God	203
On Jordan's stormy banks I stand	110
Our God, our help in ages past	339
Our life is ever on the wing	174
Prayer is the soul's sincere desire	201
Proclaim, saith Christ, my wondrous grace	29
Return, O wanderer, now return	139
Rise, O my soul pursue the path	10
Salvation! Oh, the joyful sound............*Joyful Sound*	264
Shepherd divine, our wants relieve	195
Since Jesus freely did appear	285
Speak gently to the erring ones............*Mendota*	448
Sweet is the mem'ry of thy grace	260
Sweet Sabbath-school, more dear to me....*My Sabbath Home*	156
Sweet was the time when first I felt.........*Peoria*	367
Teach me the measure of my days	86
That doleful night before his death.........*Solon*	49
That solemn hour will come for me	354
The billows round me rise and roll.........*Rolling Billows*	349
The God of love, the God of peace......... *Urbana*	351
The head that once was crowned with thorns	37
The Lord of glory is my light	404
The morning of the centuries...................*Dawn*	23
There is a fountain filled with blood........*Cleansing Foun*	22
There is a house not made with hands	109
There is a land of pure delight	106
There is a little, lonely fold	314
There is a name I love to hear	266
There is an hour of hallowed peace	130
There is an hour of peaceful rest .... *Woodland*	379
This is the day the Lord has made	377
Though darkness turn the skies to night	407
Thro' all the changing scenes of life	287
Thy life I read, my dearest Lord	76
'Tis by thy strength the mountains stand..*Land of Rest*	427
To whom, my Saviour, shall I go	317
Upon the pillow of thy love	100
Was Jesus tempted like as we.................*Brown*	361
We join to pray, with wishes kind	286
What glory gilds the sacred page	263

	Hymn No.
What is the chaff, the word of man....................................322	
What shall I render to my God..359	
What though the arm of conquering death.......................87	
When all thy mercies, O my God.....................................259	
When blooming youth is snatched away...........................81	
When floating on life's troubled sea................................318	
When I can read my title clear..............*Ninety-Fifth*..........4	
When waves of trouble round me swell..........................352	
Where could I go but unto thee..............*Broadway*............316	
While thee, I seek, protecting power.......*Rochester*...........405	
While through this ch'ging world I roam...*Wales*...............128	
Whom have we Lord in heaven but thee........................403	
Why do we mourn departing friends.......*Dublin*................74	
Why should our tears in sorrow flow.......*Dundee*.............84	
Ye little flock whom Jesus feeds....................................315	
Ye men and Angels, witness now...........*Marlow*...............31	

S. M.

A charge to keep I have..3
A few more years shall roll....................*The Pilgrim*..........380
And are we yet alive..............................*Sandusky*..............45
And can'st thou, sinner, slight..............*Phoebe*..................147
And let our bodies part..435
And must this body die...67
Assist thy servant, Lord........................*Lake Enon*...........190

Blest are the sons of peace..434
Blest be the tie that binds......................*Gerar*................433

Come, we that love the Lord..356
Commit thou all thy griefs..417

Dear Savior, we are thine..347
Destruction's dang'rous road..............*Butler*..................453
Did Christ o'er sinners weep.................*Lottie*.................187

Far from my heavenly home.......................................418

Give to the Lord thine heart..150
Go to thy rest fair child............................*Morn*...............65
Grace! 'tis a charming sound..................*Salem*................280

Have mercy, Lord, on me..188
How charming is the place..281
How gentle God's commands..................*Home*.............416

METRICAL INDEX OF HYMNS AND TUNES.

                                                                                     Hymn No.

I give myself to God...............................*Clinton*..................303
I have a home above..112
It is not death to die..447
If through unruffled seas..346

Jesus, who knows full well..191

Laborers of Christ, arise..357
Let sinners take their course...454
Lord, at this closing hour......................*Ninety-Third*........444
Lord, what a feeble piece..66
Lo, what a pleasing sight.....................*St. Thomas*.........445

Make haste, O man, to live..455
My soul, be on thy guard.........................*Laban*..................2
My soul, repeat his praise...279
My soul, with Joy attend.........................*Albion*...............355
My times are in thy hand......................*Ruth*.....................345

Not all the blood of beasts.....................*State Street*........25
Now, brethren, though we part..297
Now is th' accepted time..149

Oh, bless the Lord, my soul..................*Boyleston*..........277
Oh, cease, my wand'ring soul..382
Oh, for the death of those...113
Oh, sing to me of heaven........................*Dunbar*...............111
Oh, where shall rest be found...............*Eugene*................381
Once more before we part.....................*Sweet Day*.........296
One sweetly solemn thought...............*One S. S. thought*...123
Our heavenly Father, hear..227

Raise your triumphant song..278
Rest for the toiling hand..383

Teach me, my God and King............*Golden Hill*..........225
The day is past and gone......................*Vesper*..................93
The day is past and gone...94
The Lord my Shepherd is......................*Shirland*.............323
The Lord who truly knows..226
Thy laws, O God, are right..283
To God the only wise...282

What charming words are these.....................................446
When on the brink of death...348
With humble heart and tongue..192

Ye sinners, fear the Lord..148

Metre 4......8, 7.

Hymn No.

Art thou in thy spirit lowly		180
At the door of mercy sighing	*Crystal Fountain*	179
Be not anxious for the morrow	*Oakland*	410
Blessed Bible, how I love it	*Fount of Glory*	333
Brother, thou hast left us lonely	*Bro. Sweetly Rest*	80
Call the Lord thy sure salvation		366
Can my soul find rest from sorrow	*The Penitent*	176
Come, thou fount of every blessing	*Nettleton*	268
Come, ye sinners, poor and needy	*Greenville*	151
Far from mortal cares retreating		334
God is love, his mercy brightens	*Effie*	42
Hail! my ever blessed Jesus		269
Hark, the voice of Jesus crying	*Joppa*	16
Hark, what mean those holy voices	*Dixon*	33
In the cross of Christ I glory	*Charleston*	364
I would love thee, God and Father	*I would Love Thee*	409
Jesus Christ our Lord and Saviour		412
Jesus, grant us all a blessing		221
Jesus, hail! enthroned in glory		272
Jesus, I my cross have taken	*Autumn*	330
Jesus, while our hearts are bleeding		79
Lamb of God, we fall before Thee		177
Let me go where Saints are going	*Abner*	120
Let thy grace, Lord, make me lowly		219
Listen to the gentle promptings	*Talmar*	449
Lord, a little band and lowly		270
Lord, I hear of showers of blessing	*Even me*	234
Love divine, all love excelling		178
Oh, the blessedness of leaning		411
Oh, the bliss of loved ones resting	*Eden*	384
One there is above all others	*Ovio*	27
Praise the Lord, ye heavens adore him		273
Savior, breathe an evening blessing	*Evening Hymn*	92
See, above time's clouds and shadows		332
Shall we meet beyond the river	*Shall we Meet*	121
Sinners, will you scorn the message		152
Sister, thou wast mild and lovely	*Mount Vernon*	78
Sweet the moments rich in blessing	*Divine Compassi*	271
Take my heart, O Father, take it		220
Tarry with me, O my Saviour	*Evening*	218

	Hymn No.
Weary pilgrim, why this sadness	331
What a friend we have in Jesus......*What a Friend*	38
With my substance I will honor	365

Metre 5.......7s.

As the sun doth daily rise		399
Blessed fountain full of grace	*Aletta*	24
Cast thy burden on the Lord	*Mercy*	43
Cast thy burden on the Lord	*Delaware*	329
Children of the heavenly King	*Lincolnshire*	371
Come, my soul, thy suit prepare		216
Come, said Jesus' sacred voice		400
Come, ye thankful people, come		423
Day is breaking in the sky	*Chatham*	294
Depth of mercy, can there be		185
Faint not, Christian, though the road		328
Fear not, brethren, joyful stand		44
Hear me, Saviour, while I pray	*Josie*	235
High in yonder realms of light	*Eltham*	117
Holy Spirit, faithful Guide	*Holy Spirit F. G.*	390
Jesus, lover of my soul	*Allen*	304
Lord, we come before Thee now		217
Mary to the Saviour's tomb	*Martyn*	374
Now the shades of night are gone	*Trusting*	168
O, the agonizing prayer	*Gethsemane*	61
People of the living God	*Ennius*	441
Praise, O, praise our God and King		422
Praise to God, immortal praise	*Nuremburg*	421
Saviour, bless thy word to all		401
Saviour, teach me day by day	*Purity*	215
Sinner, art thou still secure		186
Softly fades the twilight ray	*Eve*	102
Softly now the light of day		103
Take my life and let it be	*Yarbrough*	184
Tell us sinner, tell us why	*Lancaster*	155
They who seek the throne of grace		236
To thy pastures fair and large	*Hendon*	398
To thy temple we repair		372
Wake the song of Jubilee		372
We are traveling on our way	*We are Traveling*	327
Welcome, welcome day of rest	*Welcome*	161

Metre 7......8, 7, 4.   Hymn No.

Angels from the realms of Glory............*Happy Zion*.........32
Father, in my life's young morning........*Gorton*...............222
Guide me, O thou great Jehovah..............................223
In the vineyard of our Father..............................308
Jesus, when my soul is parting............*Arthur*...........306
On the mountain's top appearing............*Zion*...............46
Saviour, like a Shepherd, lead us............................224
Zion stands with hills surrounded...........................307

Metre 11......11s.—4 lines.

Farewell, my dear brethren, the time is...*Expostulation*......298
How firm a foundation.........................*Portuguese Hymn*. 39
'Mid scenes of confusion and creature......*Sweet Home*.........232
Though faint, yet pursuing, we go on......*Lyte*..............325
Why sleep ye, my brethren, come let us...*Huger*...............452

Metre 14......7, 6.

Go thou in life's fair morning..............................145
I lay my sins on Jesus.......................................26
I need thee, precious Jesus.............*I Need Thee*........189
In heav'nly love abiding...................................275
I thank the Lord my Maker.............*Salvation*..........426
Lord, I care not for r............Pec........*Is my Name Writ*.408
O God, the Rock of Ages.................*Webb*..............274
O when shall I see Jesus................*Missionary Hymn*. 14
Remember thy Creator.....................*Manoah*............144
There is a land immortal..............*Heavenly Desire*...118
Thy love, O Holy Father.....................................276

Metre 17......7s.—6 lines.

Rock of Ages, cleft for me...............*Toplady*............305
Safely through another week.............*Sabbath*.............157

Metre......26 6s. and 4s.—7 lines.

My faith looks up to thee...............*New Haven*.........233
The God of harvest praise...............*Harvest*.............429

Metre 27......6s. and 4s.—8 lines.

I'm but a stranger here...................*Dothan*............104
Nearer, my God, to thee..................*Bethany*............419
Wash me, O Lamb of God.....................................420

Metre 33......11, 10.—4 lines.

Hymn No.
Come ye disconsolate where...............*Come ye Discon.*..... 47
Hail the blest morn when the...............*Zion's Glad Morn*. 34
Rock of my strength to thee... 48

Metre 55......10s.—4 lines.

Abide with me; fast falls the eventide......*Enon*................... 97
Again the day returns of holy rest...........*Holy Rest*............160
As pants the wearied hart for cooling sp...*Forty-second Ps'lm* 302

12s. and 8s.

I will sing you a song of that b'tiful land..*Home of the Soul*...122
When the harvest is past, and the Sum......*Boaz*.....................457

Not Classified.

Child of sin and sorrow.........10s. and 4s...*Ava*......................153
Follow the path of Jesus.........7, 6 and 5...*Bound Brook*......... 15
God be with you...................9s. and 8s...*God be With You*..299
Great God! what.....................Pec. 8, 7...*Monmouth*............375
Holy Sabbath evening............6s. and 5s...*Holy Sabbath E*...162
How bright is the day..........M. 52, 9, 8...*Mifflin*.................126
I have a Saviour, He's......11s, and 12s...*I am pray. F. Y*...231
In seasons of grief.........11s., 4s. and 12s...*Alaska*................326
Lamb of God, w.........M. 13. 7s. and 6s...*Turin*.................... 52
My days are gliding swiftly by..Pec. 8, 7...*Shining Shore*......389
Oh, how happy are......M. 20. 6s. and 9s...*O How Happy*...... 5
O think of the......Pec. M. 8s. 9s. and 6s...*The Home Over T.*124
Saw ye my Sav...Pec. M. 10s. 7s. and 9s...*Saw ye my Sav*...... 60
There's a b'tiful, b'tiful land..9s. and 6s...*Home of the Blest*..114
The time for toil is past.........10s. and 6s...*Bringing H. S*......385
To-day the Saviour calls.........6s. and 4s...*Amoy*..................146
When shall we meet again...Pec. 6s. 5s...*Unity*.....................443

INDEX OF TUNES.

	Hymn No.
Abner 4	120
Alaska 11s and 12s	326
Albion S. M.	355
Aletta 5	24
Allen 5	304
Amoy 6s and 4s	146
Angel Band C. M.	116
Arlington C. M.	7
Arthur 7	306
Athens C. M.	141
Autumn 4	330
Ava 10s and 4s	153
Avon C. M.	87
Azmon C. M.	54
Baca L. M.	394
Balerma C. M.	57
Barr C. M.	142
Beaufort L. M. D.	456
Bethany 6s and 4s	419
Bethlehem C. M.	1
Boaz 12s and 8s	457
Bound Brook 7, 6 and 5	15
Boylston S. M.	277
Bridgewater C. M.	291
Bringing home our sheaves. 10s and 6s	385
Broadway C. M.	316
Brother, sweetly rest 4	80
Brown C. M.	361
Butler S. M.	453
Cana C. M.	284
Canaan C. M.	127
Charleston 4	364
Chatham 5	294
Cleansing Fountain C. M.	22
Clinton S. M.	303
Come ye Disconsolate 33	47

	Hymn No.
Coronation C. M.	255
Cross and Crown C. M.	376
Crystal Fountain 7	179
Dawn C. M.	23
Dayton C. M.	402
Dearest Tie C. M.	442
Delaware 5	329
Divine Compassion 4	271
Dixon 4	33
Dothan 6s and 4s 8 lines	104
Downs C. M.	21
Dublin C. M.	74
Duke Street L. M.	243
Dunbar S. M.	111
Dundee C. M.	84
Dunlap's Creek C. M.	138
Eden 4	384
Effie 4	42
Elida C. M.	173
Elizabethtown C. M.	193
Elkhart C. M.	358
Elm Street L. M.	11
Eltham 5	117
Ennius 5	441
Enon 55	97
Eugene S. M.	381
Evan C. M.	98
Eve 5	102
Evening 4	218
Evening Hymn 4	92
Evening Twilight C. M.	319
Even Me 4	234
Expostulation 11	298
Federal Street L. M.	53
Forty-second Psalm 55	302
Fount of Glory 4	333
Freedom L. M.	288

INDEX OF TUNES.

Tune	Hymn No.
Gerar S. M	433
Gethsemane 5	61
Give me a Foothold C.M.D.	206
God be with you 9s and 8s	299
Going Home L. M	115
Golden Hill S. M	225
Gorton 7	222
Gratitude C. M	169
Greenville 4	151
Hamburg L. M	158
Happy Day L. M	30
Happy Zion 7	32
Harvest 6s and 4s 7 lin	429
Hattie L. M	68
Heavenly Desire 14	118
Heber C. M	108
Hebron L. M	95
Hendon 5	398
Herald L. M	132
Hick's Farewell C. M	300
Holy Rest 55	160
Holy Sabbath Eve 6s & 5s	162
Holy Spirit, faithful 5	390
Home S. M	416
Home of the Blest 9s & 6s	114
Home of the Soul 12s & 8s	122
Howard C. M	28
Huger 11	452
Hursley L. M	386
I am Praying for you	231
I need Thee 14	189
Is my name written 14 Pec.	408
I would love Thee 4	409
Joppa 4	16
Josie 5	235
Joyful Sound C. M	264
Juniata L. M	88
Laban S. M	2
Lake Enon S. M	190
Lancaster 5	155
Land of Rest C. M	427
Lawrence C. M	338
Lincolnshire 5	371
Lottie S. M	187
Lyte 11	325
Magruder L. M	309
Maitland C. M	17
Manoah 14	144
Marlow C. M	31
Martyn 5	374
Mear C. M	75
Memphis C. M	199
Mendota C. M	448
Mercy 5	43
Mifflin 52	126
Migdol L. M	424
Missionary Chant L. M	62
Missionary Hymn 14. D	14
Monmouth P. M	375
Morn S. M	65
Mount Vernon 4	78
My Helplessness L. M	18
My Sabbath Home C. M	156
Naomi C. M	196
Nettleton 4	268
New Haven 6s & 4s 7 lin	233
Ninety-Fifth C. M	4
Ninety-Third S. M	444
Nuremburg 5	421
Oakland 4	410
O how Happy 20	5
Old Hundred L. M	246
Olivet L. M	239
One Sweetly Solemn S.M.	123
Ortonville C. M	261
Ovio 4	27
Parting Hand L. M D	295
Peoria C. M	367
Peterboro C. M	163

INDEX OF TUNES.

Hymn No.		Hymn No.
Phoebe S. M.............147	Tampico C. M..............313
Pilgrim C. M............... 35	The home over t Pec. M...124
Portguese Hymn 11......... 39	The penitent 4..............176
Prayer C. M................207	The pilgrim S. M..........380
Purity 5.....................215	The rolling bill'ws C.M.D.349
	The solid Rock L. M.......324
Rantols L. M.............171	Toplady 17..................305
Repose L. M..............391	Trusting 5..................168
Rest L. M................. 72	Turin 13.................... 52
Retreat L. M..............436	
Rochester C. M............405	Unity 6s and 5s............443
Rockingham L. M..........341	Urbana C. M................351
Rolling billows C M.......349	Urvilla L. M................208
Ruth S. M.................345	Uxbridge L. M............. 119
Sabbath 17.................157	Varina C. M. D.............105
Safety C. M................335	Vesper S. M................. 93
Salem S. M.................280	
Salvation 14...............426	Wales C. M.................128
Sandusky S. M............. 45	Ward L. M..................135
Saw ye my Savior Pec. M. 60	Warwick C. M...............166
Shall we meet 4...........121	Waverly L. M...............413
Sharon L. M...............211	We are trav'l'g on our w 5...327
Shining Shore Pec. 8, 7....389	Webb 14....................274
Shirland S. M.............323	Welcome 5..................161
Solitude C. M.............202	Wells L. M.................154
Solon C. M................. 49	Welton L. M................ 40
Star of Day L. M..........125	Weston L. M................251
State Street S. M......... 25	What a friend 4........... 38
St. Martins C. M..........258	Whiteside L. M. D.......... 6
St. Thomas S. M...........445	Windham L. M..............450
Sweet Day S. M............296	Woodland C. M..............379
Sweet Home 11.............232	Woodworth L. M............181
Sweet hour of pr. L. M.....228	
Sykes L. M.................237	Yarbrough 5................184
Talmar 4...................449	Zion 7..................... 46
Tamar C. M................430	Zion's glad morning 33... 34

INDEX OF FIRST LINES OF HYMNS.

	No.
Abide with me fast falls the eventide.	97
Above the trembling elements.	198
A broken heart, my God, my King	182
A charge to keep I have	3
A few more years shall roll	380
Again the day returns of holy rest	160
Alas! and did my Savior bleed	57
Alas! what hourly dangers rise	194
All hail the power of Jesus' name	255
All praise to Thee, the Triune God	247
Almighty Sov'reign of the skies	254
Amazing grace, how sweet the sound	360
Am I a soldier of the cross	7
Amid the splendors of thy state	370
And are we yet alive	45
And can'st thou sinner slight	147
And let our bodies part	435
And let this feeble body fail	77
And must this body die	67
And now my soul, another year	173
Angels from the realms of Glory	32
Another day has passed along	159
Another year, another year	171
A pilgrim through this lonely world	35
Art thou in thy spirit lowly	180
As children dwelling in their home	51
As Jesus died and rose again	378
As on the cross the Savior hung	58
As pants the weary heart for cooling springs	302
As the sun doth daily rise	399
Asleep in Jesus! blessed sleep	72
Assist thy servant, Lord	190
At Jesus' feet I take my place	338
At the door of mercy sighing	179
Awake, awake the sacred song	256
Awake my soul, awake my tongue	239
Awake my soul, in joyful lays	243
Awake my soul, stretch every nerve	9
Awake my tongue, thy tribute bring	253
Awake, ye saints, and raise your eyes	131

INDEX OF FIRST LINES OF HYMNS.

	No.
Before thy face with lifted hands	18
Behold a stranger at the door	451
Behold the glories of the Lamb	258
Behold the lilies of the field	394
Behold the Savior of mankind	59
Behold the sure foundation stone	319
Be not anxious for the morrow	410
Be strong, my soul, in God most high	363
Bless, O my soul, the living God	244
Bless'd Redeemer, how divine	439
Blessed Bible, how I love it	333
Blessed fountain full of grace	24
Blest are the sons of peace	434
Blest be the dear uniting love	300
Blest be the tie that binds	433
Broad is the road that leads to death	450
Brother, thou hast left us lonely	80
By cool Siloam's shady rill	336
Call the Lord thy sure salvation	366
Can my soul find rest from sorrow	176
Cast thy burden on the Lord	43
Cast thy burden on the Lord	329
Child of sin and sorrow	153
Children of the heavenly King	371
Christ in the night he was betrayed	53
Come, children, learn to fear the Lord	143
Come gracious Spirit, heavenly Dove	211
Come hither all ye weary souls	132
Come, Holy Spirit, calm my mind	237
Come, Holy Spirit, heavenly Dove	200
Come, humble sinner, in whose breast	138
Come in ye blessed of the Lord	28
Come, let us all unite to praise	265
Come, let us join our friends above	430
Come let us join our souls to God	8
Come let us now forget our mirth	107
Come, my soul, thy suit prepare	216
Come, O my soul, in sacred lays	245
Come, said Jesus' sacred voice	400
Come, thou fount of every blssing	268
Come, we that love the Lord	356
Come, ye disconsolate	47
Come, ye sinners, poor and needy	151
Come, ye thankful people, come	423

INDEX OF FIRST LINES OF HYMNS.

                                                                            No.

Come, ye that love the Savior's name...291
Commit thou all thy griefs...417

Day is breaking in the sky...294
Dear Father, to thy mercy seat...204
Dear Jesus, ever at thy side...313
Dear Savior, we are thine...347
Deem not that they are blest alone...388
Deep are the wounds which sin has made...19
Depth of mercy, can there be...185
Destructions dang'rous road...453
Did Christ o'er sinners weep...187
Dismiss us with thy blessing Lord...214

Faint not, Christian, though the road...328
Farewell, my dear brethren, the time is at...298
Far from affliction, toil and care...82
Far from mortal cares retreating...334
Far from my heavenly home...418
Father in heaven, upon thy word...230
Father, in my life's young morning...222
Father, I stretch my hands to thee...199
Father of mercies, bow thine ear...229
Father, whate'er of earthly bliss...196
Fear not, brethren, joyful stand...44
Follow the path of Jesus...15
Fond parents, calm the heaving breast...85
Forever here my rest shall be...54
Fountain of grace, rich, full and free...396
Fountain of mercy, God of love...428
From all that dwell below the skies...251
From thee, my God, my joy shall rise...108

Give me a foothold on the rock...206
Give me to know thy will, O God...197
Give thanks to God, He reigns above...425
Give to the Lord thine heart...150
Glory and thanks to God in heaven...312
Glory to thee, my God, this night...96
God be with you till we meet again...299
God is love, his mercy brightens...42
God is our refuge and defense...309
God is the refuge of his saints...395
God moves in a mysterious way...402
God of my life, my morning song...165

INDEX OF FIRST LINES OF HYMNS.

	No.
Go thou in life's fair morning	145
Go to thy rest fair child	65
Grace! 'tis a charming sound	280
Great God, in vain man's narrow view	250
Great God, preserved by thine arm	167
Great God! we sing that mighty hand	172
Great God! what do I see and hear	375
Guide me, O thou great Jehovah	223
Hail! my ever blessed Jesus	269
Hail, sovereign love that formed the plan	311
Hail, sweetest, dearest tie that binds	442
Hail the blest morn	34
Happy the man that finds the grace	387
Hark, from the tomb a doleful sound	75
Hark, the voice of Jesus crying	16
Hark, what mean those holy voices	33
Have mercy, Lord, on me	188
Hear me, Saviour, while I pray	235
He dies, the Friend of sinners dies	456
High in yonder realms of light	117
Holy Sabbath evening	162
Holy Spirit, faithful guide	390
How blest the righteous when he dies	73
How bright is the day when the Christian	126
How charming is the place	281
How condescending and how kind	50
How did my heart rejoice to hear	293
How firm a foundation	39
How gentle God's commands	416
How happy are these little ones	83
How happy every child of grace	376
How precious is the book divine	36
How sweet, how heavenly is the sight	432
How sweet the name of Jesus sounds	262
How vain is all beneath the skies	119
If through unruffled seas	346
I give myself to God	303
I have a home above	112
I have a Savior, He's pleading in glory	231
I heard the voice of Jesus say	141
I lay my sins on Jesus	26
I'll bless the Lord from day to day	292
I long for God the living God	1

INDEX OF FIRST LINES OF HYMNS.

	No.
I love to steal awhile away	101
I'm but a stranger here	104
Indulgent Father, by whose care	99
Indulgent God of love and power	437
I need thee, precious Jesus	189
In evil long I took delight	21
In heavenly love abiding	275
In memory of the Savior's love	56
In mercy Lord, remember me	98
In seasons of grief to my God I'll repair	326
In the cross of Christ I glory	364
In the vineyard of our Father	308
In this lone hour of deep distress	69
In Thy great name, O Lord, we come	267
I owe the Lord a morning song	169
I thank the Lord my Maker	426
It is not death to die	447
I will sing you a song of that beautiful land	122
I would I were content to be	335
I would love thee, God and Father	409
Jerusalem my happy home	127
Jesus, be endless praise to thee	64
Jesus Christ our Lord and Savior	412
Jesus, dear name, how sweet it sounds	135
Jesus, grant us all a blessing	221
Jesus, hail! enthroned in glory	272
Jesus, I my cross have taken	330
Jesus, lover of my soul	304
Jesus, my Savior, let me be	209
Jesus, the spring of joys divine	41
Jesus, the very thought of thee	358
Jesus, thou art the sinner's friend	207
Jesus, thy blood and righteousness	20
Jesus, when my soul is parting	306
Jesus, while our hearts are bleeding	79
Jesus, who knows full well	191
Just as I am without one plea	181
Laborers of Christ arise	357
Lamb of God, we fall before Thee	177
Lamb of God, whose dying love	52
Let me but hear my Saviour say	344
Let me go where Saints are going	120
Let sinners take their course	454

INDEX OF FIRST LINES OF HYMNS.

No.

Let thy grace. Lord, make me lowly	219
Let us adore the eternal Word	55
Life is the time to serve the Lord	154
Listen to the gentle promptings	449
Long as I live, I'll bless thy name	284
Lord, a little band, and lowly	270
Lord, at this closing hour	444
Lord, bless thy saints assembled here	436
Lord, for the mercies of the night	170
Lord, how delightful t'is to see	438
Lord, I care not for riches	408
Lord, I hear of showers of blessings	234
Lord, in the morning thou shalt hear	166
Lord, in thy presence here we meet	431
Lord, we come before thee now	217
Lord, what a feeble piece	66
Lord, when I count thy mercies o'er	369
Lord, when together here we meet	301
Love divine, all love excelling	178
Lo, what a pleasing sight	445
Majestic sweetness sits enthroned	261
Make haste, O man to live	455
Mary to the Saviour's tomb	374
'Mid scenes of confusion and creature	232
Must Jesus bear the cross alone	17
My days are gliding swiftly by	389
My dearest friends, in bonds of love	295
My dear Redeemer and my Lord	13
My faith looks up to thee	233
My Father, God! how sweet the sound	368
My God, my Father, blissful name	340
My God, permit me not to be	212
My God, the spring of all my joys	362
My God was with me all the night	164
My heavenly home is bright and fair	115
My hope is built on nothing less	324
My latest sun is sinking fast	116
My op'ning eyes with rapture see	158
My soul, be on thy guard	2
My soul, repeat his praise	279
My soul, with humble fervor raise	241
My soul, with joy attend	355
My times are in thy hand	345

INDEX OF FIRST LINES OF HYMNS.

	No.
Nearer my God to thee	419
No more, my God, I boast no more	392
Not all the blood of beasts	25
Now, brethren, though we part	297
Now, gracious Lord, thine arm reveal	175
Now is th' accepted time	149
Now the shades of night are gone	168
O for a closer walk with God	193
O for a thousand tongues to sing	257
O God, the Rock of Ages	274
O happy day, that fixed my choice	30
O happy is the man who hears	321
O land of rest for thee I sigh	105
O Lord, I would delight in thee	406
O love, beyond conception great	249
O praise the Lord, 'tis sweet to raise	252
O render thanks to God above	248
O Savior, welcome to my heart	353
O the agonizing prayer	61
O thou who camest from above	343
O weary wanderer, come home	142
O when shall I see Jesus	14
Oh, bless the Lord, my soul	277
Oh, cease, my wandering soul	382
Oh, come, loud anthems let us sing	240
Oh, could I find from day to day	205
Oh, could our thoughts and wishes fly	129
Oh, deem not they are blest alone	415
Oh, do not let the word depart	134
Oh, for a faith that will not shrink	337
Oh, for a heart to praise my God	202
Oh, for the death of those	113
Oh, hallowed is the land and blest	424
Oh, happy soul that lives on high	320
Oh, how happy are they	5
Oh, how I love thy law	350
Oh, sing to me of heaven	111
Oh, that I could forever dwell	342
Oh, the blessedness of leaning	411
Oh, the bliss of loved ones resting	384
Oh, think of the home over there	124
Oh, what amazing words of grace	140
Oh, where shall rest be found	381

INDEX OF FIRST LINES OF HYMNS.

	No.
Once more before we part	296
Once more my soul, the rising day	163
Once more we come before our God	203
One sweetly solemn thought	123
One there is above all others	27
On Jordan's stormy banks I stand	110
On the mountain's top appearing	46
Our God, our help in ages past	339
Our heavenly Father, hear	227
Our life is ever on the wing	174
People of the living God	441
Praise God, from whom all blessings flow	246
Praise, O, praise our God and King	422
Praise the Lord, ye heavens adore him	273
Praise to God, immortal praise	421
Praise waits in Zion, Lord, for thee	289
Prayer is the soul's sincere desire	201
Proclaim, saith Christ, my wondrous grace	29
Raise your triumphant song	278
Remember thy Creator	144
Rest for the toiling hand	383
Return, O wanderer, now return	139
Rise, my soul pursue the path	10
Rock of Ages, cleft for me	305
Rock of my strength	48
Safely through another week	157
Salvation! Oh, the joyful sound	264
Saviour, bless thy word to all	401
Saviour, breathe an evening blessing	92
Saviour, like a Shepherd lead us	224
Saviour, teach me day by day	215
Saw ye my Saviour	60
Say, sinner, hath a voice within	133
Shall we meet beyond the river	121
Shepherd divine, our wants relieve	195
Since Jesus freely did appear	285
Sing to the Lord with joyful voice	288
Sinner, art thou still secure	186
Sinners, will you scorn the message	152
Sister, thou wast mild and lovely	78
See, above time's clouds and shadows	332
So fades the lovely blooming flower	70

INDEX OF FIRST LINES OF HYMNS.

	No.
Soft be the turf on thy dear breast	88
Softly fades the twilight ray	102
Softly now the light of day	103
So let our lives and lips express	12
Some day the word will come	11
Speak gently to the erring ones	448
Sun of my soul thou Saviour dear	386
Sweet hour of prayer, sweet hour of prayer	228
Sweet is the mem'ry of thy grace	260
Sweet meditation on the Lord	414
Sweet Sabbath-school, more dear to me	156
Sweet the moments rich in blessing	271
Sweet was the time when first I felt	367
Take my heart, O Father, take it	220
Take my life, and let it be	184
Tarry with me, O my Saviour	218
Teach me, my God and King	225
Teach me the measure of my days	86
Tell us sinner, tell us why	155
That doleful night before his death	49
That solemn hour will come for me	354
The billows round me rise and roll	349
The billows swell, the winds are high	310
The bosom where I oft have lain	68
The day is past and gone	93
The day is past and gone	94
Thee we adore, eternal Lord	242
The God of harvest praise	429
The God of love, the God of peace	351
The head that once was crowned with thorns	37
The heavens declare thy glory, Lord	290
The Lord my Shepherd is	323
The Lord of glory is my light	404
The Lord who truly knows	226
The morning of the centuries	23
The time for toil is past, and night has come	385
The time is short ere all that live	91
There is a calm for those who weep	125
There is a fountain filled with blood	22
There is a glorious world on high	89
There is a house not made with hands	109
There is a land immortal	118
There is a land of pure delight	106
There is a little, lonely fold	314

INDEX OF FIRST LINES OF HYMNS.

	No.
There is a name I love to hear	266
There is an hour of hallowed peace	130
There is an hour of peaceful rest	379
There's a beautiful, beautiful land	114
They who seek the throne of grace	236
This is the day the Lord has made	377
Though darkness turn the skies to night	407
Though faint, yet pursuing, we go on our way	325
Though love may weep, with breaking heart	90
Thou only Sovereign of my heart	391
Thou strong and loving Son of Man	397
Thro' all the changing scenes of life	287
Thus far the Lord has led me on	95
Thy laws, O God, are right	283
Thy life I read, my dearest Lord	76
Thy love, O Holy Father	276
Thy presence, gracious Lord, afford	208
Thy ways, O Lord, with wise design	393
'Tis by faith of joys to come	413
'Tis by thy strength the mountains stand	427
'Tis midnight; and on Olive's brow	62
To-day the Saviour calls	146
To God the only wise	282
To thy pastures fair and large	398
To thy temple we repair	372
To whom, my Saviour, shall I go	317
Upon the pillow of thy love	100
Was Jesus tempted like as we	361
Wake the song of Jubilee	373
Wash me, O Lamb of God	420
We are traveling on our way	327
Weary pilgrim, why this sadness	331
We join to pray, with wishes kind	286
Welcome, welcome day of rest	161
We've no abiding city here	40
We now have met to worship thee	6
We pray for those who do not pray	210
What a friend we have in Jesus	38
What charming words are these	446
What glory gilds the sacred page	263
What is the chaff, the word of man	322
What shall I render to my God	359
What though the arm of conquering death	87

INDEX OF FIRST LINES OF HYMNS.

	No.
When all thy mercies, O my God	259
When blooming youth is snatched away	81
When floating on life's troubled sea	318
When I can read my title clear	4
When I survey the wondrous cross	63
When on the brink of death	348
When shall we meet again	443
When the harvest is past, and the Summer is gone	457
When waves of trouble round me swell	352
Where could I go but unto thee	316
Where two or three with faithful heart	440
Where two or three, with sweet accord	238
While life prolongs its precious light	136
While now thy throne of grace we seek	183
While thee, I seek, protecting power	405
While through this changing world I roam	128
Whom have we Lord in heaven but thee	403
Why do we mourn departing friends	74
Why should I murmur or repine	341
Why should our tears in sorrow flow	84
Why should we start and fear to die	71
Why sleep ye, my brethren, come let us arise	452
With humble heart and tongue	192
With my substance I will honor	365
With tearful eyes I look around	137
With thankful hearts we meet, O Lord	213
Ye little flock whom Jesus feeds	315
Ye men and Angels, witness now	31
Ye sinners, fear the Lord	148
Zion stands with hills surrounded	307

www.ingramcontent.com/pod-product-compliance
Lightning Source LLC
Chambersburg PA
CBHW020243240426
43672CB00006B/623